FIC
TRO

Trout, Richard.

Czar of Alaska.

$15.95

61205

DATE			

Czar of Alaska

Czar of Alaska
The Cross of Charlemagne

MacGregor Family
Adventure Series
Book Four

a novel by

Richard Trout

Pelican Publishing Company
GRETNA 2005

Library of Congress Cataloging-in-Publication Data

Trout, Richard.
Czar of Alaska : the Cross of Charlemagne / by Richard
E. Trout.
    p. cm. -- (MacGregor Family adventures ; bk. 4)
    Summary: While in Alaska, the MacGregors encounter
an unusual new threat from ecoterrorists and must work
desperately to save the state from a disaster that would
impact United States security and the balance of power in
the world.
    ISBN-10: 1-58980-328-0 (alk. paper)
    ISBN-13: 978-1-58980-328-2 (alk. paper)
    [1. Alaska--Fiction. 2. Terrorism--Fiction. 3. Ecology--
Fiction. 4. Adventure and adventurers--Fiction.] I. Title.

PZ7.T7545Cza 2005
[Fic]--dc22

                                              2005002838

Printed in the United States of America

Published by Pelican Publishing Company
1000 Burmaster Street, Gretna, Louisiana 70053

For Virgil and Gwen Trout,

the inspiration for my imagination

Contents

Acknowledgments

A special thanks to Dr. Neal Coates, Professor
Bertha Wise, Lt. Col. Jeff Mager, USAF (ret.), Capt.
David Morton, USN (ret.), and Mr. Joe C. Zorger,
civilian aviation specialist, for their invaluable
input into this series.

Czar of Alaska

Prologue

The Bavarian Alps
December 5, 788 A.D.

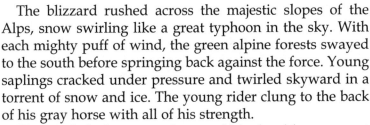

The blizzard rushed across the majestic slopes of the Alps, snow swirling like a great typhoon in the sky. With each mighty puff of wind, the green alpine forests swayed to the south before springing back against the force. Young saplings cracked under pressure and twirled skyward in a torrent of snow and ice. The young rider clung to the back of his gray horse with all of his strength.

The wool cloak wrapped around his shoulders was not enough to prevent the cold of the storm from penetrating right to his bones. His teeth chattered as he stared through the scarf around his face into the blinding white of the snow. For an instant he thought he saw a shadow that he recognized, but realized it was just a large boulder. He held his breath for a moment. The ice crystals on his beard rubbed his face raw, but he couldn't feel the pain. His skin was icy cold, and all feeling was nearly gone.

The gray steed trudged one step at a time, instinctively knowing that if she stopped, she and her master would surely die. Her long eyelashes were frozen with droplets of snow, but she moved without breaking a stride. The rider was confused by the blowing snow and the glare of the sky and had lost track of time. But even now, the gray skies showed no relief from the blizzard. The shadows of the tall trees appeared as if they were sentries at the gates of a frozen kingdom of sorts. Their movement sent chills across the rider's cold skin. He knew the cold was getting to his brain.

But as the sun began to peek over the Alps, and an eerie shadow hung over the rolling snow covered fields, the icy fog began to lift and cling to the bare branches of the trees that were silhouetted in the light. Meadows ringed with pines formed a beautiful mosaic that reached up to the slopes of the snow-covered peaks. Perched on the mountainside just a mile away was a long row of campfires that could be seen for miles until they disappeared into the hills and forests. The rider began to smile. His cheeks tingled as imaginary needles dug in from the bitter cold he had just survived.

The clanging of pots and the low rumbling of an army awakening on a cold December morning resonated across the valley. For two days, he had longed to hear these sounds. An occasional snort or neigh from a startled or anxious horse punctuated the increasing rumbling noise of men preparing for battle. At the top of the hill on the western ridge of the valley stood a very large tent that was made of the purest white linen in all of Europe. The linen had been imported from Egypt especially for royalty. The tent was three meters tall at its peak, with four corners rising two meters in height. Red and gold pennants flew from each corner. The white linen was now gray from the smoke of the campfires and the dust of many battles. Across the opening hung the coat of arms of Charlemagne, King of the Franks.

As he returned from the three-day ride, the two alert sentries could hear the heavy hoofs of his weary horse. Pulling hard on the reins, he leapt to the ground and tossed the leather straps to a soldier standing guard in front of the tent. The guard turned and shouted toward the tent.

"Captain, the blue rider has returned."

A large flap under the banner quickly opened and a tall man with a black beard stepped out. He walked over to the scout and took his right hand. Having been in the saddle so long in such frigid weather, the rider had difficulty standing as the captain of the guards balanced him. Together, they walked into the tent.

The air was heavy with smoke and dust but the warmth felt so good. A cold wind blew through the open flap where the weary scout stood, frosted breath pouring from his mouth. When he saw the King, he immediately fell to both knees and bowed his weary head. He was still breathing hard from the long ride. The captain of the guard spoke to the young scout.

"What have you seen?" the captain asked.

"Your Majesty, I have seen the Avars and Bavarians moving south toward the mountains. They will be here in two days time with 16,000 men. They carry the battle flags of Duke Tasilo and Arechis of Benevento. It seems, your majesty, that the Duchy of Benevento has become allies of the Bavarians and the Avars."

The king raised his right arm.

"Take this young man, give him a hot bath, and then escort him to the cook's tent and feed him anything in our possession he should desire. Then, after a days rest, he will join us in our march to battle. He will carry one of my swords and ride one of my horses. And when we return home victorious, he will be given an estate, with many servants, and he may choose a new bride."

In what seemed a blink of the eye, the scout was clean and feasting on roasted turkey, fresh bread, and hot soup. He slathered the goat's butter on each slice of bread and swallowed ale after each bite. He couldn't force it down fast enough, but no matter how much he ate, the hunger pangs would not go away easily. His mouth still felt cold, so he ate more soup, followed by a slice of warm turkey. The turkey was tough and chewy so he tried the soup again. His head began to ache, so he held his forehead and tried to force in a bite of bread, but his jaws hurt and he couldn't chew. Suddenly he felt ill and leaned forward, but nothing happened. He gagged a little and reached for the soup, but it was gone. Gone also were the turkey and the bread. Then he felt a jabbing pain in his right arm, and his body became limp.

The gray mare leaned over and rubbed her frozen nose across his face. She then licked his cheek with her rough tongue. The young scout opened his weary and nearly frozen eyelids and gazed into the flurry of snow that drifted overhead. There was no food, no warm fire, no cozy tent, and no king's promises. He felt the pain in his right arm again and realized he had fallen off his horse. The leather rein was still wrapped around his wrist. His cold blood had clotted where the leather was cutting into his skin.

Leaning on the other arm, he slowly began to crawl up the stirrup until he was standing. He tried three times before he could hook his boot into the stirrup and climb into the frozen saddle. The gray mare turned her head back and let out a short burst of a neigh. It was enough to encourage him to stand in the stirrup and swing into the saddle. The cold was numbing. He couldn't feel his fingers or his feet. Sharp pain began to penetrate all over his body. He reached for his face as he thought he felt a sewing needle go through his right cheek and prick his eyelid.

"I must warn the king," he thought to himself.

"I must warn the king," he said softly.

"I must warn the king," he grumbled out loud.

Then, with all of his might, he sat tall in the saddle, brushed the snow from the neck of his loyal companion, and shouted with his hoarse voice. "I must . . . I must warn the king. I must warn the king. I must warn the king," he repeated in his exhausted voice trying to keep his spirit alive.

He planted his spurs into the side of the mare, and she lunged forward in the snow. Jumping with all of her last energy, she reached the downward slope of the mountain pass and leaned into the snow-covered trail. Unable to stop her forward motion, both beast and rider sat back as hoofs began to slide. The side of the mountain began to move with them. In an instant, a small avalanche ensued and captured them within its grasp. But the downward slope was mild, and soon the avalanche was gone in a puff of snowy mist within a hundred yards. Clambering to his feet, the scout looked around for his horse. Her nose was poking up through the snow just a few feet away. Her heavy weight had caused her to sink to the bottom of the small slide.

He worked frantically to dig her out. His bleeding hands, cut even more by the ice crystals, began to leave a mixture of red and white in the snow. He got her head and neck uncovered and had to stop to catch his breath. The gray mare was laboring to breathe. The weight of the snow was crushing the life out of her. As he quickly began to dig again, he heard something coming up the trail. Not wanting to stop digging, he tried looking over his shoulder. He heard the snorting of horses.

"Help me! Please, someone help me!" he shouted.

Within a couple of minutes a column of the king's army appeared behind him and four men leapt from their horses and ran over to him. They reached out to pull him up but he pulled loose.

"No! I won't leave her. She saved my life, and when I tell you what I have seen, you will agree that she has also saved your lives and the life of our king."

Still mounted on a black steed, an officer nodded. Three other soldiers joined the four men. They all worked quickly to dig out the gray mare. Within minutes the scout's horse was standing and being fed a bag of grain. She was nearly too weak to eat but managed to munch a few mouthfuls. The scout was pulled up on the saddle behind another rider so the mare could walk the last two miles to the camp without a load.

As the column approached the massive array of tents, it was not as the scout had dreamed. Icicles dangled from the sides of the tents. Men rushed around carrying wood, trying to thaw out an army that had been assaulted by the Alps' worst December storm in decades. Men who had

frozen to death in the storm were being stacked like cord-
wood near a stand of pine trees.

Two soldiers pulled the scout from the back of the horse.
The blue tunic showing from under his cloak told the captain at the door of the tent that he was the blue rider who
had been scouting to the east along the foothills of the Alps.
The scout staggered as he was dragged into the tent. There,
towering above him, were Charlemagne and seven officers.
Each was cloaked with a thick sheepskin coat. The smoke in
the tent burned his eyes.

"Your majesty, the blue rider has returned," the captain
of the guards said, still holding him up on one side.

The young scout, about seventeen, looked up into the
craggy face of the great king. Time and battles had left their
trails across his face. But his blue eyes seemed to calm the
scout enough to speak.

"Your Majesty, I've seen the Avars and Bavarians moving south toward the mountains. They'll be here in two
days with sixteen thousand men. They carry the battle flags
of Duke Tasilo and Arechis of Benevento. They have two
columns of mounted archers. Their supply wagons reach to
the horizon." The scout coughed and lost his balance but
was held upright by the captain and a guard.

"Son, you're a brave man," Charlemagne said and stepped
closer. He reached into his pocket and retrieved five gold
coins. He took the scout's hand and put the coins in his frozen
palm and gently closed his fingers. "You may have these now
for your courage. When we return home, I will give you a
hundred times this amount. Our lives are in your debt."

Charlemagne turned to the soldiers around him. "Take
this man to the cook's tent and feed him all he wants. Have
my surgeon check him over and then place him at the end
of the column. He has battled enough enemies for this campaign." Looking at each man, he continued. "Were all of
our soldiers this brave, no army would oppose us. They
would hear of our courage and be too frightened to meet us
in battle. Now do as I have said."

"Yes, my king. It will be done," the captain of the guards
said.

The captain bowed and reached down to the arm of the scout and led him out the front of the tent into the cold of the December day. It was the fifth day of December and the seventh week of the campaign. The king motioned to a general, who was standing behind him. Together they walked across the broad expanse of the torch-lighted tent to a large oak table. Draped across the table was a map drawn on the smooth side of a large sheepskin. As the king leaned across the map, his long gray beard lightly brushed its surface.

"So the blue rider comes back first," he spoke under his breath as he moved around the table. "Any sign of the red or yellow riders?" he asked without looking up.

"No, Your Majesty," the general replied.

"Then this could be good information, or it could be a trap. Our other scouts may have encountered the enemy and already be hanging from a tree. We shall proceed cautiously with the direction of the blue rider."

His steel blue eyes were sharp and sparkled in the smoky light of the tent. Picking up a small stick with a charcoal end, he began drawing lines and arrows across the map as he spoke.

"The Avars will reach the Danube River by the middle of the second day from today. With our men placed here and here," he marked an X in two places, "we'll be able to surprise them and back them into the river. I want all weapons and shields wrapped in tent cloth and all horses muzzled. No armor will be worn or carried. All riders must remove their spurs and leave all helmets behind so the sun doesn't reflect light from them or the slightest noise gives us away."

"But, my king, they will slaughter us in battle without our armor," objected the general.

"No," the king said softly but firmly. "With God's help and a major surprise, they will fall to the silence of men and the sharp edges of our arrows. We'll dive down on them as quietly as an owl takes its prey in silent darkness with her sharp talons."

The general stood straight and bowed his head to the king.

"I'll prepare our men for the long march. The trails will be treacherous after the storm, but they can do it."

Within an hour, the camp looked like a bee colony that had been poked with a stick. The massive tents were falling quickly. Buckets of snow were dumped on each campfire. By noon, the army, weary from a long campaign, was moving through the pass high in the Alps where the storm had trapped them. Word spread among the men that the end was only two days away and soon they would be going home, so they marched with a new sense of promise.

Two days later, the sun had burned off the morning haze as Charlemagne's legions topped a ridge in the foothills. In the valley below, unfettered by the winter snow, were green pastures and pine forests. Moving casually down the valley were the armies of Tasilo and Arechis. Riders were walking next to horses, armor and weapons were stowed on wagons, and cook tents were being set up near a grove of trees. A smile came across the king's scarred and pitted face, showing a near perfect row of teeth.

"Praise God, we've caught them by surprise. On my signal, sound the horns for the attack."

"But, Your Majesty. The men are exhausted . . ."

The king turned and stared the officer straight in the eyes before he could finish his sentence.

"Christ is on our side," he shouted as his big chestnut mare pranced in anticipation, sensing the enthusiasm of her rider. "We cannot fail!"

The young officer with the dark flowing beard pulled hard on the reins. The stallion reared back on two legs and then sped across the ridge. At the same moment, the king's men were reaching the point of no return.

Charlemagne sat tall in the saddle and peered at his men, who were unwrapping their swords and weapons. The horses began to squeal and pull at their halters the minute their muzzles were taken off. The king pulled his long sword from the leather sheath that was decorated with gold and silver braid.

"Sound the battle charge," he shouted to the royal

trumpeter. A brass horn came out of a satchel and the trumpeter's jaws puffed out as he blew. The tone of the horn reverberated through the valley. Then another horn sounded, and then another, until the sounds were lost in the distance. The line of horsemen moved ahead of the foot soldiers down the hill into the valley.

A mile away, the Bavarians and the Avars were marching slowly alongside the river, still unaware of the coming onslaught. The rushing rapids of the river had blocked the sounding of the horns just as Charlemagne's general had predicted. It had been the right moment.

When Charlemagne's army reached the pine forest, they were only a quarter mile from the enemy. Swords were drawn. It was only then that the Bavarians and the Avars could hear the rumble of the horse's hoofs on the padded ground of pine needles. Gone was the clanging of metal swords and axes of an expected battle. Present was the grunting of weary men running through the forest; attacking with an adrenaline rush they had carried for two days.

The captain of the royal guards was in the lead on a tall black horse that was trimmed in red silk braids. The first surge of Charlemagne's foot soldiers met the Bavarians, who were now backed up to the river. Hand to hand, swinging heavy swords, axes, and the weapon of Satan himself, the mace, Charlemagne's soldiers pushed forward. As the mace was swung through the air, the skilled attackers held firmly to a twelve-inch wood handle. A two-foot chain was attached to the end and then to a metal ball covered with razor sharp spikes. Blood filled the air and was inhaled like water droplets as the mace found its home and ripped flesh and muscle, and crushed bone.

The Avars were unable to organize a defense as the horsemen charged through, cutting a path of blood and pain. The charging horsemen held ten-foot-long jousting lances and easily severed men in half or lifted them off the ground like dolls on a stick. The king entered the forest with his sword drawn and ready as he saw the Bavarian royal colors fall. A group of ten of Charlemagne's Royal

Guards provided an escort as they charged through the battle zone. Suddenly, a wounded Bavarian soldier stood and
swung his sword at the passing king, who quickly deflect-
ed it with his own and plunged it into the soldier's heart.
For a brief second, the smell of pine filled the king's nostrils
before they were invaded by the wretched odors of battle
and death as men were eviscerated and bowels emptied on
the forest floor.

Charlemagne could now see the Duke of Bavaria fighting for his life. Sword drawn, the duke beheaded one of his
attackers in a downward stroke from his horse. As
Charlemagne drew close, his foot soldiers fell back, leaving
the duke and the king alone in a circle formed by the Royal
Guard. The deep blue eyes of the Bavarian duke were
filled with hate and at the same time, resignation, that the
battle was indeed lost. Blood dripped from his brown
beard and his azure blue cloak. His armor hung from the
saddle and dragged on the ground, a result of the surprise
attack.

As the future Roman Emperor, Charlemagne, and the
duke stared coldly at each other, the king moved his big
chestnut horse to within three feet of the duke. The
duke's sword was still held firmly and was pointed at the
king. Charlemagne took his own sword and gently leaned
over toward the duke and wiped the blood off the blade
and onto the duke's blue blouse. The duke's eyes winced
and his body stiffened as the blood of his own soldier
touched his garment and soaked through to the skin. As
if a great spirit had just left his body, the duke bowed his
head and dropped his sword to the ground. It stuck point
first in the thick forest floor and swayed gently back and
forth.

Charlemagne put his long sword away and signaled to
his Royal Guard. Again the horns were brought from their
satchels, and the trumpeter's cheeks puffed out mightily.
The horns began to sound through the forest, and soon the
fighting began to stop as each foot soldier and cavalryman
began to realize either their defeat or victory was at hand.
The overwhelming forces of Charlemagne standing over

the corpses and injured revealed who was the victor. The groans of the wounded and dying reverberated through the hardwood forest. Three Royal Guardsmen escorted the Prince of the Avars on foot as he cursed and spat. Charlemagne dismounted and walked up to the prince as the Royal Guards made him kneel. Reaching inside his cloak, the king pulled out a cross that hung from a thick chain around his broad neck. The Bavarian duke was dismounted and was made to kneel next to the Prince of the Avars.

Taking the cross from his neck, Charlemagne approached his defeated enemies. As he lifted the cross toward the sky, the sunlight, peeking through the forest canopy, reflected off the rubies, emeralds, and pearls, set in a massive gold frame.

"God Almighty has given us this victory," the king spoke boldly.

Continuing his oratory, the king faced the captive duke and prince.

"Do you, the Duke of Bavaria, surrender all of your kingdom, your body, mind, and soul to our Lord Jesus Christ of Nazareth?" Charlemagne asked.

The young duke looked up at the legendary king and spoke softly.

"Yes, mighty king, I surrender."

At that moment, the duke closed his blue eyes, fully expecting to feel the cold steel of a sword across his neck. But there was only the sound of the Holy Roman Emperor, Charlemagne, moving in the tall grass to face Prince of the Avars.

"Do you, the Prince of the Avars, surrender your kingdom, your body, your mind, and your soul to our Lord Jesus Christ of Nazareth?"

The prince, blood dripping from a wound in his shoulder, looked up with anger and disdain and shouted, "I do not and I will . . ."

But before he could finish his sentence, the king dropped the cross, and a guard pushed a sword through the heart of the prince. A gush of air rushed through his throat, followed by a flow of blood. His body shuddered as he fell dead on the pine needle carpet.

Charlemagne turned to the young Duke of Bavaria, who fully expected a sheath of steel to be pushed through his spine, as well. At the same moment, a priest arrived by horse with a guard on each side.

"Holy priest, take this pagan lump of clay," Charlemagne spoke as he gestured with the cross, "and baptize him in this river. Let it be known that the Christian Duke of Bavaria is forever a servant of Christ and a loyal ally, and that I restore to him all of his property and riches."

The young duke fell prostrate at the feet of Charlemagne and spoke out boldly.

"Your Majesty's name will be exalted, your enemies are my enemies, and my children will be your children."

The king leaned over and touched him on the shoulder and said, "Rise. We have many lands to conquer for Christ."

As the Bavarian duke rose, he took the outstretched hand of the king that held the magnificent cross. He kissed the cross softly. A droplet of blood from the corner of his mouth fell onto an extremely large pearl set at the base of the cross.

As the smoke from the flaming battle arrows began to clear, the army of Charlemagne began setting up their camp next to the river. Screams of the injured and dying reverberated through the valley. Horses fed hungrily on the rich meadow grass in the forest clearing. Men were pouring pails of cold mountain water over their dirty and aching bodies.

Once inside his hastily erected command tent, the king again took the gold cross from around his neck and handed it to the priest beside him. It was a ritual that occurred every day.

"It's from this cross that I draw my first breath at the beginning of each day and my resolve to serve God at the end of the day. In the heat of battle, all I have to do, Holy Priest, is hold it for a moment and my spirit is renewed," Charlemagne said solemnly.

The king turned and walked into his private room of the big tent as two guards walked in and stood next to the tent doorway. The old priest took the cross and held it close to his chest as the king disappeared.

"I will guard it with my life, Your Majesty," the priest said, and tucked it inside his robe and left the tent.

1

White Out

Wednesday, November 10, 1999

---◖▬▬◗---

The first blizzard of the year swept across western Alaska from the Bering Sea and dumped tons of ice and snow onto the Alaska Peninsula. As the raging Arctic wind crossed the Shelikov Strait, it sucked up moisture and unleashed a torrent of white powder on Kodiak Island, home to fifteen thousand Alaskans and three thousand bears. Chris MacGregor held on to the reins of the dogsled with one hand while adjusting the hood on his parka with the other. He quickly wiped the ice off his goggles with his right hand before again grabbing the straps with both hands. The lead dog jumped through the snow, with the others following behind. The new snow was wet and was easily pressed down into a rut. Heather held on tight to the reins of her sled as she steered the dogs into the path being plowed by her older brother, Chris.

"Way to go, Heather," R.O. shouted over the roar of the wind. He held on tight as he sat in the sled, getting a face full of snow from the dogs' kicking up the fresh powder.

Heather only nodded and kept her eyes glued on the trail ahead as Chris blazed onward. Chris strained to see his sister and brother, but the fur on the parka blocked his view. He could hear the barking of the dogs and hoped Heather and R.O. were still attached to the sled somehow. He knew he couldn't stop unless one of them fell off. When they had left Trader Jim Gailey's lodge that morning for a fun sled trip through the forest, the weather report had called for a mild arctic front with only a few inches of snow. But when the arctic blast tangled with a cold front from the Bering Sea, it grew into a major winter storm from Nome to Anchorage. One of Trader Jim's dog handlers had suggested the path to take to ensure their safety from the large bear population, but he didn't realize that the kids had other plans. Chris had long since lost the trail and was now relying on the dogs to take them to Three Saints Bay.

Yesterday's dog sledding lessons were simply a crash course on how to hang on as the dogs led the way. Thrown in was an hour on how to escape a bear attack with the help of a Colt Anaconda .44 magnum pistol. With Chris being an experienced hunter and outdoorsman and eighteen years old, Trader Jim felt it would be better if he carried a gun, just in case he encountered one of Kodiak's famous grizzlies that had wandered away from its bear cave this early in the winter.

Chris again wiped the ice off of his goggles and made a slight turn and craned his neck to see his fourteen-year-old sister, Heather, and his twelve-year-old brother, Ryan, whom everyone called R.O. He sighed a frosted breath of relief as he saw them through the cloud of snow behind him. Heather was leaning over the sled and seemed to be as one with the dogs, kicking at just the right time to establish the rhythm that would carry the sled forward just as the lead dogs pulled in the snow. She had learned in her brief lesson that to kick out of rhythm would pull the sled back against the dog harnesses, and she looked like a natural at it. R.O. was seated in the sled and let out a whoop of joy as the sled cleared a small rise and lifted into the air a few inches.

Chris thought immediately what his mother, Mavis, was going to say. If he could keep his brother quiet, his parents would never know. But he knew that was unlikely. R.O.

had a tendency to share his excitement with everyone he met, and usually at the wrong times. Heather, on the other hand, was very sophisticated, as she would like to think. She didn't need for anyone to know anything and much preferred her privacy and anonymity. But that was difficult with two famous parents.

Dr. Jack MacGregor, a noted zoologist, Texan, and authority on endangered species, was their father of whom they were quite proud. Dr. Mavis MacGregor, a published paleontologist from London and their mother, had also accompanied them in their recent adventures in the Cayman Islands, East Africa, and Egypt. So Heather learned to live in the limelight and also in their shadow. She preferred the latter.

"Mush, Mush!" Chris yelled through the whine of the storm.

The beautiful huskies responded with an added leap into the snow. Their eyes were wild and determined. Their pink tongues were hanging out as they built up heat from their efforts at pulling and running. Chris's dad had known Trader Jim, the owner of the dogs and sleds, for nearly twenty years, having worked on several wildlife projects. Chris was sure that if the owner had known of the severe weather change, he would have never turned three kids from Texas loose in a wilderness with his prized dogs.

"Ryan," Heather shouted. "I hate this weather. I'm getting ice down my neck."

"Pull up your parka," R.O. replied and tugged on his own fur-lined hood. He looked back to see several locks of Heather's blond hair dangling free and coated with ice crystals. Her beanie, knitted by her English grandmother, was soaking wet. The wind blew with a fury and sent waves of snow across them as if they were ocean waves on the beach in Grand Cayman.

Chris watched carefully ahead trying to see a trail through the dense wilderness forest, as the ice and fog worked against him constantly. The white shrouded trees loomed along the trail, and for a mile seemed to slow down the wind. But each time they reached a hill and changed elevation, the cold blast would hit them dead center and drive the chill deep into their bones. After an hour of heavy wind, snow, and ice crystals, the dog teams began to labor. Chris could feel it in their harness and knew that a rest stop was needed. Peering through the forest, he found what he was looking for, a cabin. The blue metal roof was coated with wet snow that was forming a large bank on both sides, but a blue onion-shaped dome pierced the snow, giving the building a starkly beautiful appearance. As Chris tugged at the harnesses and pulled on the friction brake, the dogs started to slow down.

Heather realized she was suddenly gaining on Chris and pulled back hard.

"He's slowing down, Heather," R.O. shouted.

"I know it. Just be quiet and hang on," she shouted back.

R.O. shouted something but she couldn't hear it clearly. Her concentration was focused on bringing the sled to a halt without turning it over in the deep snow. A big flake of snow hit her goggles and she instinctively blinked. Her lead dog moved up quickly next to Chris' sled dogs in a short race to the cabin. The dogs labored as they plowed through the snow. The sleds soon dug to a stop next to the cabin, and the dogs instinctively looked at Chris as if asking what was next.

He motioned for Heather and Ryan to follow him as he stepped off the sled into the heavy snow. With each step, his boots seemed to be pulling off of his feet, until he came to the big front door of the building. Glancing around the outside, he couldn't tell whether it was a seasonal cabin used for hunting and fishing or something else. The dome on top made it look like a church of some kind. He didn't really care at the moment. It was just a place to escape the blizzard. As he approached the massive door, he noticed the big padlock that dangled from the brass fittings. Walking to the shuttered window next to the door, he tugged with all his strength. He felt the restraint that only a bolted window would have.

"What's up, big brother?" R.O. said as he trudged up from behind kicking snow as he walked.

"Door's locked. Window's bolted," Chris replied.

"How do we get in?" Heather asked as she took her last two big steps in the snow.

"Give me a minute," Chris replied and trudged back to the sled. The dogs were now resting with a thin layer of snow forming on their coats. Their pink tongues were still hanging out of their mouths, and their frosted breath created a mini-cloud around them.

In a couple of minutes, Chris returned with a navy-blue shoulder pack and handed it to Heather.

"Here, hold this," he said.

Chris unsnapped the plastic latches on the side and reached deep in the pack. He pulled out a green zippered case. He pulled off his left glove and handed it to R.O. From inside the case, he retrieved the brushed stainless steel Colt Anaconda .44 magnum revolver.

"You guys step back and cover your faces in case I get some splinters flying," Chris said.

They had been with Chris enough to know when he was serious about something and complied immediately. Taking aim from three feet away, with both hands wrapped around the gun, Chris pulled the trigger. The big Colt barked like a small cannon. The smooth recoil from the gun slightly pushed Chris' hands up in the air. Taking a step closer, he just barely had to push the door and the lock mechanism broke free from the jam and the door swung open. R.O. and Heather turned around quickly.

"Way to go, dude," R.O. said with a smile on his face.

"Now, go unharness the dogs and get them in here," Chris said.

Without a word, R.O. and Heather walked as quickly as they could through the snow. Chris put the gun back in its case and dropped it down into the pack. Stepping into the dry room, Chris first noticed a large stone fireplace on one end of the cabin. Thanks to the owner, there was a lot of wood stacked neatly next to it. There were two doorways leading to other rooms and stairs leading to a loft overhead. But it was dry, and that was what they needed. He carefully stacked four logs in the fireplace, tore off some dry bark, and placed it next to the logs for kindling. Dropping his gloves on the floor next to the pack, he retrieved from his pocket a lighter, which he always carried in the wilderness, and lit a piece of the dried bark and laid it carefully on one of the logs. The fire quickly spread to the dry wood.

"Hey, cool," R.O. said as he ran through the door with a team of dogs right behind him. Two of them were barking as if this were fun.

Heather's dogs ran in front of her and joined the other huskies. She pulled the parka hood down from her head and yanked off her goggles. Reaching up and touching her wet matted hair, she frowned.

"My hair's a mess," she said.

"Let me see if I have some mousse in my pack," R.O. smarted off.

"Stuff it, Ryan," she barked back and squinted her eyes.

"R.O., don't take off your gear yet. You're coming with me. We're going to unload the two packs from my sled. Trader Jim said there was dog food and some boots for the dogs if we hit some ice," Chris said. "Heather, watch the fire. Don't let it go out. Here's my lighter," he said and tossed it to her. She caught the lighter and walked over to the fireplace.

As Chris opened the door, a gust of wind pushed it out of his hands, and an avalanche of snow from the roof slid to the ground, creating a five-foot wall just in front of him. Undaunted, he stepped into the white snow bank and pushed with both hands, stepping higher each time. After a few feet, he was out of the bank and walking toward the sleds. He dusted off the new six inches of snow and pulled the quick release to the tarp on the sled and yanked it back. There he found two large plastic duffle bags. Pulling one off the sled, he turned to hand it to R.O., but there was no R.O. to hand it to. So he threw it over his right shoulder and began the short walk to the cabin, where he heard a familiar giggle. Noticing a red glove and brown boot sticking out of the drift around the cabin, he let out a heavy sigh.

He reached out and gave a yank on the hand, and R.O. popped free of the bank. Chris stared him straight in the face but didn't say a word.

"O.K., I know," R.O. said, already knowing the meaning of the stare.

"Go get the pack off the sled," Chris said.

"Roger, Chris. Pronto I go." R.O. started out in a run and got bogged down quickly. By the time he had pulled out the second pack, Chris had returned. Another gust of wind rushed down through the forest dumping still more ice and snow on the cabin. R.O. and Chris carried opposite ends of the pack through the snow and into the now warming cabin. Dropping the pack to the floor, Chris pulled his hood down and took off his goggles. He glanced across the room to find Heather sitting on her parka in front of the fire with her bare feet pointed toward the flames.

"Be careful. You can blister your feet pretty quick doing that," Chris said as he took off his parka.

"Chris, I swear. Sometimes you're worse than Mom," Heather said and then smiled.

Ryan dumped his coat and was digging out the two twenty-pound bags of dry dog food from the sled packs. As he poured it on the wood floor of the cabin, the huskies began to munch it up, looking toward Ryan as he continued to dump it out. The first bag went quickly. As he opened the second bag, Chris stepped out the door and retrieved a bucket full of snow. He had found some metal buckets under the sink in the primitive kitchen in the next room. He walked across the cabin and set the bucket next to the fireplace. The snow began to melt. Retrieving another bucket from the crude kitchen, Chris poured water from the melting snow into the cool bucket and took it over to the dogs. Several moved in and pushed each other to get a drink.

"Ryan. Go get another bucket in the next room and get more snow. These dogs need a drink after the run we put them through," Chris said.

R.O. did as he was told and for the next hour the focus was on feeding and watering the animals that had pulled them through the still-raging blizzard. When the dogs had stopped drinking, Chris stripped off his parka and dropped it next to Heather. Next off came the boots and soon Chris, Heather, and Ryan were all lounging in front of the fire while the storm continued to rage.

"Mom is sure going to be mad," Ryan said as he bit into a frozen candy bar.

"I'm sure of it." Heather said. "She said yesterday, when she and dad flew on to Anchorage, not to mess around but catch the next plane off Kodiak. It was your big idea, Chris, to go dog-sledding for a few hours," she said sarcastically. "I can't believe you talked Trader Jim into it. Mom is sure going to give him a piece of her mind. I can hear her now. 'Jim, you let three children go dog-sledding in bear country in the middle of winter," Heather mimicked in her mother's British accent and then laughed.

"Well, I . . ." Chris began.

"There's no well about it," Heather scolded. "You're taking the rap for this one all by yourself, big boy. I'm out of it. Totally devoid of responsibility, as adults would say."

"Me, too. And I like that adult thing, Heather," R.O. added and crunched on his candy bar. "Dude, did we bring any pop?" he said to Chris.

"No, and I'm not dude. But there are a few bottles of water in the pack," Chris replied. He had already begun feeling bad, so he didn't respond further to their comments. He just sat quietly by the fire, looking around the big room at the wooden paintings on the walls. He got up and walked over to one and touched it.

"These are really old," he said.

"I think they're icons of some kind," Heather said.

"Yeah, I know. This must have been a church or something. The dome on top, these icons all over the walls," he said as he walked to another, noticing the faded colors of the faces and robes of the people on the icons.

"Saints, I think," he said trying to remember the history lesson where he studied them. He shivered from a cold draft that hit him and walked back to the fire.

"Ok, what's the plan?" Heather asked and dug through the pack looking for food.

"We wait for the storm to stop, harness up the dogs, and move on toward the coast. We should only be about five miles away," Chris replied. "I suggest we all get a nap. It's about eleven o'clock," he said, as he looked at his diving watch. "With a little luck, we should be able to leave around noon or just after."

The trio didn't need the suggestion to tell them they were tired and needed a nap. The dogs were already curled up like big balls of black, tan, and white fur across the cabin floor. A couple had dumped their bladder and the rank smell of urine floated through the air. Heather wrapped her muffler securely across her face so she couldn't smell it. Ryan was fast asleep while Chris at first just lay there and listened to the wind howling through the cracks of the cabin. It was amazingly warm inside, and soon Chris fell asleep.

An hour passed quickly, and suddenly Chris opened his eyes. For a second, he couldn't remember where he was but then remembered as he gazed into the dwindling fire. The room had gotten colder despite all the warm bodies, human and animal, scattered about. He sat up and looked around. One of the lead dogs was up walking around with its nose high in the air. Instinctively, Chris sensed something but couldn't tell what it was. Then it hit him. It was a rank odor that surpassed anything the dogs could give off. It was strong, and then it was weak again. Quickly he pulled on his snow boots and stood up.

"Heather, Ryan," he said softly. "Wake up."

Heather looked up and didn't say anything when she saw Chris' face.

"Ryan, get up," Chris said again and nudged him with his right foot.

"O.K.," Ryan said loudly.

Chris leaned over quickly and put his hand over R.O.'s mouth.

"Sshh. Don't talk." Chris looked him straight in the eyes.

Ryan shook his head up and down in agreement.

"Put on your boots and parka. Quick. Then harness the dogs together. But do it quietly," Chris whispered.

But it was too late. Two more dogs were already on their feet, their noses high in the air. One of them barked and then began to growl. Immediately all the dogs were up and restlessly running around the cabin. Several were barking.

A loud bang was heard at the back of the cabin.

"Quick, let's bolt the front door," Chris said and ran across the cabin. He grabbed the big two-by-six-inch timber and dropped it into the metal brackets blocking the door.

"What is it?" Heather shouted over the barking of the dogs.

"Grizzly," Chris replied as he ran back to his pack and pulled out the Colt revolver.

"Cool. I've never seen a grizzly before," Ryan said and zipped up his parka and slipped his goggles over his head.

There was another big bang in the back of the cabin. Chris walked carefully to the back room just as a boarded window was hit again. Two planks gave way and snow blew into the room in force. Chris froze in his tracks as he saw a grizzly paw reach in and feel around. But it was no ordinary bear paw. The rangers at Trader Jim's had been talking about a few of the old grizzlies that had gotten to twelve feet in height and developed into a dangerous threat to humans and bears alike. This paw could have easily belonged to one of them. It was twelve inches across, with eight-inch claws. Coming to his senses, Chris turned and ran into the next room.

"We've got to get out of here fast. Line up the dogs. Put the leader dogs in front. You two get on each side and hold on to your lead dog. I'll take mine. When I swing open the door, take off in a run and don't look back. No matter what you hear or what I do, don't look back. Just keep running."

"Chris, what's wrong? You're not telling us something," Heather said.

"Just do what I say to do and we'll be at the coast in two hours. Now. Get ready," Chris said and put the Colt in his front coat pocket and barely zipped it closed. Heather and Ryan quickly lined up the dogs that were agitated from the smell of the bear and fought to be harnessed. Another loud boom could be heard from the back of the cabin. Chris slid the beam off the door.

"We've got to go!" Chris yelled and swung open the door.

The lead dogs bolted through and tried to turn to go around the cabin toward the bear, but the three MacGregor kids held on tight and steered them toward the sleds. As they reached the sleds, they frantically worked to find the harness connections in the fresh snow. Another loud boom was heard from the cabin, followed by a crashing noise. The dogs were barking wildly as the last one was lashed into place. The giant grizzly bounded out of the cabin door on the run.

"Oh, my gosh!" shouted Heather in terror as she stared at the mammoth bear.

"Ryan, take my sled," Chris shouted.

R.O. jumped from Heather's to Chris's in one step.

"Now both of you, get going," Chris shouted again.

"Chris, we can't leave you," Heather argued.

Chris reached into his pocket and pulled out the Colt Anaconda and fired one round into the air. The dogs jumped forward in a run, and the sleds pulled out of the snow and surfaced on top. In a few strides, the dogsleds were on their way. Chris knew that his extra weight and Ryan riding with Heather would have slowed them down enough for the bear to catch them. Turning toward the grizzly, he lowered the Colt and pointed toward its two-foot-wide head. The leviathan of a bear lunged with massive strokes through the deep snow toward the sleds, just missing Heather by two feet. Chris could hear her scream through the gale wind still blowing, her blond hair trailing in the wind.

Pursuing the sleds for thirty yards, the grizzly stopped and looked toward Chris. Chris glanced to his right and began running in the deep snow toward the trees. The bear turned and ran quickly in the same direction. After a few steps, Chris realized his escape attempt was futile, so he stopped and turned to face the angry bruin. He breathed in deeply as he raised the Colt and aimed at the head of the bear. He judged the distance at one hundred feet. It was too far for accuracy, given his inexperience with a high-caliber pistol. But if he waited longer, he might not have time for a second shot. He cocked the hammer and for a second held his breath. He pulled the trigger, and the gun bucked up in the air. The big bear stumbled and plowed headfirst into the snow, leaving a trail of red behind him.

Chris pulled back the hammer again. He thought his heart had stopped. The falling snow matted down his hair, and he suddenly noticed his hands were cold. In the rush of leaving the cabin, he hadn't put on his gloves or cap. He held the gun steady for a full minute before he lowered it and released the powerful hammer. He took a deep breath and started walking through the snow toward the giant grizzly. After a few steps he stopped and listened. He couldn't hear anything, so he walked closer to the bear. He was awed by its size. It was definitely one of the old grizzlies the rangers had been talking about. As he looked down at the bear, he noticed that he had shot it in the head. But when he looked closer, he realized the bear was still bleeding. It was still alive.

He stepped back and readied the Colt again. The bear breathed in deeply and rolled to one side. Chris could see that the bullet had glanced off the side of the skull and had simply delivered a knockout punch rather than a fatal blow. He pulled the hammer back on the Colt and aimed it at the head of the bear. As he pointed the gun at the grizzly, he thought about what he was doing and lowered the revolver. He released the hammer and stepped back. The grizzly, he tried to reason, was no longer a threat. He would probably never see another human, and so he needed to get out of there.

He ran through the snow back to the cabin and went inside. He gathered up his navy backpack and picked up his gloves. He saw R.O.'s knit cap lying on the floor and grabbed it. As he ran back to the door of the cabin and went outside, Chris quickly glanced back toward the fallen grizzly and saw that it was gone. A cold chill went down his neck. He tried to unzip his parka and pull out the Colt, but the hammer got hung on the corner of the pocket. A heart-stopping growl echoed over the cabin as the giant grizzly staggered around the corner, dizzily crashing headfirst into the side of the cabin. Chris stepped backward but tripped in the snow and fell on his back. The grizzly stood up with its head level with the eaves of the cabin, and growled. Big strings of slobber rolled out of its mouth.

As it walked on hind legs toward Chris, it wobbled right and left.

Chris yanked hard at the gun in his pocket and ripped the nylon as the Colt came out. Pulling the gun up, Chris pointed it at the bear just as an avalanche of snow came off the house on top of him. Rolling to one side to avoid the snow, he pulled the trigger. The bullet ricocheted on the thick log walls of the cabin, causing more snow to dump from the roof, but this time onto the bear. Chris struggled to his feet while clinging to his backpack in his right hand and the Colt in his left hand. Lunging out of the snow, he found the dog tracks and sled ruts and began running. He looked back and could see the bear's paws waving about in the snow. He estimated he had a three-minute head start and hoped the grizzly would be in enough pain and confusion not to follow. He slung the pack on his back, gripped the gun tightly, and began to run.

After five minutes of running, his lungs began to hurt from the cold air. The snow had stopped falling, the sky was turning blue, and the sun was peering through the clouds. Still frightened, he turned and pointed the Colt toward the trees. When he couldn't hear anything, he turned back toward the trail and again began to follow the ruts that the sleds had made. Then he heard something. It was the barking of dogs. In another minute, he could see a dog sled coming toward him at high speed. It was Heather.

As the lead dog came to a stop, Heather bounded off the sled and jumped into his arms.

"We were so scared. I had to come back for you. When I heard the third shot, I knew you were still alive and might be able to escape," she said and hugged his neck hard.

"Where's Ryan?" Chris asked as Heather stepped back.

"He's waiting over the rise," she replied.

"Good, let's get out of here," Chris said and tucked the gun back into his torn coat pocket. The walnut grips of the Colt hung out next to the broken zipper.

Suddenly, tree branches cracked as the giant grizzly burst from the forest and landed on the sled, crushing it flat on the runners. Heather screamed and jumped into the snow next to the dogs. With twelve-inch paws swinging wildly, the grizzly wrestled with the sled as if it were a mortal enemy. Still groggy, dizzy, and confused from the head wound, it fought with great ferocity. The dogs barked and growled and tried to run, pulling hard at their harnesses.

Chris struggled to one knee and pulled the Colt from his pocket. His first shot was at the chain attaching the dog harnesses to the sled. It ripped apart as if it were paper, setting the dogs free. They quickly bolted from the mangled sled and ran toward Ryan up the trail. The angry grizzly stood on its hind legs and hovered over Heather. Chris pulled the trigger in rapid succession three times, with the hammer hitting on the last round and two empty chambers. Chris held his breath, but the final bullet had found its mark straight through the heart of the grizzly.

The grizzly stood still and then fell backward, landing again on the sled. The creature was dead. Chris stood up slowly. Heather got up and joined him. They hugged and looked at each other. A full minute passed as they embraced and looked at the giant bear.

"Why didn't you shoot the bear first?" Heather asked.

"I don't know. I guess I lost count of the bullets. I wanted to save the dogs, too. Sorry," Chris replied.

"I'll forgive you and thanks for the day trip, big brother," Heather said and then smiled.

Chris let out a heavy sigh.

"Let's go find R.O. He'll be mad he missed this," Chris said and smiled.

"Boy, I'll say. He'll complain all the way to Anchorage," Heather replied and moved in alongside Chris on the trail.

For a moment, they relaxed and tried to calm down. But little did they know that the day's excitement was not over yet.

2

The Flying Beaver

---⬭---

"Man, I'm sure glad to see you," R.O. said. "The dogs came over the rise but no Heather. I was getting worried after I heard the gun go off three more times."

"We're here, but we've got to keep moving. We'll try to hook up the dogs to make a double team, " Chris said as a light rain began to fall and the sun disappeared. "This weather is unbelievable."

"Will that work?" Heather asked and wiped the rain off her goggles. Sleet pounded her face between the raindrops. She pulled her parka hood over her wet hair. "I absolutely hate this weather? Massive snow, cold, wind, then rain and sleet."

"We've got to work quickly. There must be a trail under this snow, but it will all ice over on top," Chris replied as he worked to harness the dog teams together.

"Yeah, like skiing on ice in late March at Angel Fire," R.O. said.

"I would prefer New Mexico right now," Heather added.

Soon the teams were harnessed together and all three kids were crammed onto the sled. After a long push by Chris, the dogs got their rhythm and pulled through the snow down the hill toward the shoreline just four miles away. The rain continued, with moments of sleet and an occasional flurry of snow. The run to the coast took forty-five minutes.

"We're heading toward that group of buildings next to the pier," Chris shouted. "Must be the marina Trader Jim was talking about."

Nothing more was said until they neared the rocky beach and stepped off in about six inches of fresh powder next to the marina.

"Seems like everything we find is out of season," Heather said as she walked toward the log building with the long jetty reaching out into the bay.

"R.O., help me unharness the dogs," Chris said.

Heather walked down the snow-covered path toward the first big building. In a few minutes, sixteen dogs were running around enjoying their freedom. None strayed too far, already having learned that the kids carried food.

Chris and R.O. walked up to the front door where Heather was waiting.

"Locked?" Chris said.

"Nope, just checked it and all we do is turn the knob and walk in," Heather smiled and led the way. Two dogs ran up to the door, but R.O. closed it before they could get in.

"You guys have to stay out this time. No messes in this cabin," R.O. said.

The modern cabin had several rooms with large picture windows that framed the mountains behind them and the sea on the other side. Trendy furniture filled the rooms, and one of Trader Jim's four big screen televisions was stationed on one wall. But the décor had a definite feminine touch, the work of Trader Jim's wife, Cina, who was quite the decorator.

"I could take these digs and I love this china," Heather said and dropped her wet parka on the floor as she stared at the intricate outdoor designs on the porcelain plates inside the large hutch.

"Me, too," R.O. said and disappeared into another room.

Chris found the kitchen and opened the refrigerator. It was empty and hot. He entered the big room overlooking the pier just as R.O. walked in from the other side with a box of cheese crackers.

"Where did you find those?" Chris asked.

"They were in a box on a big table. There's some dry cereal and stuff, but I thought these were the best," R.O. replied and crunched down on a couple more.

Heather made a beeline to R.O. and snatched the box out of his hand.

"Hey, those are mine," R.O. complained as crumbs fell out of his mouth.

"They belong to all of us," Chris said and took the box from Heather. He quietly doled out the crackers and each MacGregor ate a welcome treat.

"Now what?" Heather asked as she walked across the room and looked out the big glass windows toward the Three Saints Bay.

Chris sat down on a long couch sectional and laid his pack on the tile and iron table in front of him. Retrieving a small black pocket calendar, he studied it carefully for a couple of minutes and then spoke.

"There is a passenger plane leaving the city of Kodiak for Anchorage at 6 P.M. That's the one we have reservations on. Our ride to Kodiak leaves from Old Harbor at 3:30. It's now 1:30. We've got two hours to get a boat and get to Old Harbor."

"I saw two boats in the boathouse at the end of the pier," R.O. said.

"You did not," Heather replied and squinted at him.

"Yes, I did. Look, follow me." R.O. jumped up and walked quickly into the room where he had retrieved the crackers. Chris and Heather followed. "See." R.O. pointed out the picture window toward the tiny boathouse.

"There are two boats out there. I couldn't see them from the other direction," Chris said and paused. "O.K. let's go. It's eight miles across the peninsula to Old Harbor, and there is no way the dogs could pull in this weather and on ice. But if the sea stays calm, we could make it on time."

Within minutes, the three MacGregor kids were headed down the dock. Chris had stopped for only a moment to open a small maintenance shed for the dogs to have shelter if they needed it. Walking down the short stairway to the boathouse, Chris opened the door and stepped inside. Heather and R.O. crowded in behind him.

"Cool," R.O. said and jumped over the gunwale into a thirty-foot whaler.

"Let's just hope there's fuel around here," Chris replied and started looking around the boathouse.

"Here are some jerry cans. Let me check them," Heather said.

She quickly unscrewed the caps and got a whiff of the gasoline.

"It's gas alright," she said and rubbed her nose.

"I've told you a hundred times never to smell for gas or chemicals from a container. Let it waft into the air and then smell," Chris scolded.

Heather just rolled her eyes. "Chris, I swear."

Chris grabbed two cans and climbed over the gunwale of the boat. Heather picked up another one and followed. In another minute all three cans were emptied into the gasoline tank on the boat. Without saying a word, Chris walked to the controls and turned the key that was still in the ignition. The engine sputtered and belched out a blue cloud of smoke.

"P.U., that stinks," Heather said and coughed.

The next try of the ignition fired up the engine, and more smoke bellowed out and filled the small house.

"R.O., pull the chain on the door and then get in," Chris yelled over the noise.

R.O. crawled out of the boat and ran down the walkway inside the boathouse and reached the big wooden sliding door. He grabbed the chain that controlled the counter-balance and gave it a pull. Nothing happened. On the second try, he jumped two feet up on the chain and grabbed with both hands. His weight freed the door from the icy grip of the storm and the counter-balance began to drop. The door jerked upward and rolled on its tracks over the boat. Chris put the whaler in reverse gear and started moving backward when the door quickly reversed itself and began to fall.

"The door's coming down," Heather screamed and instinctively put her hands on her head.

Chris jammed the throttle forward and the twin motors pulled deeper into the water as the boat quickly moved backwards.

"Jump," Chris yelled at R.O. as the boat whisked by him. R.O. looked up at the swiftly moving door coming down and lunged into the front of the whaler, landing hard on the wood flooring. The boathouse door missed the front of the whaler by only a few inches and came to a halt just above the waterline. Chris quickly eased off the throttle and the boat drifted backward for a moment. He switched the gear to forward and stood up behind the wheel that was mounted in the middle of the boat. Heather and R.O. joined him on each side. No one spoke, but all put on their gloves and goggles and adjusted their parka hoods over their heads. Their coats were wet on the outside but dry on the inside.

Chris looked up at the sky and couldn't find the sun as the whaler began to gain forward motion. He looked at his watch and tried to gauge his speed. From the map, he knew he had to go three miles down Three Saints Bay to reach the passageway between Kodiak Island and smaller Sitkalidak Island. Then they had to turn northeast for eight miles. Without any problems, he figured, they would just make it.

The rain had stopped and a light snow had begun to fall. Heather sat on a chest mounted on the side of the boat and gazed out across the bay.

"This is just beautiful," she said. "I wish Mom and Dad could see it."

"They've seen it before," Chris said.

"I know, but not with us. I like for us to see things together. It's more meaningful," she replied.

"Hey, look at that," R.O. said and pointed to the shoreline.

There were two large grizzlies scavenging up and down the rocky beach.

"Must be looking for a last free meal before hibernating for winter," Chris said and then frowned.

The three miles to the end of the bay passed quickly, with the whaler reaching a speed of about 20 knots per hour. Chris looked ahead and noticed a heavy fog rolling in as they approached the end of Three Saints Bay.

"We didn't need this," Chris said.

R.O. and Heather knew exactly what he meant.

"Ryan, break out your compass and your flashlight," Chris said.

"Roger," R.O. replied and started digging into his pack.

"Give me a reading," Chris said.

"You're heading due south," R.O. replied.

"O.K., Heather. In thirty seconds I want you to start the timer on your watch. I'm going to turn to a heading of 40 degrees northeast."

A few seconds passed before Heather spoke, as she pushed the timer on her swim-team watch that she had worn for four years.

"Ten, nine, eight, seven, six, five, four, three, two, one, mark," Heather said as she looked through her goggles at her watch.

"R.O., give me a reading," Chris said and turned the wheel on the boat. They entered the strait, clearing the end of the peninsula just as the fog engulfed them. Within seconds, all they could see were each other and both ends of the boat. The waves from the Gulf of Alaska and the recent storm had reached all the inlets and bays and began to rock the boat. Having slowed to ten miles per hour, Chris pushed the throttle forward to gain speed and settle the boat in the choppy seas.

"One twenty, 90 degrees, 80, 70, 60, 50, 40, you're there, Chris," R.O. said and looked up at him.

Chris stopped spinning the wheel and the boat leveled out of the turn and gained speed.

"We are headed 40 degrees northeast," R.O. said, rechecking the compass.

"O.K. team, we made the turn. Now we just hang on for thirty minutes at this speed and we should see the lighthouse at Old Harbor," Chris said.

"Won't we hit something?" Heather asked with a worried expression on her face.

"I checked the map. There aren't any shoals or small islands in the strait. We shouldn't have any problems."

"Look, there's somebody else out here in this soup," R.O. said and pointed forward.

Suddenly out of the fog appeared a row of lights sitting sixty feet off the water's surface. It appeared as a bodiless monster floating through the fog.

"Oh, my," Chris said and yanked hard to starboard on the wheel of the whaler. "It's a big fishing boat. Hang on. We're going to collide."

Chris shoved the throttle all the way forward, and the small whaler jumped in the water and tore quickly across the surface, cutting through the soupy fog. Then the bow of the fishing boat pierced the fog just yards away. The big fishing boat just clipped the back of the whaler, ripping both motors off into the sea. Chris struggled with the wheel but felt the rudder cables snap. He had no control. The small whaler bounced off the side of the fishing boat, spinning in a circle before being left behind in the fog and the wake. Chris, Heather, and Ryan held on tightly to the now useless wheel until the boat was free from the encounter as the big fishing vessel moved southwesterly in the strait, its crew not even knowing that it had bumped anything more than a floating log.

"Are we taking on water?" Chris shouted as he left the wheel to explore the damage.

When he got to the transom, he could see the gaping hole where the two big outboards had once been mounted. The gas tank was ruptured, and fuel was pouring into the boat with a mixture of salt water from the sea. Soon his boots were covered.

"We've got to work fast. Look in all the storage bins for something that can help us. Life jackets, anything." His mind was working fast. He knew their survival time in the cold seas would be limited to only minutes.

Heather and R.O. worked frantically, searching the entire boat and throwing fishing gear everywhere.

"Anything, anything at all," Chris shouted and dug through a rear compartment.

"Nothing up here but a small trolling motor and fishing gear," Heather said and returned to the wheel to hang on in the bumpy seas.

"A trolling motor?" Chris turned and rushed to the storage

box. He leaned over and lifted the motor and laid it on the deck. He looked it over carefully. Looking back into the box, he found the battery cables that attached to it. Moving swiftly to the rear of the boat, he carried the motor and cables and set them on the deck. With a swift kick he knocked the ice off the handle over the battery compartment next to where the motors had been attached.

"I hope they're still here," he said and opened the compartment. "Yes!" he shouted.

R.O was leaning over him.

"What can I do to help?"

"Hook these cables to the battery," Chris replied. "Don't make any sparks or it could explode."

"Gotcha," he said and did so in hurry.

Chris took the trolling motor and dropped it over the transom and tightened the fastener so it was stable. Water was still leaking into the boat, along with the gasoline mixture. Chris turned and checked the cables to the motor then secured them in place. He looked at Heather and R.O.

"Cross your fingers," he said and flipped the switch on the motor. He then turned the throttle button and the prop began to hum. The whaler started moving.

The three cheered in unison as Chris steered the whaler through the choppy waters at about four miles per hour.

"I need a compass reading, Ryan," Chris said.

R.O. pulled out the compass. "We are headed south by southeast."

"O.K. Making a turn, tell me when we are at forty degrees northeast again," Chris said, trying to see through the dense fog.

"Chris, we've got a problem," Heather said calmly.

"What is it?" Chris replied.

"We're at forty degrees, Chris," R.O. said.

"Good. Heather, what is it," Chris said.

"We're still taking on water," Heather replied.

Chris looked down and could see water seeping in the through the hole in the transom. He could smell the gasoline.

"O.K.," he muttered. "Think, think."

"R.O., check the compass. The trolling motor is mounted

nearer the starboard side, so I'll have a tendency to steer northwest."

"Roger that. Bring us starboard about ten degrees, that's it. You're back," R.O. said and stared at the compass with his flashlight in the other hand as Chris made the slight adjustment.

"Listen," Heather said.

"I heard it," Chris replied. "It's an airplane and it's flying pretty low. It's flying so low that the fog has got to be only a couple of hundred feet off the water. It's fading."

"Wait, it's making a turn," Heather shouted.

"We can't keep the water out forever and the batteries are bound to go down soon," Chris said to Heather and Ryan. "I've got an idea. Hand me that heavy fishing line."

Heather quickly brought him a spool of line she had found. Chris tied the end of the line on the handle of the trolling motor. He ran the line to the wheel and tied it firmly and cut it with his big pocketknife. He then went back to the transom and checked the leaking gas tank. He ran back to the wheel, took the small ax mounted on the side of the boat next to the fire extinguisher, and returned to the transom. Leaning over, he quickly stood up.

"Ya'll come help me. I'm going to lean over and puncture the gas tank below the waterline. Hang on to my legs so I don't fall in."

Heather and Ryan positioned themselves closely and each grabbed a leg.

"Watch the ax on the back swing," Chris shouted as he leaned over.

The first swing splashed the icy cold seawater into his face, stinging his eyes. The ax had barely penetrated the remainder of the shell over the gas tank. Chris held his breath with each swing as he chopped away at the fiberglass-and-wood shroud. On the fifth blow, the tip of the ax penetrated and gas gushed out into the water. Chris stood up quickly. He was soaking wet from the waist up.

"Stand back," he shouted. Taking his metal butane lighter from his pocket, he struck it and it fired up immediately. He leaned over and with a light toss dropped it into the ocean. The gushing gasoline rising to the surface four feet behind the boat ignited just an instant before the lighter hit the water's surface and a ball of flame roared across the water. The trailing gas floating on the water's surface ignited, and the fire raced the two hundred yards the whaler had traveled since the accident. The clean water next to the boat protected the gas tank from exploding.

"Jessica, did you see that?"

"Yeah, Dad. It was a streak of light through the fog, for sure. There's somebody down there that needs help. Let's check it out," Jessica said.

"I'm looking at the surface radar to find out what's floating down there while you bring her around for another pass," the copilot said and started flipping toggle switches to illuminate the radar screen.

The DeHavilland Beaver, an amphibious aircraft, soared 1,000 feet above the water and about 800 feet above the rolling fog. After a tight circle, Jessica lined the aircraft parallel with Shelikov Strait and reduced altitude to 500 feet.

"What's the radar tell us, Dad?"

"Jessica, I can't see anything but what appears to be a large boat, probably a trawler headed southwest about three miles and moving away from us. There's a small blip drifting free in the channel. No, it looks like it's under power and moving very slow. It's moving too fast for a log and too slow for anything with much power. Someone needs help," Trader Jim said.

"I agree," Jessica replied and dropped to just above the fog at 210 feet.

"We should pass over them just about now," Jim said.

"Wow, did you hear that?" R.O. said. "They must have seen the fire."

"Good, but how do we communicate in this fog?" Heather asked worriedly.

"I don't know. But these Alaskan bush pilots are some of the best in the world. They'll come get us. I'm sure of it," Chris replied.

He then turned to look at the aft section of the boat.

"I hope it's soon," he said with a worried look on his face. He was shivering from the cold, wet clothes stuck to his body.

The water had risen to about a foot in depth and was now across one-third of the deck and rising faster.

"The hole in the gas tank must be filling with water as the gas is running out," R.O. said and stepped closer to the wheel.

"Did you find any life jackets up there?" Chris asked calmly.

"Yes, there were two," Heather said and picked one up.

"You two put them on. I'll tear a cushion free and hang on to it. When this thing goes down, we'll have about ten minutes in the water before it's all over," Chris said solemnly with a lump forming in his throat.

Throughout their journeys in the Cayman Islands, East Africa, and the Nile River, Chris had never placed his brother and sister in such danger before. He fastened them tightly into their life jackets.

"I haven't heard the airplane go by again. Do you think they gave up?" R.O. asked and pulled off his goggles.

"O.K. Dad, we're going to drop into the fog in about fifteen seconds. I'll make an instrument landing. But we'll have to use the altimeter to get us within ten feet of the surface of the ocean. If it's too rough, I'll have to abort and pull up. We should be within about two hundred yards of the craft. So in we go," Jessica replied and gripped the wheel tightly.

"One hundred. Ninety. Eighty. Seventy. Sixty. Fifty," Jim read calmly. "Thirty. Twenty. You're at ten."

"I see water, choppy but doable. Hang on for a bounce — make that two bounces. That's it, sweetheart, settle in, caress that ocean gently, we're in. Whew. Now just pray for no floating logs or debris," Jessica said as the Beaver cruised along like a boat.

"Don't worry. Everything on this planet has been prayed over in the last minute," Jim laughed. "Straight ahead, watch out!" he shouted.

"Chris, look." Heather screamed as the wing of the Beaver passed over the now half-sunken whaler. The MacGregor kids were standing knee deep in icy water.

"Three kids. Did you see that?" Jessica said.

"Yup. They're my kids all right. I was hoping they made it to Old Harbor with my dogs. I'm sure glad I second-guessed them and talked you into flying today," Jim said.

"Me, too. Let's turn this around and get the side door open. It'll be tricky getting in close to them," Jessica said.

The Beaver circled around in the fog and got within twenty yards. Trader Jim opened the side door and hollered through the fog.

"Chris, stay put. We're going to get as close as we can."

"Don't worry." Chris gave the first smile he had offered all day. Heather and R.O. were too cold to cheer but smiled anyway.

Jessica drove the DeHavilland Beaver right up to the sinking whaler. R.O. and Chris threw their three packs to Jim, who stowed them quickly. Heather was the first on board.

"Take off those wet boots and socks right away. You'll get frostbite," Jim said and reached out and took R.O.'s hand.

Chris looked around the sinking ship and shook his head. He took one step up on the gunwale and leapt into the flying Beaver. As he did, the rear of the whaler dropped out of sight and the nose of the boat pointed straight into the air, just missing the tip of the right wing.

"Too close for comfort, young man," Trader Jim said and closed the door. "Take off your wet clothes and get buckled in tight. We still have to get out of this soup."

"Thanks, Trader Jim," Heather said between chattering her teeth. She had stripped out of the wet parka, gloves, boots, and socks. R.O. was just a second or two behind her in the process. Chris, wet nearly all over, shed down to a thermal undershirt and leggings. The heat in the cabin was starting to build up again as the plane cut through the waves.

"O.K. Dad. Now comes the fun part. We've got to gain airspeed in choppy water with practically zero visibility. Check the surface radar again," Jessica said to her copilot.

"Just the fishing boat, now about six miles away.

Nothing coming at us," Trader Jim replied.

Jessica again pointed the aircraft down the middle of the channel at exactly forty degrees northeast and set the flaps. Visually checking the wings for ice, she pushed the throttle forward, and the Beaver began to cut through the waves. The fog rushed by the cabin windows like a painted wind.

"Oh, my," Heather said.

"We'll be all right," Chris said calmly but gripped his seat belt tightly just the same.

"This is awesome. Wait till I e-mail Drew about this. He won't believe it," R.O. said.

"I'm thinking the whole Nevius family won't believe it. You know how his mother, Judy, won't let him hang out with you because she thinks you are way too reckless. If you tell them this, you'll never see Drew again," Heather said nervously as she looked out the window.

"At least I have a friend to write to," R.O. quipped and looked away with the satisfaction of having the last word.

Chris ignored the conversation as he usually did and kept his eyes glued out the window.

"O.K., coming up on 75 knots. Any second she'll leap off the surface like a ballerina into her leading man's arms," Jessica said and smiled.

"You always did enjoy ballet and dance lessons," Trader Jim said.

"Sure did, Dad. I should have been a dancer instead of a bush pilot and fishing guide," Jessica replied. "But I wouldn't trade it now for anything."

The Beaver finally let go of the water and leapt into the air. Within seconds, the sun burst through the cockpit window.

"Whew. Hallelujah!" Jessica said, pulling the Beaver into a steep climb.

Trader Jim and the MacGregor kids all began to clap and cheer. Jim turned around and spoke.

"It's time to meet your rescuer, kids. This is Jessica, the oldest of my three daughters. Jessica, let me introduce Heather, Ryan, and Chris MacGregor. Their parents are longtime friends of mine."

"Thanks, Jessica," Heather said.

Chris and R.O. joined in the thanks.

"Well, it was my dad, Trader Jim, who called me around noon and said he thought a rescue might be in order. We figured we would pick you up at the end of Three Saints Bay on the shore at the marina. Didn't figure for a minute you would take a boat and head up the coast in a storm. You guys are more fearless that I thought. That qualifies you for Alaskan citizenship." Jessica laughed.

"I've got a GPS tracking system for my dogs in their collars. When you guys stopped and started and the storm hit, I figured it was going to be a long day, and I sure didn't want to do a lot of explaining to your parents. In the storage box behind the seat, you'll find sandwiches, hot chocolate, cookies, and some blankets. I knew we would find you, but I had no idea that we would take it down to the wire," Jim said and breathed a deep sigh of relief.

After a few minutes of visiting and telling Jessica and Trader Jim about the accident, the gasoline trail, and Chris' idea to signal them, the kids were overcome with exhaustion.

"Chris, just relax. We're going to refuel in Kodiak and then take you three on to Anchorage. We should get there about seven o'clock," Jessica replied.

"Can you let us tell my parents about all of this?" Chris asked, hoping he knew the answer. He could choose the time and the right place and control the reaction better, he thought. Jim sat for a minute and then replied.

"O.K., son. You know your parents, but you take the heat if they get mad I didn't tell them right away," Trader Jim replied.

"That's a deal," Chris said, smiling for only the second time that day.

The Beaver made a turn to line up with the lights of Kodiak. Cook Inlet lay beyond where once sailed mighty ships that explored these waters for nations hungry for adventure and treasure. While kings waited at home to count their gold and silver, many sea captains and sailors counted their freedom on the high seas, the clean salty air, and the beautiful stars of the night as the only treasure they would ever need.

3

Captain Cook Inlet

———————————○———————————

The flight took less time than expected with the help of a tailwind that had pushed the early winter storm across the Gulf of Alaska. The DeHavilland Beaver seemed to effortlessly conquer all the turbulence the storm had and broke free on a northeasterly path toward Anchorage. The MacGregor kids changed clothes, napped, and ate all the food that Trader Jim had brought on board. Heather quickly made a blanket tent over her head to change. Trader Jim's lodge manager had already driven across Kodiak Island in an all-terrain vehicle equipped for heavy snow and located all but one of the dogs. He figured that one would show up later or become dinner for a hungry bear.

"O.K., kids, wake up. We'll touch down in about five minutes," Jessica said. She turned the Beaver to line up with the landing zone in the Anchorage harbor where at least fifty other amphibian aircraft had already set down for the night. The landing was smooth, and soon the Beaver was being tied up at a water-level pier. Trader Jim was the first off and stretched after the tight quarters of the aircraft. Being a husky outdoorsman type of guy, he loved to fly with his daughter but hated the small seats of any airplane. He would have rather been on his sixty-foot boat cruising across the Gulf of Alaska. Next off the Beaver came R.O., then Heather, Chris, and finally Jessica.

"I'll take the kids up to the marina and get them a taxi. I'll meet you at the restaurant in about thirty minutes," Trader Jim said to Jessica.

"Are you flying back tonight?" Chris asked.

"No, we're going to take care of some business in town tomorrow and then fly back in the afternoon. It's been a long day," Jessica replied.

With a solemn look on their faces, the three kids turned to face the two Alaskan wilderness adventurers.

"We can't thank you enough," Chris started. "I mean, I've always been able to figure out how to get us out of a jam, but today . . ."

"Don't worry about it. What works in other places around the world, sometimes doesn't work up here on top of the world. Alaska's got its own set of rules for survival. The point is, we're all here and that's what counts," Trader Jim said.

Heather stepped forward and hugged him and then turned to Jessica and did the same. Within minutes, the three kids were in a taxi headed for the downtown hotel where they were supposed to meet their parents. The short trip only took about ten minutes. As they slowly walked into the lobby, they noticed a tall, auburn-haired woman walking toward the coffee shop. She was dressed in leather pants and vest, with a yellow silk blouse. Her auburn hair was accented with a pearl hair comb on one side.

"Mom," Heather said softly.

Chris smiled. He always admired how beautiful his mother was.

"That's our mom," he said.

R.O. took off and ran across the lobby toward her.

"Mom, Mom," he yelled.

Mavis MacGregor wheeled around in stride in her boots with four-inch heels and looked toward the charging R.O.

"Ryan O'Keef MacGregor. Where have you been, laddie?" she said in her strong accent.

Ryan lunged toward her, and she leaned over to embrace him.

Heather and Chris walked up from behind, trying not to be noticed by the already staring hotel guests.

"Mom, you won't believe what . . ." R.O. started.

"Mom, it's so good to see you," Heather interrupted in an adult fashion and pecked her mother on the cheek. Mavis gave her a hug and big kiss. Heather didn't pull away. She then turned to Chris, and as she always did, looked him straight in the eye for a full three seconds.

"And how are you?" she asked and gave him a hug.

"I'm fine, Mom. Looks like we made it back just in time for dinner," he replied.

"Not dressed and smelling like the three of you do. What happened? Is that petrol I smell? Did your flight arrive late? And did you fall in a creek on the way from the airport, too?" Mavis said. She stepped back and looked at them individually. "And who dressed the three of you this morning? Flannel shirt, khaki pants," she started down the row. "Turtleneck, doesn't match your pants, dear."

Heather cocked her head in disbelief at the scrutiny they were getting. "And you, young man. Did you dress this way to go from the Lodge to the airport in Kodiak? I would have been thoroughly embarrassed to be sitting next to you. I would indeed." Mavis looked down at R.O. with her hands on her hips. "Chris, next time," she paused. "Oh, well. Get going."

"Mom, you look pretty," Heather said.

"Ditto that, Mom," R.O. said.

"Thanks. Your father is taking me out for dinner and if you can get up to the room and change clothes, you can go, too. Your bags are already there. And do take a quick shower. We'll be in the coffee shop with some of the people your dad came to see. Now hurry," Mavis said and strode toward the café.

The MacGregor kids took the plastic card key that Mavis had given them and headed for the elevators.

"Ryan. I told you. Not a word about what happened until I'm ready," Chris said.

"I wasn't going to say anything. I was just going to tell her about the flight over," R.O. replied.

"She doesn't know about the Beaver and the flight over, dummy," Heather said and gave him a menacing stare.

"Look, just wait and you'll get a chance to tell it all. Understand?" Chris said.

"Roger," R.O. replied as the elevator doors opened.

"Dr. MacGregor, what we want you to understand is that the Arctic National Wildlife Refuge can't take any development. It's a very fragile environment. The tundra is unique to the North Slope and the home of millions of wildlife," the scientist said.

"I understand the arguments against oil exploration," Dr. Jack MacGregor began. "I'm aware of the studies conducted about the migration of the two major caribou herds, the Porcupine River Herd and the Central Arctic Herd. I'm also aware of the . . . oh, hi, honey." Jack stood and turned toward Mavis as she walked up.

"The kids are here. I sent them up to the room to clean up and join us for dinner," Mavis said.

"Good, let me introduce Dr. Jacques Sevé from Montreal. He's with the International Confederation of Organizations for Nature. You know, they're referred to as ICON. This is my wife, Dr. Mavis MacGregor. She's a paleontologist."

"My pleasure, Dr. MacGregor," Dr. Sevé said and sat back down.

"Please to meet you," Mavis replied.

"A British subject, I presume?" Dr. Sevé said and stirred his glass of ice tea.

"I was once a British subject, but I'm now firmly an American citizen with a lot of British family," Mavis said and smiled.

"I was saying, doctor," Jack continued. "I'm firmly aware of the wildlife that is present in the Arctic National Wildlife Refuge. The eighty thousand caribou that migrate through the region have been thoroughly counted and studied ever since it became a protected area in 1960. With the coastal region of the Wilderness only sixty-five miles from

Prudhoe Bay, there were another hundred or so scientists that made a new study when the Trans-Alaska Pipeline was built in the seventies," Jack said.

"Then, Dr. MacGregor, I am puzzled why you are here to help the oil companies destroy the pristine land of the Arctic National Wildlife Refuge," Dr. Sevé said.

Jack shifted in his chair at the accusation that he would do anything that would destroy wildlife.

"Dr. Seve', obviously you don't know me. You can read my books, attend my lectures, and follow me around all day if you like, and you will discover that there is nothing in my life that would lead anyone to believe that I would destroy anything associated with wildlife or the environment. Yes, I do have a pro-hunting stance because that's the only way that governments are going to raise enough money to protect wildlife and the environment without creating a burdensome tax on the general population and subsequent resentment," Jack said, trying to calm down. He picked up a cup of coffee and took a sip. "Legal hunter's bullets and guns have saved thousands more animals than they ever killed since sound programs and conservation laws were introduced to North America and parts of Africa."

"But, Dr. MacGregor, who is funding your travels around the world? Is it not the oil companies? Are they not the beneficiaries of your presence? When the esteemed Dr. Jack MacGregor comes to Alaska, the whole world of conservation and environmentalism takes notice," Dr. Sevé said.

"I came to Alaska at the request of a friend of mine. It was not part of my original plans to write my new book. And yes, he works for an oil company as their chief biologist. And yes, they are paying my hotel bill and my airplane expense to come to Alaska. Were you willing to do the same to get me to come and give an unbiased view of the situation?" Jack asked. "Money for wildlife research is very scarce and I, like hundreds of other scientists, accept donations from wherever we can ethically find them."

"My husband has unquestionable integrity, Dr. Sevé," Mavis interjected. "In the last five months alone, he has made great contributions to the endangered species problems of the Caribbean, East Africa, and the Nile River. While we were in Italy the last three months, he represented the United States at several environmental conferences in Europe and Russia. To say that he is being paid off by the oil companies is absurd," Mavis said politely.

"My apologies, if I sounded insulting," Dr. Sevé said. "But I was only stating the rumors that I've heard."

"Your rumors are just that, rumor and lies. But that still doesn't mean that I'm here to indict the oil companies either. They've made their mistakes. The Exxon Valdez spill is the most obvious. I'm here to give objective analysis and advice, enjoy Alaska for a few days, and then head over to China for a couple of weeks with my family." Jack took another sip from his coffee cup.

"Well, we will meet again after you have toured ANWR and had time to research the situation. Please keep an open mind," Dr. Sevé said and stood up.

"I will do that doctor," Jack said and offered his hand as he stood up.

"My pleasure, Dr. MacGregor. *Au revoir,*" Dr. Sevé said as he nodded toward Mavis and left.

"A pompous little man," Mavis said as Jack sat back down and Dr. Sevé was out of sight.

"Yes, but very powerful in the environmental movement. Right now, he is the head guru that beats the drum for all the eco-soldiers out there," Jack replied.

Dr. Sevé walked through the lobby and out to a waiting car. The Saab sedan was sitting at the curb and purring quietly. When he got in on the passenger side, the young woman behind the wheel pulled out into the evening traffic.

"Our good Dr. MacGregor is going to be a problem. I feel his mind is already made up and we are in for another setback. I will contact all of our member organizations tomorrow and tell them that we will need to put pressure on Washington once again," Dr. Sevé said.

"Is he really that powerful?" the young woman said.

"Yes. His books are read not only by politicians and scientists but also by families around the warmth of their hearth. He is a folk hero of some sort. His views occupy much of the center on most issues, only shifting left or right on a few. He is more dangerous than you can imagine. He is not a threat to the right or the center, but only to us. We must apply more pressure as soon as possible. If MacGregor comes out in support of the oil companies, our efforts in Alaska will be set back for years, if not decades. Our only hope would be to gain control of some of the tribal corporations. We already have people in place across Alaska, Canada, and Norway who will infiltrate their tribal governments," Dr. Sevé said.

The young lady winced at the last statement and gripped the steering wheel tightly. She glanced over to Dr. Sevé and then down the road. She knew that plans were being made that very night to thwart Dr. MacGregor's activities and make a statement about the Alaskan environment that the world would not soon forget.

"Hi, Mom," R.O. said and walked into the coffee shop.

Chris and Heather followed right behind, all dressed in clean jeans, flannel shirts, and different parkas that still had the cleaner's tags on them.

"I'm glad we brought along a second set of coats," Heather remarked and took a sip of her dad's coffee.

"You're too young to get that habit, young lady," Jack said and pulled the cup back.

"Are you kidding? She drinks five sodas a day now," R.O. said.

Heather just looked the other way to ignore him.

"Time to eat? I'm starved," Chris said and pulled up a chair.

"Yes, but not here. We're going to a local restaurant that specializes in different ways to prepare salmon. You know, over on Kodiak Island they have some of the biggest salmon catches in the world. I bet the fishing fleet is enormous," Mavis said and took a sip of coffee.

All three kids looked at each other and then away quickly.

"Big ships, too," R.O. said and immediately got a kick from Chris under the table.

Within minutes the MacGregor clan was crammed into a taxi and on its way across Anchorage for their dining adventure. And a tame adventure it was compared to diving the Cayman Wall, trekking across the Serengeti, or crawling through a Pharaoh's tomb. The family dinner was filled with chitchat and occasional remembrances of Italy. Before long, all were tucked into bed in the four-room hotel suite and fast asleep. On the other side of Anchorage in a cabin nestled in the foothills, five people met and decided how they would deal with Dr. Jack MacGregor and improve their chances for blocking the oil companies. They weren't excluding any options.

4

Tastes Like Reindeer

Mavis MacGregor was up at dawn, packing and calling in a light breakfast for her family. Sorting through ten suitcases, backpacks, and shoulder bags, she quietly ferreted out clothes they had purchased in Italy, from those they had brought from Egypt, from those that had made the trek from Dallas. All the outdoor survival gear went into one pile while all the more tame "civilian" clothes went into another.

Reaching the bottom of her own suitcase, she found a leather box and smiled. As she opened it, the gleaming sapphire crystal of her Rolex Explorer reflected the light of the small lamp next to her. She remembered last wearing it the day she, Heather, and R.O. had left Nairobi on her search to find Chris, Jack, and Rebecca in the Serengeti. She casually slipped the diamond-studded dress watch off her dainty wrist and set it in the leather box. The Rolex slid on smoothly and she smiled again.

"Mornin', babe," Jack said sleepily as he walked into the outer room of their suite. "What's up?"

"Just packing. Did I wake you?" she asked.

"Nope. Got tired of lying in bed. After three lazy months

61

in Italy, I'm ready to get back into action. I can only take hotel beds so long, and eight hours a night is way too much sleep for me. Any coffee yet?" Jack said and sat down on the divan.

"Just ordered a pot along with some bagels, sausage links, and some cereal. Should be here pretty soon. I said 6:15. Might as well stir the brood and get them going. We've got to catch the flight at ten o'clock. I checked and the weather at Denali is perfect for a flyby, so we'll make it to the dinner at the Lodge easily by late afternoon."

Jack leaned over and kissed her softly. "You are super efficient, Dr. MacGregor," he said.

"I know," she said and smiled.

There was a knock at the door.

By seven o'clock, all five MacGregors were crammed into the small sitting room of the suite wearing flannel pajama pants and tee shirts. Chris had on a tee shirt that advertised an Italian racing company, Heather had one that promoted a fictional surf board company in Malibu, while R.O.'s was his oldest and most ragged Dallas Cowboys shirt. All three could have been typical teenagers around a breakfast table anywhere in America rather than a trio of experienced adventurers on a world-wide trek.

"O.K. Now here's the procedure for the day," Mavis announced and took a sip of coffee.

"I want the last sausage," R.O. interrupted and reached across and snatched it out of Heather's hand and bit down on it before she could take it back.

"You pig," Heather snapped and glared at him.

"Eyes here and mouths closed," Mavis said sternly.

R.O. made a face at Heather as he chomped on the sausage link. Chris took a bite of cereal and looked up, oblivious to the continual sibling interchange.

"Now, guys, listen to your Mom. She's been up working on our luggage and knows what and where everything is," Jack said and made eye contact with all three kids.

"I want everyone to take ski clothes, parkas . . . the 40-below ones . . . snow boots and hiking boots, four changes of underwear, and ten changes of socks."

"Mom, that's nasty," Heather interrupted. "Socks and underwear should match. I'm not wearing dirty underwear, no way."

"I didn't say that, sweetie. We're only going to be gone for three days max. But extra socks in the snow and ice are important. You know that. What are you thinking? Anyway, I want full survival packs made-up with compasses, thermal tops and bottoms, field knives, metal butane lighters, and two days of dried rations."

"How about some Taco Surprise?" R.O. asked Heather, who just frowned, remembering her days on the Serengeti Plains of East Africa during the summer.

"Wow," Chris said and looked up from his toasted rice cereal. Mavis stopped talking in mid-sentence. "I thought we were just going to a tribal dinner and fly over Denali. What's with all the mountain gear?"

"Well, your father and I have a little surprise for you. Seems like we've been invited to a ranger camp at the National Park at the base of Denali if the weather permits."

"Cool," R.O. shouted out quickly. "Are we climbing to the top?"

"No," Jack said firmly. "Not on the mountain, just around the mountain."

"But we are going to spend a half-day at the ranger camp and then chopper back that evening. So you need to pack everything I've mentioned plus anything you feel you want to take. Limit the weight to thirty pounds," Mavis said and took a sip of coffee.

Soon the breakfast meeting was over and all five MacGregors were busy packing, showering, dressing, and organizing the suitcases and packs that would be left in Anchorage and not touched again until their departure for China in a few days. By 7:45, they were all in the lobby, each standing next to a backpack and one large duffle. Cargo pants, hiking boots, colorful parkas of orange and blue, knit toboggans, sunglasses, and utility belts for the wilderness was the fashion statement. Tourists stared as they walked by this unusual looking family who felt more comfortable diving the Cayman Wall and climbing Mt.

Kilimanjaro than going to Disneyland, even though R.O. said he wanted to go back every year for the rest of his life.

"O.K., mount up," Jack said and smiled. "Our ride is here."

The gear and bags were thrown in the rear of the hotel shuttle, and soon they were on their way to the airport. By ten sharp, the twin-engine DeHavilland Otter was cruising at 10,000 feet and heading due north toward 20,320-foot-tall Mt. McKinley in the heart of Denali National Park.

"What's Denali mean?" Heather asked R.O.

"It means 'high one'. The native Alaskans named it that long before a prospector named it Mt. McKinley," R.O. said.

"You get high marks for geography, Ryan," Mavis said. "By the way, have any of you finished your papers on the Vatican? I told you when we left Italy that I would give you a two-week extension, and two weeks is up in five days. After that, it means more work and less play. I want the papers on the Renaissance in two weeks. Chris, the book on Michelangelo is in the hotel. When we get back, you can start that one. Heather, your additional assignment was Italy's role in the Axis alliance with Hitler."

"Wow, did I get lucky or what," Heather said under her breath.

"And, sweets, why don't you make that a ten-page paper instead of five," Mavis added after hearing the remark.

"Mom," Heather said quickly.

"You know the rules. Your homework is your ticket to stay with the family for the whole trip. You miss an assignment and it's off to Georgia with your aunt," Mavis said.

"Off to prison, you mean," R.O. mouthed without anyone hearing him.

All three kids rolled their eyes but knew well that their mom was serious about staying on schedule with homework during their year out of school. Mavis was calm but stern. Taking the three kids out of school for a year meant extreme discipline when it came to homework. The three months in Italy had allowed the kids to get ahead in their studies and cover what would have taken six months in a regular school classroom back in Texas.

"I've got my Vatican paper finished, Mom." Chris said. "When we get back, I'll go to the hotel business office and plug in my laptop and print it out for you."

"Same here, Mom," Heather said and smiled at R.O.

"Me, too, " R. O. said. He looked out the window at the Alaskan landscape, avoiding eye contact with everyone.

"Well, good. If I find that anyone is fudging the truth here, then I guess I'll have to go back to the physical science lessons," Mavis said.

"Well, mine's almost finished. Just give me a day or so and I'll be through," R.O. said quietly, still looking out the window.

"Very good. When we get back, you have one day." Mavis said and looked out her window at the winding river below. The snow-covered landscape was dotted with patches of brown and blue. Jack had his head buried in a small book titled *Drilling Methods in Arctic Conditions.*

"Look left. There's Denali," Chris said.

Everyone craned to see the mammoth peak on a cloud-less day.

"Awesome," R.O. said.

"It is definitely impressive," Mavis said as Heather crawled into her lap to look out the window with her.

The DeHavilland Otter touched down at 11:30 at Denali Field, which had a cleared landing strip at Wonder Lake Lodge. The heated runway left it clear in good weather with an alternate snow packed runway next to it for ski planes in winter. Within a few minutes the MacGregors were walking across the tarmac, each bearing his pack and heavy duffle.

As they reached the lodge, two black Hummers came to a stop amid a congestion of Land Rovers, Toyota Land Cruisers, and seven more Hummers. In Alaska after September, it was the only way to travel most roads, of which there were very few.

"The others must already be here," Jack said as he stepped out. Two young Alaskan native boys ran from the lodge to help them with their luggage as they neared. Within minutes, they were all standing in the lobby of the rustic lodge that had been assembled like a toy house of logs. The immense room was decorated with oil paintings of Alaska, bear rugs, giant moose heads, and Indian artifacts and clothing.

"My, my," Mavis said and walked over to a totem pole that was standing thirty feet high in the lobby.

"Bet I could climb it," R.O. said to Chris.

Mavis wheeled around on the heel of her snow boots and looked R.O. in the eyes without so much as a tiny smile.

"The rules apply, Ryan O'Keef MacGregor." R. O. stood up tall and looked up at her.

"No leaving the premises without Chris or Heather. No climbing of any kind and that includes totem poles and mountains. No approaching wildlife, no running in the building, and no snowmobiling without an adult. Got it, mister?"

R.O. swallowed hard and looked around, hoping he hadn't been embarrassed.

"Got it, Mom."

"Thank you," Mavis said and walked toward an original oil painting of Mt. McKinley.

"Looks like you're on a short leash again," Heather said sarcastically and followed Mavis.

"I hate her," R.O. said.

"No you don't. You just let her get to you, and she knows it and does it every chance she gets. If you didn't show that it bothered you, she would stop doing it." Chris said.

"O.K., boys, let's get the gear up to our rooms. Fourth floor, rooms 410 and 412," Jack said and picked up a backpack and a duffle.

Mavis and Heather wandered around the lodge taking in the beautiful Native American art and artifacts while Jack, R.O., and Chris hauled all the gear upstairs via a large elevator. The altitude was taking its toll, and soon all five MacGregors were scattered across the two rooms' beds and couches napping before the dinner that evening.

The afternoon was consumed with reading, doing homework, resting, and watching satellite television. By seven o'clock, all were dressed again and walking down the giant wooden stairway to the main floor. The glass windows on each landing looked southwest toward Mt. McKinley and the slight curve of the Alaskan Range that eventually reached all the way to the Aleutian Islands, having started in the southeast near Wrangle. Old black and white photographs of gold miners and early adventurers dotted the walls of each stairway, making it an enjoyable tour of eighteenth and nineteenth century Alaska. As they reached the main floor, the noise of the crowd could be heard. The snow-packed parking lot was filled with more four-wheel-drive vehicles, and a couple of dozen more airplanes were lined up at Denali Field. The sun was no longer visible on the horizon.

Flannel shirts of all colors and plaids decorated the room, accented with leather coats, denim pants, and unusual hats. The variety of hats consisted of fur, leather, fabric, some with silver, turquoise, and a couple with gold nuggets. The MacGregors stood at the bottom of the steps and surveyed the conference attendees. The overwhelming number of persons with brown or reddish skin told the story of the presence of the native Alaskan leaders, while others had the rugged and square jaws of the fifth- and sixth-generation Alaskan settlers who came from all over the world to tame this last frontier.

Nestled in one corner were three men wearing the robes of the Russian Orthodox Church. The tallest of the three had a red beard that reached the middle of his chest. He was obviously the elder. The others had black beards that barely reached their collars. Mavis noticed them and motioned to Jack.

"The Russians brought priests with them when they colonized Alaska. I've heard there are remnants of the Russian Orthodox Church in some parts of the state," Jack said.

"Yeah, Dad. We were in one of their buildings when the grizzly tore through the back window," R.O. said. "It was a monster, but Chris shot it with the .44 magnum."

"What?" Mavis said and looked puzzled, her eyes getting wider.

"There you go making up stuff again, little brother,"

Chris chided. "I told you that was just a video game and to leave it alone."

Mavis looked at the two of them while Heather walked a few feet away trying to avoid the coming storm. Two men walked over to the MacGregors and the subject was dropped.

"Dr. MacGregor, Mrs. MacGregor, and these must be the kids," the tall outdoorsman said as he reached out with a calloused hand and welcomed everyone. R.O. looked at his own hand afterward, expecting to see cracks or cuts from the man's rough skin.

"Senator McMillon, a pleasure to see you again," Jack said.

"Just call me Lynn. I'm not inside the beltway tonight," the senator said, referring to Washington D.C.

"Definitely a far cry from the Senate conference rooms in D.C. to the lodge in this beautiful wilderness. I can see why you fight so hard to keep control of it here in Alaska and not in Washington," Jack said.

"Your country is so beautiful and untamed," Mavis said. "I told Jack that we should have brought the kids up here years ago, but somehow we always vacation on an island with a coral reef or something. You know, one of those family things."

"Well, you're here now," the senator replied. "Let's mingle around. We start the talks in the morning. The Feds aren't here yet. They always arrive late. But all of the tribes are represented, and we're lucky the weather held out for us to meet here rather than in Fairbanks, which was plan B. We will fly up to Prudhoe Bay tomorrow and then take a fly-over of the Arctic National Wildlife Refuge the day after. But tonight is get-acquainted night, with no formal seating, just a large buffet, lots of small tables, and plenty of friendly conversation. We've scheduled all the yelling and fighting for later," he said and smiled.

Jack and Mavis nodded, knowing full well his meaning. Lumber, mining, conservationists, environmentalists, tribal corporations, citizens groups of Alaska, oil companies, and the U.S. government all had direct or indirect interests in the Arctic National Wildlife Refuge (ANWR), and fighting was exactly what would happen before the dust settled in three days.

Jack and Mavis shuffled off with Senator McMillon and two people who said they were with the Yupik and Athabaskan tribes, leaving Chris, Heather, and R.O. standing alone.

"I'm hungry," Heather said and turned to find the source of the rich smell of the buffet.

"Ditto that," R.O. said and started walking through the crowd.

"Better keep close," Chris said and followed R.O.

In a couple of minutes they were standing in front of a buffet table that measured twenty feet in length. Their eyes were getting bigger by the second as the aroma of five kinds of meats, over a dozen cooked vegetables, fresh fruit, and stacks of freshly baked rolls wafted in their direction. R.O. couldn't wait a second longer and grabbed a roll and took a big bite.

"Let's get plates and begin," Chris said and steered him to the end of the table. Adults were still standing around talking and sipping on drinks and hadn't attacked the food yet.

"What's that?" R.O. said and pointed to something that resembled sliced brisket barbecued on the grill back home in Texas.

"That's caribou," a voice from behind them said.

They all turned and saw a native Alaskan boy who was a little taller than Heather and dressed in jeans and a long flannel coat over a white tee shirt.

"Caribou, sounds interesting," Heather said and smiled at the boy.

"Yes, it's common around here, and I take it you three are not from Alaska?" the boy said and smiled back at Heather. "He's cute," she thought to herself and blushed.

"Texas," R.O. said first. "We're from Texas."

"I'm Chris MacGregor, and this is my sister, Heather, and my brother, Ryan," Chris said and offered his hand.

"R.O.," Ryan corrected.

"Nice to meet you. My name is Roy Nageak. I live in Barrow on the edge of the Arctic Ocean."

"I'm impressed," Heather said and blushed again, this

time touching her right hand over her mouth. No one noticed.

"That's pretty cool," Chris said. "What brings you to the lodge?"

"My father's the representative for the Inupiats on the regional corporation board. Other than that he's a whaler."

"A whaler? I thought whaling was illegal," R.O. said and forked some caribou.

"It's not if you're native Alaskan and have a permit, which we are and we have," Roy said and glanced at Heather. She looked away quickly and then down at the floor.

"Why don't you eat with us and we'll talk more," Chris said and picked up a blue pottery plate with the design of Mt. McKinley on it.

"Good idea," Roy said and stepped in behind him.

After about a five-minute cruise through the buffet line with two plates each full of meats, vegetables, and bread, the four kids wandered over to a round table near the window with a view of Mt. McKinley.

"I wish it were still light. The mountain would be a beautiful sight," Heather said and sat down next to Roy. A waiter brought over the soda and water they had ordered and set them down. R.O. was fast into the food.

Roy took a bite and looked at Chris.

"So, what are you three doing up here with your southern accent? Heather said a few words that I don't recognize," Roy said and took a drink of soda.

"Our dad is a zoologist with a specialty in endangered species and population dynamics. He works with corporations and governments trying to develop plans that would preserve wildlife while at the same time benefit human populations. He was asked to come to this conference by someone in the oil industry to get his opinion about caribou migration and ANWR," Chris replied.

"Sounds good. But what about Heather?" Roy asked and nodded to Heather who tried to hide the fact she had just taken a big bite of meat.

"Well, other than being weird, she talks like our Mom

sometimes. She's English, and Heather gets it mixed up with American," R.O. said and stuffed an entire roll into his mouth. "I just think she tries to show off," he continued with food sticking out of his mouth.

"You're disgusting and embarrassing," Heather said quickly and looked down at her food.

"This is pretty good stuff. Caribou you said," Chris said and looked at Roy.

"Yeah, it's billed as caribou. But I would bet a hundred bucks it's really reindeer. Tastes like reindeer to me. There's something about the flavor. They may have a Kutchin cook. They're from northeast Alaska and cook with spices that make everything taste like reindeer. Bet that's what it is even though it's tender like caribou. Reindeer meat is stringy and can be tough," Roy said.

"That's kind of like grass-fed beef back home in Texas," Chris said. "Grain-fed is always more tender."

"What year are you in school?" Heather asked, tiring of the food talk.

"I'm in the eighth grade," Roy replied.

"I am, too," Heather said.

"What are you doing tomorrow, Roy?" Chris asked.

"Well, I'm just hanging around here for a couple of days while my dad does this conference. It's too dark to stay at home. It's only light about four hours a day right now. Why?"

"We're taking a helicopter to the ranger camp at the base of Mt. McKinley tomorrow. Since my dad isn't going, we have an extra seat. Would you be interested in coming along?" Chris asked.

"Sure," Roy replied.

"Did you bring some snow gear?" R.O. said and swallowed hard.

"Inupiat live in snow. All of our clothes are snow gear. I have boots, parkas, the whole works." Roy smiled.

Chris and Heather grinned with him and R.O. turned red, but for just a second, and popped out of the chair and headed back to the buffet line, which was now becoming busy.

Heather reached over to Roy and tugged at the leather

cord hanging around his neck. A carved piece of ivory emerged from his shirt and fell free.

"That's beautiful. What is it?" she asked.

"It's a carving of a narwhal. It belonged to my great grandfather, who was also a whaler. The spirit of the narwhal protects me when I am on the ice. It knows that we need its brothers for our way of life and will help us find them," Roy said and took it off and handed it to Heather for a closer look.

"I think it's beautiful," a voice said from behind.

"Hi, Mom," Chris said and took a bite of the caribou.

"Who's your friend?" Mavis asked and pulled up a chair.

"This is Roy Nageek," Heather said, mispronouncing his last name.

"Nageak, like Nag E ack," Roy said, sounding it out.

"Well, Roy Nageak, I'm Mavis. Nice to meet you."

"Mom, Roy is here with his dad and has nothing to do tomorrow. I invited him to go to Denali with us. I hope that was all right," Chris said looking at Mavis.

"That's good. As I understand it, we'll be flying in a big Aerospatiale, and it's only the four of us, so Roy will fit in nicely. Roy, do you . . ."

"Yes, he does," Chris cut in smiling. "He lives in the snow."

"But of course he does," Mavis said with a tinge of pink in her cheeks. "Well, I'm back to table hopping. There are scads of interesting people here, and each one has a very strong opinion about ANWR."

"As does my dad," Roy said and smiled.

"Eight sharp, Roy," Mavis said and winked at him as she walked away.

Three Russian Orthodox priests sat down at the table next to the kids and began sipping some tea. They were quietly speaking to each other, not expecting to be overheard, especially by four kids busy devouring their food.

"Father Fefelov," the youngest of the three said. "I trust your trip from Alba was good."

"Yes, thank you, Dimitri. I was able to meet Father

Macarius at the Stavroniketa Monastery. It's always a thrilling visit to the monastery that sits so high on a cliff overlooking the sea. Greece is such a beautiful land. Father Macarius has been a hermit there for sixty years. The Fathers there told me that he must be nearly one hundred years old," Fefelov said, stroking his long red beard.

"One hundred. A long life dedicated to God," Father Kristov said.

"They believe he came to the monastery during the Second World War in an effort to hide from the Germans. And then he adopted the ways of the Brotherhood and simply stayed," Fefelov said.

"Was it a fruitful visit?" Dimitri, the youngest of the three priests, asked.

"I think so, hopefully, but I'm not sure. I have yet to analyze my notes and compare them to my research from my Vatican visit. My work with the Office of Sacred Artifacts first produced a solid lead on the cross about twenty years ago. I've been chasing leads around the world since then," Father Fefelov said. "It seems that it was last seen in the possession of a Father Cyril in Sophia, Bulgaria."

"Father Cyril, as in Cyrillic alphabet?" Dimitri said.

"Yes. It's a popular name in the Balkans used in honor of St. Cyril," Father Fefelov said. "Interpretations of a twelfth century manuscript kept referring to a cross belonging to the Holy Roman Emperor. It referred to him as the Great Emperor of Christ of the North. That was a new reference for Charlemagne I have seen nowhere else in history until an assistant to Pope John Paul II allowed me into the Vatican Library last summer. I was allowed to examine certain documents related to historical events and I trusted no one with my mission.

"I first found a reference to the Great Emperor of Christ of the North and a cross that was kept by the order at Ravenna, Italy, the last capital of the Roman Empire. It also mentioned King of the Franks. Then I stumbled across another reference that was in the diary of a Vatican priest visiting the Holy Church in Sophia, Bulgaria. If I hadn't been knowledgeable of the history of the Orthodox movement, then it would probably have slipped by. The priest noted that he saw a shrine below the floor of the church wherein a magnificent bejeweled but mysterious cross was placed," Fefelov said and sipped some tea.

"How did that lead you to Mt. Alba and Father Macarius?" Father Dimitri asked.

"My notes from the Vatican Library said that when the Ottoman Empire expanded across Eastern Europe, many of the shrines and precious artifacts of the church were moved or hidden. The artifacts and shrines at Sophia were moved by a Father Alexy, who later turned up in Russia, ministering to the court of Czarina Catherine II. It was from this court that two priests were commissioned to go to Siberia. And from there the priestly order is believed to have accompanied the first Russian colonists to Alaska.

"Since the fall of the Soviet Union, all precious artifacts in Moscow and St. Petersburg have been catalogued and accounted for. There is no mention of the cross or anything resembling it. All of the eastern European orders have accounted for items of religious significance in their possession since the Iron Curtain fell in 1989. That leaves only the Russian Orthodox Church in Alaska," Fefelov said. "I had no idea that I would find a trail that led from Rome to Moscow to our own beloved state. But Father Macarius had come from Russia to Greece. As I said, the others there think he was hiding from the Nazis."

"Well, we have our work cut out for us," Father Kristov said. "I will start immediately contacting the oldest of the priests in Alaska and try to work backward in time. If they are like most priests, they harbor a strong oral heritage and maybe some hidden manuscripts. I hope their memories serve them both on the history and where they hid things."

"I will represent the church tomorrow at the conference. Moral integrity is important among these proceedings and our presence will dictate that standard. Very few here share our faith, but all believe in the morality of right and wrong, even if they don't always practice it. My presence will be a strong reminder that God is watching and listening, too. Father Dimitri, you will fly to Anchorage to begin your search back in time in early Alaska. You should start with the Anchorage branch of Alaska State Library Archives. Father Kristov and I have already combed the archives in Juneau. We may have missed something. We have come so far, we can't stop now," Fefelov said and each man nodded in agreement.

Across the room, two men sat at a table.

"There's Dr. MacGregor now," Jean Claude said in his native French.

"*Oui*, so that's MacGregor. That's his wife coming to sit next to him?" Yves asked. "Attractive woman, she is."

"*Oui*, very," Jean Claude agreed.

"But soon it will be to her benefit when she has to find a new husband," Yves responded.

"I told you, Yves. I will not tolerate any violence. I only want to discredit Dr. MacGregor so that his findings for oil exploration will be dismissed easily," Jean Claude snapped back.

"My contact with the conference has given me the itinerary for the MacGregors. Dr. MacGregor will be here for two days in meetings. On Friday, tomorrow, he will fly to ANWR on a plane provided by the Northern Alaskan Oil Company. It will be a fly-over of ANWR and then he will land at Kaktovik if the weather is clear. There are no fronts expected over the Arctic for four days, so they have a window of good weather to fly. After that, he is tentatively planning a tour of the Trans-Alaska pipeline on Sunday and then return to Fairbanks. A news conference is scheduled for Monday, 10 A.M.," Yves explained.

"Very good. That will give us time to get people in place," Jean Claude replied. "I will stay with the conference to maintain our credibility in the matter."

"I'm going to meet with Paul and Marlena tomorrow and work out the details. The event they are planning will, as Americans say, throw water on the whole matter," Yves said in the broken English and staccato timing of a native Frenchman.

"Very good. The MacGregors are scheduled to fly out of

Anchorage for China on Tuesday. There's plenty of time. People are in place with strong loyalties just waiting for an event so they can play their part. We've had years of preparation for moments like this. Our reach is global," Jean Claude said and started to light a brown paper-wrapped cigarette.

"I'm sorry sir. This is a nonsmoking lodge," a passing waiter said and smiled.

"*Oui*, my apologies," Jean Claude said and put the cigarette back into the silver case.

"Patience is the key," Yves said after the waiter had left.

"I agree. If we push too soon, then we lose. Our job is to make the other side lose," Jean Claude replied and got up from the table.

Yves followed him through the crowd, nodding politely to people dressed in buckskin, furs, denim, and calico.

They had reached Jack and Mavis when Jack looked up and made eye contact.

"Jean Claude," Jack said as one of the men walked up to him.

"Jack, my old friend. It has been too long. Montreal was two years ago. This is my associate, Yves Montaigne from Paris. He couldn't wait to meet you."

"Did you hear that?" Heather said as the three priests left their table.

"I did. Sounds like a lot of intrigue to me," Chris replied and finished his dessert.

"Just boring history stuff to me," R.O. replied. "Don't tell Mom or she'll make us read about it and write a report."

"Vatican, Moscow, czars, and what was it that was missing?" Heather said.

"I didn't get that part," Chris said and got up. "We've got to go."

"Chris, you are no fun at all," Heather replied. "I mean, this could be really important."

The kids dispersed through the crowd and headed back to the room, unaware of the sinister events spiraling around them.

5

Totem Poles and Tall Peaks

R.O. left the room the next morning before everyone was dressed and immediately walked toward the lobby. When he reached the second landing, he leaned over the rail and firmly grabbed the winged edges of the totem pole. Swinging himself around to the front, he methodically climbed down to the main floor.

"Made it," he said to himself.

He looked around the lobby and could see only a couple of people and no MacGregors. He then reached for the first section of the totem pole and pulled himself up when he heard a voice.

"Shall I tell now, take a picture and save it for later, or are you going to be my slave for a week?" Heather said with her hand on her hips peering down from the second landing.

"Do what you want to do, but I am climbing this to the top," R.O. replied and began the climb.

The elevator doors across the lobby opened and out stepped Jack, Mavis, and Chris. They hadn't walked ten feet when Mavis looked up and saw Ryan halfway up the totem pole. She calmly walked over to the pole and looked up.

"Having fun, are we?" she said.

Ryan stopped, looked down, and took a big gulp.

"Yes. Yes, I am," he said and tried to smile.

"Good. Because you won't have much fun when you get down, so I suggest you stay up there for a day or two and when we get ready to leave, we'll let you know," Mavis said.

Ryan thought for a minute and then swung over the third floor landing of the massive wooden stairway and grabbed the rail. In a couple of minutes he was standing in the middle of a circle formed by the MacGregors.

"O.K. I'm toast. Do what you have to do," Ryan said and smiled, hiding the nerves churning in his stomach.

"I think we should leave him behind today," Heather piped up.

"Maybe we should have him shovel snow on the walks outside," Jack said.

"How about if he has to carry all the gear until we leave for China?" Chris said and laughed.

"No, that wouldn't be fair. He's just a twelve-year-old boy who loves adventure, and the totem pole was just too much to bear, right, honey?" Mavis said and looked down at Ryan.

"That's right, Mom. I just couldn't withstand the temptation, and I'm only twelve, you know. And since I climbed the mountain on Cayman Brac I've had this pent up desire to climb something else," R.O. said and frowned.

"Pent up desire, give me a break," Heather said and burst out laughing.

"I think the fair thing to do here, since you were aptly warned yesterday about climbing the totem pole, is to help you understand the culture behind it, who the people are and what the animal spirits represent. Really neat stuff, wouldn't you say, dear?" Mavis said and looked at Jack.

"Really neat," he replied and held back his smile.

"I noticed a book in the gift shop on the history and culture of the Alaskan natives, and I think it would be a wonderful book to read and write a five-page, no, make that a seven-page report. And I want it read by the time we get to Beijing next week, and don't forget the Vatican paper is also due. And if you choose not to do it, then it's off to Georgia with your aunt for the rest of the year while we enjoy this wonderful year of travel." Mavis stood still.

R.O. looked around and then up at the totem pole.

"If I do the paper, can I climb the rest of the way to the top?" R.O. said in a whiney voice.

"Oh sure, go for it, knock yourself out, because there's another book in the gift shop about the fishing industry in Alaska, and I think that would be very educational," Mavis said and looked down at him. Two little creases appeared on her forehead between her eyes.

"On second thought, one book will be just fine," R.O. said, knowing he had reached the end of his mother's rope.

"Honey, here's twenty dollars, would you mind going to the gift shop and purchasing the book for your younger brother?" Mavis said and handed the money to Heather.

"Mom!" R.O. said and made a face at Heather.

"I would be very happy to go find a good book for Ryan to read," Heather said and pranced away. When she had walked about ten feet, she looked back and smiled. R.O. stuck out his tongue at his sister when Mavis had turned her back to him.

Having said goodbye to Jack, the family got in a Hummer and headed for the landing strip where the Aerospatiale would pick them up. It was too cold to walk and try to juggle their packs. Roy Nageak had intercepted them as they walked across the lobby and had on a seal-skin parka and backpack. His snow boots reached up to his knees.

Soon the massive helicopter was lifting off the hard pack of the landing strip and climbing southwest toward Denali. There was very little conversation between anyone, including Roy. Everyone was awestruck by the majesty of the terrain.

The park ranger camp was found easily at the base of Mt. McKinley, a giant mountain that was much different from other tall peaks around the world. There was a lot of flat land at different altitudes that made climbing more time consuming and treacherous. While Everest and K2 were much taller, McKinley was no less challenging. Seventy lives had been lost over the years from attempts to climb her. The climb to the top could take three weeks, instead of just a few days, as was the case for Everest and K2.

"Mom, I'm feeling a little queasy," Heather said and rubbed her face with both hands.

Mavis reached up on the wall of the cabin of the helicopter and retrieved a small oxygen bottle. Connecting the breathing mask and hose to the bottle, she handed it to Heather.

"Take a few breaths on this sweetie and you'll feel better. It's just a little altitude sickness. You'll be fine in a bit," Mavis smiled and patted her hand.

The boys were glued to the window as the Aerospatiale made its final approach to the camp.

"Why can't we go higher than just the park area?" R.O. asked Chris.

"Well, I read that the winds on the mountain could reach a hundred miles an hour and the temperature can drop to seventy below during November. You wouldn't last two minutes in that kind of cold," Chris replied.

"You're right. Hiking around the park will do just fine," R.O. said.

"There won't be much hiking," Mavis said. "We're going for a ride in the park's all-terrain vehicle."

"That makes me really cold just thinking about it," Heather said.

As they stepped from the helicopter, each one looked up to the top of the mountain, trying to compare it to Mt. Kilimanjaro. Two rangers, a man and a woman, walked over to greet them as the rotor blades of the Aerospatiale came to a halt.

"I'm Dr. Richard Blake and this is Anna Hubbard," the park ranger said and took off his glove to shake hands with everyone. Anna did the same. "And the extra person is . . ." Blake said.

"Roy Nageak," Mavis said. "He's an Inupiat from the Beaufort Sea coast."

"Nice to meet you," Anna said. "Richard is the veterinary wildlife specialist at Denali, and I'm in charge of the law enforcement division. It's pretty slow around here this time of year, so we were glad to get the request to give you a little tour of the part of the park that doesn't include the mountain."

Parked next to the ranger's cabins was a large ATV with dual tracks for snow. It could easily seat eight people in comfort in its enclosed cab. Donning snow glare sunglasses and putting sunscreen on their faces, the MacGregors looked like mountaineering professionals queued up by the Snow-Cat. Heather announced she was feeling better and stepped up to the front behind Anna. Chris checked the time on his Rolex Submariner and noted that they needed to return to the ranger headquarters in about two hours.

The big ATV lumbered through the soft snow for about thirty minutes without the slightest effort. The snow-layered trees created a fairy-tale effect that thrilled everyone.

"This is the area where most of our wolf sightings take place," Richard said and pointed off in the distance.

"How many wolves are in the park?" Mavis asked.

"Not more than one hundred usually. The population fluctuates in size depending on the severity of the winter. The harder the winter, the smaller the moose herds, which then reduces the wolf population. It seems to be a strong predator-prey relationship in terms of continuing populations," Dr. Blake said.

"So they starve to death?" Heather asked.

"It's possible. But there is plenty of large game for food in Denali and other parts of Alaska," Anna replied as she drove the ATV.

"I heard that hunters shoot wolves from airplanes," R.O. said as he looked out the window.

"That's a big controversy. People who hunt for food and for sport claim that wolves are reducing the caribou and moose populations, so some have used that to justify hunting wolves from the air. Another plan moved some wolves from central Alaska to other regions so the large game animal populations could grow. But that doesn't always work.

Studies have shown that the wolves in Denali hunt the old and the sick from a herd. And some wolves have been known to return to their original home range after being transplanted elsewhere. Denali has about twenty separate packs," Dr. Blake said.

"I just can't imagine anyone shooting a wolf from an airplane," R.O. said.

"They don't shoot them from the air, R.O.," Roy said. "They run them until they get tired and then land and shoot them on the ground."

"Oh, my," Mavis said. "That seems rather barbaric. For the same reason, I much opposed the old fox and hound hunts in England, where there were fifty hounds chasing a scared little fox. Doesn't seem much different to me. Not much sport in shooting a tired animal who has lost its ability to defend itself through escape or its cunning nature."

"It's a major controversy for sure," Anna said. "It's not going to be solved easily. I'm just glad we have the laws to protect the wolves within the park. There are only about nine thousand wolves in the state, and we are losing about sixteen hundred per year."

"How do you lose them?" Heather asked.

"The number one cause of death is that they kill each other over territories and mate selection. The average wolf only lives three to four years. Then there's disease, lack of prey, and hunters," Dr. Blake said.

"I'm a hunter. There's nothing wrong with hunting," Roy interrupted. "My tribe hunts whales, seals, birds, and fish. We have a right to hunt them because it's our culture and our way of life. I would gladly stand on two feet and shoot a running animal to take its hide and meat."

"Roy, I'm sure Dr. Blake wasn't saying that about your tribe or any other tribe in Alaska. As we all know, there are good hunters and bad hunters," Mavis said.

"That's right, Dr. MacGregor. If we didn't have hunting of some animals, then the populations would get out of control and they would suffer from starvation and disease without natural predators to control populations. On the other hand, I'm not convinced that hunting wolves has a proven purpose. As a veterinary wildlife specialist, I'm well versed in the population dynamics of all the animals in Denali. But when it comes to wolves, the issue becomes clouded by emotions on both sides of the argument. I want good empirical data before I make a decision," he said.

"What's empirical data?" R.O. asked.

"Facts," Chris said. "He wants the facts, and then if you have the facts straight, emotion goes out the window. It's a matter of simple cause and effect, logic. I always like a logical approach to solving problems."

"Look, over there," Roy said.

"Good. I thought we might see the Toklat pack today. I noticed their tracks near here yesterday. They're about a hundred yards a way. We can stop and get out so you can take some photos if you want," Anna said and stopped the big ATV.

Within minutes, they were all out in the snow and Chris and Mavis were readying their cameras. Heather and Roy walked back down the track that the ATV had made to get a better view of the pack. There were four wolves chasing each other around a tree and then they would stop and growl and mouth each other in various forms of dominance displays and play.

"I don't see the alpha male today," Dr. Blake said.

"You can bet he's nearby," Anna replied.

Roy and Heather had walked a little further when Roy said he spotted a moose.

"Heather, over here," he said as he left the track and walked into the forest with Heather right behind him.

"Wow, is that a real moose?" she said as she walked behind him.

"Yes it is," Roy said. "But it looks sick or something. I mean it's just sitting on the snow. Heather, don't move," he said as he turned around.

Heather stopped in her tracks and stood looking at Roy five feet in front of her.

She heard a low growl. A chill went up her back and she suddenly froze. She looked out of the corner of her right eye and could see the big black alpha male wolf crouching, ready to attack. His canines were showing and his ears were laying back.

"Roy, what do I do?" she said softly, not moving.

"Don't move. Don't even breathe. I think he was stalking the moose," Roy replied.

Heather took a step and the wolf growled even louder and let out a sharp bark.

The pack of wolves that were playing near the tree about a hundred yards away immediately stopped and turned toward their leader. In two seconds they were on the run.

"Get back," Dr. Blake said, and the wolves passed within twenty yards of the ATV on a full run, ignoring the humans.

Mavis turned and noticed that Heather and Roy had wandered away.

"Where's Heather?" she said to Chris.

"That's the problem," Anna said and took off in a run in the snow down the track. She soon found where Roy and Heather had left the track and followed their steps in the snow on the run. She could now hear the growling male wolf a few yards ahead and could see the pack circling Roy and Heather. Quickly pulling off her right glove, she unholstered her Colt .45 automatic and chambered a round. Just as she reached the clearing, Anna quickly fired two rounds into the air. The concussion echoed through the trees and wolves scattered everywhere.

"Oh, gosh, I'm so glad you're here," Heather said and ran toward the ranger.

Roy just stood watching the wolves run between the trees and then regroup around the sick moose that would be their next meal. He understood the balance of nature better than all of them.

"Heather, what do you think you're doing?" Mavis said out of breath as she ran up.

Chris came up on the other side of the trees with Dr. Blake and R.O.

"Looks like we interrupted the big male's stalking of the moose," Dr. Blake said.

"I agree," Anna said. "He wasn't going to intentionally

hurt you. In the summer, he probably wouldn't have even growled at you but would have just run away. I imagine they're all pretty hungry, and that moose represented a lot of needed calories for this pack."

"He could have eaten Heather. I would have had a great story to tell when I got back home. I mean, how many kids do you know have had their sister eaten by a wolf?" R.O. said.

"Ryan, you are so sick," Heather replied in disgust.

"Ryan, you tempt my dark side too many times," Mavis said sternly, breathing heavily from the run through the snow.

"Time to head back," Chris said as he looked at his watch.

Ranger Hubbard holstered her Colt and led the way back as Dr. Blake watched the wolves move in on the helpless moose. The laws of nature would be the order of the day in the wilderness of Denali. Within thirty minutes, they were back at the Ranger headquarters, where the helicopter was beginning to warm up.

The Aerospatiale lifted off and everyone waved to the rangers, who were going back into their cabin to prepare for a storm that was coming. The rangers were happy that this might be the last storm they would endure before leaving Denali alone to herself for several months while they retreated to Anchorage for a peaceful winter. They would have to return in March for the beginning of the climbing season.

The helicopter seemed like a normal ride for everyone as the pilot headed for the promised fly by of Cathedral Mountain just southwest of the park headquarters before turning around and heading back to the lodge. All was smooth for nearly twenty minutes when suddenly an alarm went off. Chris looked up toward the instrument panel and saw the orange flashing light. He unbuckled his seat belt and stepped across Mavis and slid into the seat next to the pilot.

"What's happening?" he asked, already guessing at the answer.

"Looks like we aren't bringing in enough oxygen for the engines to maintain maximum RPMs," the pilot said.

"What caused it?" Chris asked.

"I won't know until I take a look at the engine," the pilot said and pushed a button that stopped the alarm. "We'll have to set her down and check it out. I can make it to a village on the Savage River just outside the park boundary. We would be only about twenty miles from Healy and fifty miles from the lodge at Wonder Lake.

"Twenty, that's not bad. Can we call for someone to come pick us up?" Chris asked.

"Not likely. That's twenty miles of pristine wilderness, the type of wilderness that would ruin a snowmobile in about a hundred yards. You either fly in or fly out, or not at all."

Chris looked out the front of the helicopter at the jagged peaks all around. He looked back at the worried look on Mavis' face and gave her a thumbs up. She smiled and relaxed, fully trusting her son's ability to analyze any situation. She had yet to learn about the adventure in the channel of Three Saints Bay.

In a few minutes, the Aerospatiale was cruising along about one hundred feet above tree level. The trees were covered with snow, and dead ahead plumes of smoke could be seen rising from a clearing. As they got closer, rows of cabins came into view revealing a wilderness town of about fifty cabins and buildings. Chris spotted a few trucks and raised his eyebrows, not quite knowing how they got there. People were coming out of their cabins as the chopping noise of the Aerospatiale vibrated through their small village. A large outpost of some kind, possibly a trading post, sat in the center of the cabins. The pilot spotted a clearing next to a sawmill and set the aircraft down slowly. The powdered snow whipped into a miniature whiteout. A few of the villagers came walking over to the aircraft as the rotor blades slowly came to a halt. R.O. was the first one out, followed by Chris and Roy.

"Greetings," came the words from a tall man with a black beard.

"Hello," Chris said. The pilot was still in the aircraft working on the instrument panel. "Our helicopter experienced a slight malfunction, so we had to set it down to check it out."

"Better to set it down than crash it down," the man said with a smile that showed a missing tooth. "How long will you be staying?" he asked.

"We don't know, but it may be overnight before we can get another helicopter to pick us up," Chris replied.

"We don't have any hotels, but I've got a cabin I rent out to tourists in the summer. It's not much but once the fireplace is stoked, it gets real warm, and it's free," the big guy smiled once again.

Chris stepped forward and took off his glove to shake the man's big hand.

"I'm Chris MacGregor, and that's my mother, Dr. Mavis McGregor, my sister, Heather, my brother, Ryan and my friend Roy Nageak," Chris said as the entourage joined him.

"A whaler, huh. Inland no less," the man said.

"How'd you know that?" R.O. asked with a puzzled look on his face.

"His coat, boots, and necklace. Must be Inupiat."

"Exactly right," Roy said.

"I'm impressed," Mavis said.

"Been around here for thirty years. It's like reading a road map when it comes to tribes," the man said. "And I've been rude, my name is Kurt Mortensen. I've got a trapping business, tourist business, sawmill, pretty much everything you see. Most of these people here work for me or do contract work. My wife and four daughters live in a big cabin up in the trees over there."

"Four girls. How sweet," Mavis said and smiled.

"Well, I reckon you should get your things and follow me. It'll start getting dark pretty soon, and the temperature will drop pretty fast. You're lucky it's just late November and not December or January. Another month and who knows how much snow we'd have on the ground," Mortensen said and turned to walk toward a cabin about a hundred yards away.

After retrieving their packs and talking with the pilot who had radioed in the dilemma, they all decided that staying overnight would be the prudent thing to do. A mechanic would fly in tomorrow and look at the helicopter. Mavis had relayed a message to Jack so he wouldn't worry, but she knew she would miss him since he had left early for the fly-over of the Arctic National Wildlife Refuge.

Once inside the big cabin, Kurt soon had a roaring fire going. It was clean, with the typical wilderness decor of wood and animal skins. There was one big room, with two rooms off to the side. One was a kitchen and the other was a bathroom. The bathroom was a two-seat latrine.

"The general store at the end of the village has bottled water and canned goods," Kurt said. "But mind you, it's run by a couple of women who are set in their ways about things."

"Thank you so much for your kindness," Mavis said and extended her hand.

"You're mighty welcome, ma'am," Kurt said. "Well, there's more dry firewood in the back in the wood box. The stove is wood-fed and there's no running water," he smiled. "I'll rustle up some sleeping bags for you and be back in a jiff."

"Thanks," Chris said and walked him to the door.

As he walked back into the big room, he heard R.O. over-head in a loft.

"There are eight beds up here. No sheets though," he said.

"We have clothes and parkas that will do nicely, and Mr. Mortensen is bringing some sleeping bags," Mavis replied and walked over to the big stone fireplace now crackling with activity.

"I guess I'll head up to the general store and get some food and water," Chris said and zipped up his coat again and put on his gloves.

"I'll go, too," Roy said and followed Chris to the door.

"Wait for me," R.O. yelled as he ran down the wooden stairs from the landing above.

"Heather and I will wait here by the fire and sit in these nice hand-crafted chairs," Mavis said smiling.

With their snow boots back on, the boys walked through the nine-inch snow. As they approached the general store, they looked up the twenty or so steps to a porch where an eight foot-tall stuffed grizzly was standing.

"Not as big as the one you shot, Chris," R.O. said.

"You shot a grizzly?" Roy said.

"Not by choice. Well, it was by choice. Either shoot the bear or become his next meal," Chris replied.

"That's awesome. I've never done that. Where I live we only have polar bears, and only experienced hunters are allowed to hunt them," Roy said.

When the three boys reached the top step, they could see lights coming on inside as darkness began to fall. Six hours of daylight was all that Denali would get this time of year. When they opened the wooden door that had glass panes in the top half, a little bell hanging over the door began to jingle. They stopped and looked around. It was a classic outpost store with hunting gear, fishing tackle, rows of canned goods, and even some clothes hanging on the wall.

"Can I help you?" came the husky voice of a woman who appeared through a door across the room.

"Yes, we just arrived and need to buy some water and food for the evening," Chris said.

"That was your big helicopter that landed, huh?" she said and walked across the room toward them.

She stood about six feet tall with short blonde hair. She wore a red thermal shirt that buttoned from the top and denim pants. Strapped to her waist was a Colt .45 revolver with an eight-inch barrel and zebrawood handles. She walked around the counter and leaned on it.

"I'm Ginna. If you need some help, just holler," she said.

R.O. nudged Chris and kept looking at the big gun.

"Looks like your little buddy there noticed my pistol. Sonny, this is bear country and with a good shot at ten feet, I can take one out before it wrecks my store," she said and spit into a cup on the counter. "Sunflower seeds," she said and smiled.

"Thanks, Ginna. We'll look around and get some things and maybe come back in a few minutes if my mom wants something different," Chris said.

The tall wilderness woman just nodded and smiled and

spit into the cup again. "I may have to make a delivery, so if I'm not here, just bang on the door and my partner will help you. Her name is Regina," she said.

"Ginna and Regina," Roy said and smiled.

Before long the three boys had gathered up some canned meats, pork and beans, bottled water, and some homemade bread. Chris paid the $30 bill with a frown. He had forgotten that this was the Alaskan outback.

The return to the cabin was a cold one, with the temperatures beginning to drop. When they entered the cabin, the room was already warm, and they shed their heavy coats, knit caps, and gloves. Mavis and Heather were curled up in the big chairs in front of the fireplace engaged in a good mother-daughter talk, which they rarely had time to do on this global trek. They could hear the helicopter pilot snoring from the loft above.

Once Chris opened the meats, sliced the bread, and opened the big can of beans, he rummaged around and found some metal plates and spoons.

"Home sweet home," he said as he set it all out.

When an hour had passed, they were all full and sitting around the fireplace.

"Which did you like best, Mom, the potted meat or the vienna sausage?" Heather said with a smirk on her face.

"Actually, I'm a spam girl myself. Reminds me of kidney pie back in London," Mavis said.

"Mom, everything reminds you of kidney pie," R.O. said and bit off a large piece of bread.

"I liked it all," Roy said. "Didn't remind me of anything I eat everyday."

Chris just laughed and was glad they were all full and nothing bad had happened on a day when a lot could have. But there were still four days left of their adventure in Alaska, or so they thought.

6

Yukon 66

———————◯———————

The Cessna 172 amphibian circled over the small town of Stevens Village, population 104, nestled neatly against the Yukon River on the 66th parallel. The pilot scanned the river to be sure there was no ice forming this early in November because all climate forecasts suggested an early and hard winter. With the equator heating up recently and massive amounts of moisture rushing into the atmosphere, arctic weather patterns raced southward across North America putting most cities into an early fall while others skipped fall and jumped directly into winter.

The Cessna lined up with the river and slid in as gently as a mallard duck sliding to a stop on a Kansas farm pond. Taxiing over to one of the many docks, the plane nestled up against four other aircraft already at rest. Two men and a woman were standing next to a black Jeep at the end of the dock. The pilot stayed with the aircraft while the other man, of medium build with wavy brown hair and a small goatee beard and pencil-thin moustache, walked quickly toward them. As he reached the reception party, he leaned forward and hugged each one, kissing them on each cheek, as is the custom in France and many countries. A large man with a black and gray beard stood to the side.

"Yves, I trust you had a good flight," one of the men, who's name was Paul, said in French. "We'll speak English for Marlena's benefit and for our new Alaskan friend."

"*Oui,* it was very clear and turbulence was at a minimum," Yves replied. "It's good to see you again Paul."

"And how is Marlena?" Yves said and turned to the medium-height blonde with a perfect complexion and bright blue eyes. She was wearing a leather coat with mink collar and cuffs.

"I am very well and anxious to talk," she said in a heavy German accent. "This is Mickey, one of our associates in Alaska. He possesses very important information we can use as well as an honorable history with the environmental groups we've been working with the last nine months."

Yves sized up the middle-aged Alaskan with the full black and gray beard. With a slight paunch, glasses, and infectious grin, Mickey seemed very non-threatening. Yves relaxed, considering his own two colleagues were dangerous indeed and the source of more concern.

"Nice to meet you, Mickey. Well, let's have some lunch and begin our discussion," Yves said.

In about twenty minutes, the four of them were seated on the second floor glassed-in veranda of the Aunt June's Yukon Home Cooking restaurant overlooking the Yukon River and the majestic mountains beyond. The sign of an early winter was prevalent, with snow already accumulating at lower altitudes down the sides of the mountains and scattered patches along the river. Stevens Village had twice that month experienced a major arctic storm that uncharacteristically drove the temperature down from 65 degrees on one day to 10 degrees on the next.

"During our meeting at Denali, Jean Claude suggested that we merely sabotage the visit of Dr. MacGregor to try to shame the oil company that supports his visit," Yves said.

"I wasn't aware an oil company was giving him support," Marlena said and took a drink of black coffee.

"By support, I mean they paid for his plane ticket. He

makes no secret of that. But his reputation is so widespread that this by itself won't tarnish him or his final opinion. We all know that as 'hired guns' of the environmental movement, we'll sell to the highest bidder. What's to keep our opponents from doing the same?" Yves replied and glanced down at the handwritten menu through his reading glasses.

"Nothing," Paul said and looked at Marlena.

"Marlena, Paul tells me that you have made many contacts this past year in Europe," Yves said. "Would you like to tell us about them?" Yves took another sip of coffee.

"My new contacts are offering support for our efforts in Alaska. Their agenda is global, so they feel that if they can assault the United States in any form or fashion, be it even through environmental sabotage, then they are willing to help," she said.

"What are they willing to do?" Yves said.

Paul smiled as the big Alaskan Mickey sipped his coffee and leaned back in the chair.

"We all know that the world took notice of the environmental crisis in Alaska when the Exxon Valdez ran aground in Prince Edward Sound. The loss of eleven million gallons of oil in a few hours in a pristine environment was enough to initiate action against big oil. The spill stretched for 460 miles, all the way to the Aleut Peninsula. The problem is that, since then, we have only had the burning of the Iraqi oilfields in 1991 and a few lost ships that have refocused on the problem. Now we are on the threshold of drilling in the Arctic National Wildlife Refuge and except for Washington politics, nothing is standing in the way of this exploitation," Marlena said.

"What Marlena is proposing, Yves, is that Alaska needs another major disaster to focus on the environmental crisis we're facing. Not far from here is the Trans-Alaska pipeline," Paul said.

"Are you proposing sabotaging the pipeline?" Yves said.

"Yes, exactly," Marlena replied.

"The pipeline has safety valves and pumping stations that would prevent a massive loss of oil. That was built in to the design," Mickey interrupted. "Then there is the satellite monitoring. During daylight season in the northern latitudes, satellites map out and report animal migrations and human traffic near the pipeline. There are thermal indicators for dark days and nighttime. Various federal agencies have specialized geographers who know this terrain like the back of their hands and read satellite photos every day. These agencies and NASA report to the National Security Agency any aberrations. When it's dark, radio telemetry devices and GPS can also do the job."

"Your man is truly full of good information," Yves said.

"Exactly so. But if the pipeline were hit in several sections all at once, the impact would be highly meaningful. The stock market would drop, gasoline prices would sharply rise, political bickering would be everywhere as to who did it, and it would serve as a great diversion from ANWR. They would have to ask the question then how oil was going to be transported from the North Slope without an even greater security headache. The safeguards built into new exploration would be costly and might, just might, drive the project into termination," Paul said.

"But how will this impact our Dr. MacGregor?" Yves said.

"We could make the hit three days from today. That would be Sunday, the day before the MacGregor news conference," Marlena said. "This is where our big Alaskan friend comes in."

Mickey smiled.

"You see, Yves, he helped build the pipeline and knows the vulnerable locations that would do the most environmental damage," Marlena said. "He has thought of things other saboteurs would never dream of and Washington doesn't have a clue about."

"And how can we move so quickly? We haven't consulted Jean Claude or the others in Montreal," Yves said with a frown.

"There comes a time when the window of opportunity is right, and now is the time," Paul said. "It's best that Jean Claude not know. He can truthfully claim ignorance."

"How can you be ready in three days?" Yves asked.

"I projected that this action might be needed and have been planning it for months," Marlena said with a smile. "The five aircraft are in place with enough explosives to cause considerable damage."

"How did you arrange this?" Yves asked.

"My contacts were in Europe, but the explosives came from other sources in the former Soviet Union. They were brought in through fishing trawlers from Iceland to the Hudson Bay territories. We trucked them across Canada in moving vans full of furniture. Our contact with a moving company in Montreal notified us whenever a family was moving to Vancouver. From there they were flown across Yukon Territory to Alaska," Marlena said. "There are so many aircraft flying at one time in Alaska that it's difficult to track any single aircraft. The smuggling was relatively simple."

"We met Mickey about a month ago at one of our private meetings in Fairbanks with the Earth Only group. They are the ones who spike trees, plant land mines in forested areas, and paint SUVs," Paul said and smiled. "He came highly recommended and after we checked him out, we feel he can be trusted."

"That's encouraging," Mickey said and smiled again.

"O.K. Enough talk for now. I'm hungry," Yves said and motioned for the waiter in the other room.

After an hour of eating and small talk, Paul, Marlena, and Yves got into the jeep and drove away. Mickey walked over to an old, faded, blue, four-wheel-drive pickup and fired it up. A blue cloud of smoke blew out the tailpipe. In a few minutes, he was traveling southwest toward the pipeline.

"Can your Alaskan be trusted?" Yves asked in a concerned voice.

"Absolutely," Paul said. "But we plan to kill him anyway when this is done. It's better not to have any loose ends. He should have made better choices and not gotten involved with those eco-terrorists."

They all laughed.

"I don't know if Jean Claude will approve of this. He

doesn't like to be left out when it comes to major decisions," Yves said.

"He will have to get over it. The movement is leaving him behind. The days of civil disobedience and politics are over. Statements today must be bold and very loud, and that's what this action will be," Marlena said. "I can handle Jean Claude."

"Who are your pilots?" Yves asked.

"They are all environmental action people with at least ten years of work in many organizations. We ran dossiers on all of them to be sure there were no undercover agents or federal moles. They don't know their targets and won't until twenty minutes before takeoff. They arrive every third day at the airstrip, never knowing what day they will fly. They, too, will be taken care of when it is all over," Marlena said.

"We will go over the details of the attack tonight — planes, delivery system, passports out of the country. Every detail will be covered. Did you bring the money?" Paul asked.

"Yes. I got it through in a very large diplomatic pouch that Jean Claude was issued. He is Canadian government, I remind you. Even though a solid comrade of ours, he is weak. But the two million is in my two bags. U.S. $100 bills," Yves said.

"When we flash this to our pilots and our Alaskan, there will be no hesitation to complete the mission," Marlena said. "I will then funnel the money into other organizations in America before we leave."

"Here's our cabin. We rented it for a month," Paul said.

Within minutes, all three were inside along with two million dollars in U.S. currency.

Just a few miles away, the old four-wheel-drive pickup came to a stop next to a metal shack hidden on the Yukon River just twelve miles from the pipeline. Mickey got out and walked over and opened the massive padlock on the outside. Once inside, he reached inside his red flannel shirt and retrieved a Beretta 9mm automatic pistol and laid it on the wooden table. He flipped on the light switch, revealing walls that were covered with tools. He opened a wall panel and turned on the radio, setting the frequency.

"White Fox, this is Caribou," he said as he took off his dirty cap and opened the Frigidaire refrigerator that was only about five feet tall and forty years old. He retrieved a brown bottle of Henry Weinhard's root beer and screwed off the cap and took a drink.

"Go ahead, Caribou, this is White Fox," the voice on the other end said.

"Contact made. They've got the greens, when do we take it? This is going to be like shooting fish in a pickle barrel."

"Give us at least a twenty-four-hour notice when they are ready to move and we'll be ready," White Fox said.

"That's a roger. Next cycle is 18, 12, 7. Caribou out."

Mickey made a quick mental note that he would make contact again in thirteen hours as he drank more root beer. The big Alaskan walked over to another cabinet and pulled out a drawer. From it he retrieved a Ruger Super Redhawk .44 magnum revolver and Colt Python .357 magnum revolver. The Redhawk would go in the leather holster under his right shoulder, and the Python would go under the seat in the pickup. Of course, Mickey always carried the lightweight, fast-shooting Beretta 9mm either in a leg holster or under his left arm. Sometimes he just tucked it inside his overalls inside the band of his thermal under-wear. It didn't matter as long as he could get to it quickly.

"No pea shooters for this bunch. It'll take the big boys and his sidekick to get this job done. Those eco-freaks won't know what hit 'em," he said out loud to himself and smiled. He finished off the last drop of root beer and tossed it into a fifty-gallon drum that was nearly full of the brown bottles. He raised his eyebrows and smiled. "Barrel's about full, so I guess that means the job's about done." He spun the cylinder on the Ruger Redhawk to check if it was loaded, and an even bigger grin ran across his face.

Two hundred miles to the south, the next morning was again unseasonably cold. The replacement helicopter wasn't expected until after 1 P.M. Wind whipped around the cabins, creating little vortexes of powdered snow before playing out. R.O. skipped along the snow-covered path through the village, kicking up clouds of snow. Occasionally some would rise above his head and drop down the collar of his coat. He would just giggle and do it again. He finally reached the trading post and stepped inside quickly and began stomping the floor to rid his boots of the attached ice crystals and snow.

"Young man, I suggest you go back outside and do that. This is not a cow barn nor are you a wild animal," said the tall brunette behind the counter.

"Yes, ma'am," R.O. acknowledged and stepped back outside quickly.

He began to stomp on the porch but noticed he had already knocked off most of the ice and snow inside. He finally gained the courage to go back in. As he closed the door behind him, he looked across the big room toward the counter and noticed the brunette was not there.

"Looking for me," said someone from his right, behind a row of shelves filled with bread, donuts, and pastries of all kinds.

Startled, R.O. quickly replied. "Yes, yes I was," he said and blushed.

"Did I surprise you?" she said.

"Yes. Just a little," R.O. replied.

"Good. You made quite a mess on my wood floors. Now we're even," she said and walked toward the counter.

R.O. followed her and stopped in front as she stepped behind the counter. He leaned forward and stared at the big jar of dill pickles sitting next to long glass tubes full of red licorice.

"Are you Ginna?" he asked.

"No, I'm Regina. Do you want me to go get Ginna?" she asked.

"No, I was just trying to figure you both out. Where's your pistol?" R.O. asked.

"I don't carry a gun. I'm Regina. Not Ginna," she said and smiled.

"I carry the gun," Ginna said as she walked into the room. The heavy boots she wore made solid thuds on the varnished wood.

R.O. turned and stared as she approached the counter.

"So Ginna packs the pistol?" R.O. said, trying to sound mature. "So why doesn't Regina pack one, too? I mean, aren't you afraid of bears?" He looked back at Regina.

"I don't have to. I've got this," Regina said and reached under the counter where she pulled out a Weatherby 7mm rifle.

"Wow, that's just like mine," R.O. said and smiled.

"Your folks let you have a large game rifle?" Ginna asked and pulled out the Colt .45 from her holster. She spun the chamber and emptied all the shells on the counter before she laid the gun down next to it.

"If you own a Weatherby 7mm, then you should be able to handle this old Colt," Ginna said.

"I wouldn't want to unless it was an emergency or something. My parents don't let me handle handguns. I haven't had a handgun training class, and they said I have to wait until I'm eighteen like my brother Chris. Safer that way," R.O. said and nodded his head as he eyed the big revolver. "I use my Weatherby for big game in Africa and for the mule deer out in West Texas where my family likes to go hunting. Handguns are for adults, not kids."

"Big game in Africa?" Regina said and smiled. "I used to live in Johannesburg, South Africa."

R.O. thought that for the first time he noticed a slight accent of some sort. But it wasn't strong like his mother's central London English accent and he was so used to her accent that he often missed the British, Australian, or South African accent of some people.

"You must be a good shot," Ginna said as she reloaded the Colt and holstered it.

"That's right, Regina," R.O. said as he looked up at the tall blonde.

"No, I'm Ginna, she's Regina," she replied.

"I'm sorry. I mean Ginna and Regina is kind of confusing.

I mean if I knew your last names, I could probably get it right," R.O. said.

"It's Ginna Bloom," she said.

"And Regina Hartley," Regina added to the end of Ginna's sentence.

"So Regina is from South Africa and Ginna is from I don't know where," R.O. said, trying to sound adult.

"Ginna is from nowhere, she is going nowhere, and it's really none of your business," Ginna said and folded her arms across her chest, wrinkling her blue denim shirt.

"I see. Well, I'm from Texas and proud of it. I think people should be proud of where they come from and not be secretive about it," R.O. said.

"Well, young man. It's none of your business where I come from, and I must remind you that you're in my village, standing in my store, and I have the Colt .45, not you," Ginna said and then smiled.

"Well, I guess you're right . . . uh, Ginna," he hoped he guessed right.

"What can we get for you?" Regina said and fished two long sticks of red licorice out of the bottle and handed them to R.O.

"Nothing. I just wanted to get out of the cabin until the helicopter picks us up. I can only take so much of my family," he said and took the licorice. "Thank you very much."

The door opened behind him as Chris and Heather walked in.

"I figured we'd find you here," Chris said and walked up to the counter. "I hope you haven't been pestering anyone."

"He's been just fine. We've been talking about guns and such and find your little brother to be quite knowledgeable for such a young age," Ginna said and put a handful of sunflower seeds into her mouth after spitting out a wad of hulls.

"Yes, he knows a lot. He learned it from our dad on hunting trips," Chris replied.

"And he blows off a lot, too," added Heather.

"Well you wouldn't know a Weatherby from a weather vane," R.O. said.

"O.K. guys," Chris said firmly. "Let's get back to the cabin and wait there."

"See ya, Ginna and Regina," R.O. said as he opened the door.

"Goodbye," Regina said.

Ginna just winked at him and then spit some sunflower seed hulls into the trashcan behind the counter.

Once outside, R.O. grabbed for the snow first and pelted Heather in the face. In two long strides, she tackled him and brought him to the ground. She then sat on him and packed snow around his head.

"Mom's going to be real ticked when you both show up wet and cold," Chris said.

When they got up and turned to look his direction, he pelted them both with a snowball and took off running.

"Gotcha," he shouted and raced through the row of cabins.

"You're dead meat, Chris," Heather said, picking the snow from her hair.

R.O. launched several snow missiles, just barely missing Chris as he disappeared behind the last cabin.

"My, we are energetic this morning," Mavis said and sipped a metal cup full of coffee as Chris and R.O. ran into the cabin.

Heather walked in last with her wet hair dripping in her face.

"Oh, sweets. What has happened to you?" Mavis walked over and touched her wet bangs. She immediately turned toward the boys, who coyly sat down without any expression on their faces. Roy looked at everyone, trying to figure out what was next. Mavis turned back to Heather.

"Honey, looks like the payback will be from the both of us on this one," Mavis said and smiled.

Heather gave her a hug and reached for a dry shirt from her pack to dry off her hair.

The door creaked open and the helicopter pilot walked in.

"I was on the radio and they want to drop the mechanic and fly you all back to the lodge. So get your gear ready to leave around noon." He immediately left.

"Three more hours," Heather whined.

"Good. Maybe we can find more wolves or bears to eat you," R.O. fired off at his sister.

"Well, I'm going to lie by the fire and just relax. I have a feeling we won't have much downtime the next few days," Mavis said.

Around 11:45, the pilot reappeared at the cabin.

"The other helicopter will be here in a few minutes," the pilot said. "They were finally able to locate a replacement chopper nearby."

"You heard him. Get your packs together and head out to the helicopter to transfer your stuff," Mavis said and put the coffee cup down as they heard the other helicopter make a flyby of the village looking for a place to land.

In ten minutes, the MacGregors and Roy were standing in the clearing transferring their gear to the smaller helicopter. Mavis turned and noticed Heather just standing perfectly still with her mouth slightly open.

"Heather, let's get cracking, girl," Mavis said.

Heather didn't move and didn't even look in Mavis' direction.

Mavis turned to see what had so distracted Heather and a slight smile crept across her face. Standing next to the new chopper was a tall young man in his early twenties with coal black hair, tan face, and striking features. The young man started walking toward them. In a minute he was standing in front of Mavis and Heather.

"Good morning," he said.

Heather's blue eyes were locked on his soft hazel eyes.

"Good morning," Mavis replied. "Thanks for coming to get us."

"Not a problem, ma'am," he replied. "I'm B.A. Luff. I subcontract with the Porcupine River Trading Company."

"Don't worry about the fare, young man. I am sure the officials with the symposium will take care of it," Mavis said.

Heather was still speechless.

"I'm Dr. Mavis MacGregor, and this is my daughter, Heather. Heather," Mavis said, taking Heather out of her trance.

"I'm happy, no I'm Heather, but I'm happy to meet you," Heather replied and began to blush.

"I bet you are," R.O. said from behind her.

Heather quickly glanced over her shoulder, sending R.O. her finest drop-dead look.

"I'm Chris MacGregor, and this is Roy Nageak," Chris said.

"Hey, Roy. What brings you to the trees, man?" B.A. said as Roy walked up.

"Hey, B.A. I'm just tagging along for a little excitement. You haven't been up to the ice in a while. What's the deal, B.A.?" Roy asked, giving B.A. a high five, low five, and a funny handshake with fingers and thumbs wiggling and twisting.

Mavis, Chris, Heather, and R.O. just looked at each other as these two obvious friends caught up on recent events.

"Well, let's get loaded. I'm on a timetable," B.A. said and walked back to his red Bell 407 helicopter that had a moose with wings painted on the doors.

"Cool chopper, B.A.," Roy said as he followed him. "You got it painted just like your Cessna. Awesome. And you have the flying moose on this one, too."

"Can't give up the flying moose, Roy. That's my sign. Someday I'll own a dozen of each and charter all over Alaska, and maybe by then you'll be old enough to fly one for me," B.A. said and draped his arm across the shoulders of the young Inupiat Eskimo.

"Well, if you can convince my father that I don't need to be a whale hunter, that would be a good plan," Roy replied.

In fifteen minutes the red Bell 407 helicopter, also known as Flying Moose 2, lifted off, sending a cloud of snow spinning around the cabins before it was high in the bright blue sky. Soon, the MacGregors were again in awe of the beauty of Alaska. By 12:30, they would be safely back at Denali, not knowing that even greater challenges awaited them over the next forty-eight hours.

7

Kayak Island

The twin Cessna 310 cruised above the Gulf of Alaska on a northwesterly course at 8,000 feet. The pilot minded the aircraft as the man in the right seat surveyed the navigational map and kept peering out the window. The skies were mostly clear, but the darkening horizon hinted that a storm was on the way, and it would be a good thing to find a place to land in the next few hours.

"That should be Kayak Island dead ahead. It fits the shape and we've been flying about forty-five minutes from Yakutat at 270° west. Our map reading could fool us but the GPS never lies. Good job, Father," the man said and looked out the window to the blue Gulf of Alaska below.

"Thanks, but remember, I said call me Vitorio. I know there are others out there looking for the cross and we don't want to accidentally tip them off," the priest said in his Italian accent as he adjusted the aircraft.

"O.K., Vitorio," Januz Lemanski said and tipped his khaki hat.

"Now, Januz, when we land we must first locate the lighthouse. From there we can ask around for the ruins of the village. I certainly hope the leads we got yesterday on Baranof Island weren't false," the priest said.

"Well, Vitorio. As an archaeologist and dealer in antiquities of all kinds, I have to tell you that I have had ten times as many false leads as I have good leads. That's part of the business and the game. And I do love the game. I am just fortunate you decided to team up with me when I was in Moscow. To tell you the truth, I didn't know the Vatican still had secret agent priests wandering the globe looking for religious artifacts," the archaeologist said.

"As a matter of record, the Vatican doesn't. As I mentioned before, I don't exist and whatever I find won't exist, either," the priest said. "I don't understand why you won't believe me when I tell you that I'm working alone."

"Alone or not, just don't go back on your word about the cross. The archives in St. Petersburg clearly stated that Charlemagne's cross was placed in a wooden box with other artifacts of equal or greater value. You get the cross to take back to Rome or whereever. I get the box and everything that's in it. Understand?" the archaeologist said and looked over at the priest flying the aircraft.

"I said that we had an agreement before we ever left Russia. And then you asked me again two days ago when we met in Sitka. For the third, and might I add, last time, we have a deal. I don't renege on my word," the priest said as he banked the plane into a right turn over the island. "But there is still no guarantee that whatever was with the cross in Russia ever came to Alaska."

"We'll see, my dear father. We'll see," Lemanski said and peered out the window.

As the Cessna glided across the island, a primitive airstrip was spotted next to a small metal building. After a couple of circles overhead, the aircraft approached for a landing. The aircraft sat down smoothly, as was the reputation for this fine workhorse of the sky. The plane came to a stop next to a metal building that had an old, faded, red 1952 Ford pickup parked next to it. A short man with blue coveralls, long unkempt beard, and scraggly long hair emerged and stood silently in front of the plane as the two men stepped out.

"What can I do for you, gentlemen?" the man asked and spit tobacco on the ground.

"We're looking for Father Justin, the Russian Orthodox priest who takes care of the lighthouse," the archaeologist said and then waited.

"That'd be about three miles up that way," he said and pointed north. "What do you want with him? You don't look like the Coast Guard fellows that come by once a year to check out the lighthouse. In fact, you don't look like nobody I ever seen before," he said and spit on the ground again, splattering tobacco spit on his old cracked boots.

"We're hear to talk to Father Justin about an important matter," Vitorio said.

"What'd that be?" the man asked and didn't move.

"That would be between Father Justin and the two of us. Not you," Januz said gruffly, stepping toward the man.

"Suits me fine. Just curious. Don't get no visitors this time of year. Just the Father and me. Wildlife types come here in the spring and count bears and foxes. We get a few planes in here during the summer months. You know, wilderness weirdos wanting a taste of the wild. Kind of silly if you ask me. If they like the wilderness so much, why don't they just leave the city and move out here. That's what I did. Lived in L.A. for thirty years. Nothing but hot concrete and foul-mouthed teenagers," the man said.

"I'm sure we'd love to hear more about your life experiences, but we're short on time, sir. We didn't get your name," Vitorio said.

"You don't need my name," the man said. "The feds don't even know my name. Why would I give it to two strangers?" the man said and pulled back his coat, revealing a Smith and Wesson .357 magnum revolver in a leather holster. "Just call me Bob. Bob works," he said and spit on the ground again. "Bob's worked for a long time."

"O.K. Bob, can you take us to see Father Justin?" Vitorio said.

"Will do. Why didn't you just ask?" Bob said and walked toward the old Ford.

Vitorio and Januz looked at each other and followed him to the red truck. The three men climbed into the Ford amidst tools and oil rags. The truck started immediately and purred like a kitten without the slightest exhaust cloud coming from the muffler pipe.

"Nice truck," Vitorio said, trying to humor Bob.

"Yeah, it is. I work on it all the time. When I'm not fixing stuff at the lighthouse for Father Justin or running my little fishing boat, I work on the Ford. Bought it in Anchorage and had it shipped over here when I moved out here a few years back. Just one road on the island and it's only five miles long. But it saves me walking," Bob chattered, obviously not getting to talk to too many people.

In just a few minutes, they stopped in front of the lighthouse. Next to it stood a small white Orthodox church. There was a whitewashed picket fence on the north side.

"Want me to wait or I could come back in a bit?" Bob said.

"Would you mind coming back in about thirty minutes?" Vitorio said.

"I'll be here. But you fellas better plan on flying out before long. Remember there's a little storm that'll be here in about four hours. You'll just have enough time to get across Prince William Sound and let the storm skirt right behind you out into the Gulf, at least that's how I'm readin' the weather maps on the satellite."

"You have a satellite monitor?" Januz said and raised his eyebrows.

"It's best you don't know what I got, buddy," Bob said and spit out the window.

As they entered, the Italian priest and the Polish archaeologist took notice of the dozens of lighted candles among the shrines of the church. Father Vitorio knelt quickly and then followed the archaeologist inside. A door opened at the front of the rectory, and a small man with a long white beard walked toward them.

"May I help you?" the old priest said.

"Yes, I'm Dr. Januz Lemanski and this is my associate Vitorio Luzano. We are looking for Father Justin," Lemanski said.

"I'm Father Justin. How can I serve you?" the old priest replied and smiled.

"Father," Vitorio said and stepped forward. "My associate

and I would like to talk to you about the history of your island and Aleksei Chirikov."

"Ah, Chirikov. It has been many years since someone came to my church to ask about Chirikov," Father Justin said.

Both of the other men quickly glanced at each other, worried that they might be too late.

"They come to ask about Vitale Bering and Aleksei Chirikov, the great explorers. They want to know if anyone ever found their lost campsite or the small church that they built and abandoned. It may be just a myth that they landed here and built a church. No record exists. Most who come are studying the Alutiq natives who had summer fishing camps here. Have I missed anything gentlemen?" the old priest smiled. "Because if I have, I would like to discuss it with you. It is a rare treat to have visitors this time of year."

"Father, you covered a lot of it very well," Januz Lemanski said. "But we had some other stories in mind. Do you know if Irina Baranof Yanovskii ever came to Kayak Island?"

The old priest frowned slightly and looked down.

"You ask a very good and quite original question, Mr. Januz Lemanski."

"Dr. Januz Lemanski. I'm a specialist in antiquities from Warsaw," the archaeologist replied in English with his strong Polish accent.

"I think we should have some tea and discuss this. Please follow me," Father Justin said and turned and walked away.

The two men followed him through the small door in the rectory and down a short hallway that opened into an efficiency apartment. A kettle of water was already steaming on the stove as Father Justin opened a copper canister and fetched three tea bags. He quickly retrieved three china teacups and saucers and placed them on the small wooden table in the middle of the kitchen. A yellow Persian cat lay curled up in the corner next to the heater and only looked up for a second at all the fuss.

As he poured the hot water into the cups, Father Justin spoke softly.

"Sugar or milk?"

"I'll take sugar," Vitorio replied.

"Nothing in mine," Januz said.

"How long have you been a priest?" Father Justin said and looked at Vitorio over the rim of the teacup.

Vitorio put the cup down slowly.

"How did you know, Father?" he asked.

"My son, I saw you bow, and the prayer on your lips only told me half the story. The look on your face told me the rest. Only a servant of Christ looks so humble before the cross," he replied and took a sip of tea.

"Then, dear Father, you know from my expression that I don't give a rusty nail for all the religions in the world, especially Catholics and you orthodox types," Januz Lemanski said with a smile. "I just want to own all of their treasures."

The old priest looked at him and smiled.

"Dr. Lemanski, the treasure that you seek is not the treasure in which we place our greatest value. You can have all the gold and gems that you can find and I'll gladly help you carry them to your plane. But the greatest treasure of all is hanging on the cross you saw when you walked into this church," Father Justin said and sipped on his tea again.

"And yes, Irina Baranof Yanovskii may have come to Kayak Island. I'm not for certain. Irina wanted to teach all the native Alaskans the Christian faith. So she backtracked across Alaska to all the places that the early Russian explorers had traveled. From St. Lawrence Island to the Kenai Peninsula, onward around the Gulf of Alaska to her home village on Baranof Island. She petitioned the Russian czar, Czarina Catherine II, to send priests to Alaska to help. The Russian Orthodox Church began to grow with the settlers and the natives.

Alas, as the colonies expanded and more Americans came, as well as British and Canadians, the church began to lose its stronghold. But we survive, even if in a meager form to this day. As Russian Orthodox, we are still here and we will never go away. It's not in our mission to surrender. May I get you more hot water?" he asked.

"Yes, please, Father," Vitorio replied.

"No thanks. One cup of tea is enough for me," Januz Lemanski said.

"But you didn't fly to Kayak to ask about a history lesson that any sixth grader in an Alaskan school could dictate to you. What treasure do you seek?" Father Justin said.

"Father, all I can tell you is that something of great value came to Alaska with the blessings of the czar," Vitorio replied.

"Alaska is a big country, my son. For a man to seek a treasure so small, it would truly take an army of men and decades of time," Father Justin replied and sipped his tea.

"We don't have men or time," Januz Lemanski said firmly. "We have only a few days. After that it may fall into the hands of men who will take it from Alaska and allow it to disappear forever." Lemanski was hoping inwardly that he would be that man.

"If Irina Baranov visited my island, she brought no treasures other than the Gospel of Jesus. That was enough for those here," Father Justin said and stood up.

"It's time for us to go. Thank you for your hospitality, Father," Vitorio said.

The two men followed the aged priest to the doors of the church where they left down the wooden steps. A cold breeze hit their faces.

"Looks like that storm is getting close. We better get into the air and outrun it to the west. I'm certainly glad you learned to fly when you were a priest in Africa, Vitorio," Lemanski said and walked out to the waiting pickup.

Vitorio turned to the old priest.

"Thank you, Father," he said.

"My son. Whatever it is you are chasing, it can only mean more heartache for you. I can see in your eyes the emptiness of the decision you've made. You must return to your first calling before it's too late. This pagan treasure hunter you've shackled yourself to will only bring you destruction," Father Justin said and clutched his hands.

"Thank you, Father. I'll remember your words. Goodbye," Vitorio said and walked toward the red truck.

As the truck drove away, Lemanski spoke first.

"What did the little guy have to say just then?"

"Just goodbye and best wishes. That's all," Vitorio replied.

Within fifteen minutes, they were airborne. The Cessna climbed quickly to fly over the rush of ground wind that preceded the storm. They leveled out at 10,000 feet and would arrive in Anchorage in a little over two hours.

Father Justin walked through the church back to his apartment. Opening a large cabinet where a marine radio sat, he reached down on the side and picked up a small cell phone. Punching in a few numbers, he waited.

"Hello," came the voice on the other end.

"Father Kristov, this is Justin."

"Father Justin, how are you, my old friend?"

"Not so good. I was just visited by two treasure hunters looking for artifacts from Russia. The connection they gave me was from Irina Baranof. That would put Czarist Catherine II on the throne at the time. You told me last year that if I ever were visited by such people to let you know," Father Justin said.

"Yes. You did very well, Father. What were their names?" Father Kristov asked.

"There was a young priest, Vitorio Luzano. I could tell he was from Rome. The other was Dr. Januz Lemanski, an archaeologist from Warsaw. They had come from Baranof Island and I assume the archives of the early colony either in Sitka or Juneau," Justin said as he adjusted his heavy cloak.

"That's not good news. It was Januz Lemanski that Father Fefelov encountered last summer at the Vatican Library. Where were they going from Kayak?" Kristov asked.

"Anchorage. From there, they didn't say, Kristov," Justin said quickly.

"Very good," Kristov replied.

"Be very careful. Something was not right with the young Italian priest. He seemed like a lost man, and lost men can be dangerous," Father Justin warned.

"Thank you, Father. Pray for our mission. We'll stay in touch. Goodbye," Kristov said and hung up.

He turned to Father Fefelov.

"They stopped on Kayak Island. They're two days ahead of schedule. We'll have to work much faster," Kristov said.

"But how can we do that when we are missing the vital clue that we need?" Fefelov said.

"I don't know. Maybe Dimitri can find it in Anchorage. Let's hope that God will lead him to it. Let's hope," Kristov said.

8

The Arctic National Wildlife Refuge

———————◯═════◯———————

B.A. Luff flew the Bell 407 helicopter, also known as the Sports Car of the Sky, on a northwestern course toward the great lodge at Denali National Park, where many delegates remained discussing the future of Alaska. The 407 glided smoothly above the treetops as the MacGregors looked excitedly at each and every large animal that was startled from its habitat.

"We'll be there in about ten minutes," B.A. said over the intercom. Everyone had a headset on to muffle the noise and allow for easy conversation.

"This is too cool. I love your chopper, B.A.," R.O. said.

"Thanks," B.A. replied. "I own this and also a Cessna Caravan airplane. My goal is to own an entire fleet, employ a couple of dozen pilots, and shuttle people all over Alaska."

Heather just looked at him with dreamy eyes without saying a word. Mavis noticed and smiled.

Chris was sitting in the left seat surveying all the controls and mentally rehearsing his experiences in flying. He could see Wonder Lake Lodge in the clearing ahead.

It was nearly noon and Dr. Jack MacGregor was also sitting quietly while the Aero Commander banked to the
north across the Arctic National Wildlife Refuge. Having
been in arctic conditions before, he was not surprised at the
desolate and raw beauty of the wilderness. He knew that
the arctic tundra was fragile and irreplaceable, but he also
knew of the needs of his country for the precious energy
that lay below its surface. It was a tough choice, but one he
was willing to make. Having spent Friday evening and
most of the night with the oil company experts and several
tribal representatives now had given him a different, if not
unique, insight into ANWR.

"Dr. MacGregor, would you like some coffee?" The
young woman in the red parka who was sitting across the
narrow aisle asked.

"No thanks. I've had too much already. I'm just soaking
in the view," he replied.

"It's magnificent. My company has had over thirty
years of experience drilling in Alaska and we haven't had
one single environmental mishap. Yes, our crews have the
same personal injuries from not paying attention to business, but our crews in the Gulf of Mexico have a similar
history. Oil drilling is a dangerous business. Any time you
have machinery and drill pipe moving with tremendous
force, humans can either make it happen or get in the
way," she said.

"I understand, Miss, uh, I didn't get your last name when
we boarded," Jack said.

"McKasson. Diann McKasson," the attractive young
blonde said and smiled.

"Diann, I'm from Texas. And that means drilling for oil
in the middle of ranches and farms is second nature. Some
oil companies have a reputation for safety and environmental protection, while others have a reputation for recklessness and pollution," Jack replied.

"Exactly," Diann replied. "But Northern Alaska Oil
Company has never had an environmental event. Yes,
we've had the minor tank spill or a mud pit that leaked or
a burn-off of excess natural gas. But never anything we

couldn't fix immediately. I would have to say we are the experts of the tundra drilling companies."

"You're very proud of your company," Jack smiled and glanced out at the coastline of the Beaufort Sea. "I was impressed with what I saw and heard last night at Barter Island. Your people seem to have covered everything. I was especially impressed with your wildlife biologists and their inventory of the Arctic National Wildlife Refuge. How many barrels of oil did you say could be produced?"

"Our estimates are that between six to sixteen billion barrels can be brought up. That would be enough to offset any needs we might have from the Middle East nations such as some members of OPEC. When ANWR is up and running at capacity, the United States can kiss Saudi Arabia good-bye. Our dependency would be over and the United States could, and I emphasize could, be energy self-sufficient," Diann said.

"That's impressive. If all that can be done without disturbing caribou migration or altering the state of the tundra with the exception of the drilling platform and limited roadbuilding, then as a zoologist I can't see that I can stand in the way," Jack said.

"My company will be excited to hear that, Dr. MacGregor," Diann replied and picked up her small laptop. She opened it and it turned on automatically. She quickly typed in something and a colorful website popped up. "With your permission, Dr. MacGregor, I'll pass on the message to my people in Fairbanks," she said.

"You can do that now?" Jack asked.

"Yes, this computer has the new wireless component, like my cell phone. Pretty soon all computers will be wireless. This one is a prototype my company acquired in Chicago last month at a tech convention. It works beautifully, just like my satellite telephone," she replied and began typing.

Jack leaned toward the window and looked down on the White Mountains as the Aero Commander flew in a south-westerly course toward the lodge at Denali. The bleak but beautiful mountains below were perched upon a major source of energy. Jack thought about the potential energy that was stored deep in the earth. There it had been deposited millions of years ago when life was plentiful and organic matter decayed under the pressure of the strata of the earth and slowly converted itself to the precious fuel that man now craved as much as food and water. Jack knew it was both a blessing and a curse, but he alone couldn't change the future, and the future could possibly lie below in ANWR.

The Bell 407 helicopter circled the lodge as B.A. Luff rotated the tail, turned, and set down softly on the small heliport.

"The moose has landed," B.A. said and smiled as he began turning off switches and shutting down the engine.

"Great ride, B.A.," Chris said.

"Thanks. Ever thought of taking up flying?" B.A. said.

"Yes, I have. I just earned my pilot's license last month," Chris said and immediately caught what had slipped out, but it was too late.

"You what?" Mavis said and leaned over his shoulder.

"Well, uh, I, what can I say?" Chris stuttered.

"Well, uh," Mavis said mocking him. "You can tell me what you meant by what you just said, for a start."

Chris reached deep into his coat pocket and pulled out his leather wallet. From it he retrieved a plastic card bearing his picture and the seal of the Civil Aviation Authority of Italy. The embossed green and gold card with letters in Italian told the world that Chris MacGregor was now a certified and licensed pilot. He handed it to Mavis.

"Well, I'll be a king's pauper," she said. "I have to say, I am quite impressed. That explains all those mornings when you said you were going on a long bike ride through the hills."

"I did go on a bike ride, straight to the small airport," Chris said. "I didn't lie."

"No, I guess you didn't," Mavis said and handed him the card. "How did you pay for the flying lessons? I know they aren't cheap," Mavis asked.

"I pulled the money from my savings account back in Texas. I went to the local bank and had the money wired to

Italy. I set up a small account and had the flying school draw from it over several weeks as I progressed in the school," Chris said as he took off his headset.

Everyone except Mavis and Chris were standing by the helicopter wondering what the deep conversation was all about between mother and elder son.

"Is Chris getting in trouble?" R.O. asked and looked up to Heather, who simply shrugged her shoulders.

"I think the discussion has something to do with Chris's new pilot's license from Italy," B.A. said and opened the cargo door and started unloading bags.

"Chris has a pilot's license?" R.O. said and rushed over to the door as Chris stepped out. "When are we going flying?" R.O. asked.

"Not for some time, at least until your father and I sort this out," Mavis replied as she stepped from the passenger door onto the cold ground. The skies were getting gray.

"Hey, Chris. That's really cool, dude," R.O. said and offered a high five.

Chris ignored it, knowing that reveling in front of his mother at a time like this would not be the best thing to do. Such news would have been better offered slowly in pieces over a long period of time rather than being blurted out like something R.O. would say as the thought raced through his mind like a West Texas wind.

As they reached the lodge, the MacGregor kids, Roy, and B.A. walked through the side entrance. Mavis went through the front doors and walked over to the desk and asked if she had gotten any messages. The clerk handed her an envelope. After she read it, she walked over to the kids.

"Your dad's plane will be here in a couple of hours. We're to eat together at the buffet that starts at five. So, let's head to the room and I'll order some sandwiches to tide us over until dinner," Mavis announced.

Tired from the full day they had already experienced, they headed to the rooms to eat a snack and rest.

It was 2:25 when the Aero Commander touched down on the airstrip next to the lodge.

"Diann, it's been a pleasure getting to know you, and I do appreciate the tour over ANWR and the briefing this morning. I can say that unless there are surprises about the environmental issues we discussed, then I can support your companies' drilling in the refuge. I want to reserve my final approval by saying that it's contingent upon a drilling and environmental protection plan that can be approved by the regional tribal councils. If everyone agrees, then I wouldn't hold back my support," Jack said and offered his hand across the aisle as the plane taxied to a stop.

"I'm thrilled, Dr. MacGregor. But I have to ask you one question. Did you have your mind made up before we flew over today?" Diann asked.

"No, not really. I had to overcome some personal biases as anyone would, but I was trying hard to be open-minded. There was no way an intelligent person would make a decision on just a fly-over. I wanted to meet your drilling officers and check their attitude and find out their true feelings about Alaska. I wanted to examine your drilling history and experience. I wanted to see what financial investment your company was willing to risk and whether it understands all the environmental safeguards. What I saw were a group of people who love their jobs, love the adventure, and most importantly love Alaska. I can't say I've always seen that with oil and gas drilling operations in Texas, Oklahoma, or Louisiana.

"As I said, there are some good ones and some bad ones. From the transportation of drilling equipment, drill pipe, drill collars, and mud pits, all the way to the extraction of the crude, I felt your people were treating the operation like a surgeon would a patient, slowly, carefully, and efficiently. I can't ask for more," Jack said and unbuckled his seat belt.

"Can I quote you on that?" Diann said and smiled as she typed furiously into her laptop computer.

"Sure, but no embellishing, please," Jack smiled.

"Roger that, Doctor," she replied.

Soon they were standing on the tarmac of the small airfield, and Diann turned to Dr. MacGregor.

"Now, don't forget. We have a date Monday at the press conference in Anchorage," she smiled.

"I won't forget," Jack said.

"Thanks," Diann replied. "Till then, stay warm. Winter has arrived early this year, I'm afraid. Our drilling crews have been on alert for the past two weeks. That's Alaskan weather. Never know when the Arctic weather patterns are going to rush across the pole and surprise you. Take care," she said as she walked away.

Jack thought for a minute how Diann's vivacious personality and love for flair reminded him so much of Mavis. He was looking forward to seeing Mavis. He turned to see R.O. waving from the small hangar on the edge of the runway.

"Hey dad," R.O. shouted as he walked over to him with his satchel slung over his shoulder.

"Hey, R.O.," Jack said and leaned over and gave him a big hug. "How was your trip to Denali, big guy?" Jack asked.

"It was way too cool, Dad. I mean I have never seen so much snow in my life. It was unbelievable. Heather and Mom did great, and the air was so thin I had to take big breaths to breathe. The snow was like, you know, those little styrofoam peanuts that come in boxes, you know, for padding, that just float on air and stick to you? You know what I mean?" R.O. asked. "And then Heather almost got eaten by a wolf."

"She what?" Jack asked.

"Heather and Roy walked away from the track toward a dying moose and were attacked by a pack of wolves. I mean the big black one nearly got her, Dad," R.O. said as they walked along.

"Whoa, pardner," Jack said and stopped walking toward the lodge. "So you just got back?" Jack asked.

"No. We've been here a couple of hours up in the rooms. Mom said you would be in by 2:30, and we were in the lobby just hanging out when B.A. said that he thought the Aero Commander was the plane you were on. He knows the pilot who flies for the oil company," R.O. said.

"Who's B.A.?" Jack said.

"He's the guy who flies the helicopter who got Chris into trouble for getting a pilot's license while we were in Italy," R.O. said. "The same pilot who picked us up after our helicopter crash-landed in the village in the forest near Denali."

"B.A. what? What pilot's license? Who crash-landed what?" Jack asked.

"The one that Chris got in Italy from doing all those bike rides and transferred money from the bank in Texas to a bank in Italy," R.O. said. "Dad, come on, keep up. I've got stuff to tell you."

"Well, I suggest you save it until we're inside the lodge and I have a chance to speak with your mother. Deal?" Jack asked with a frown on his forehead.

"Well, O.K. Deal," R.O. said and turned to walk beside his father the remaining two hundred yards from the airstrip to the lodge.

As they entered the lodge, Jack saw his family all slouched around the couches and chairs in the lobby outside the dining room. Jack noticed that Heather was talking to a nice-looking young man, and Chris and Mavis were in a deep discussion. Roy was asleep on a separate couch with his fur parka pulled up over his head. Mavis saw Jack and immediately stood up and walked his direction. They embraced and kissed.

"Ooh. I hate that," R.O. said as he looked away.

"Well, it appears you were in a deep discussion with young Lindbergh, I see," Jack said and smiled warmly.

"I'll see you later, Dad," Chris said and walked toward the gift shop.

"Oh. You know already. But of course, our number two son and his motor mouth is suppressed by nothing, not even Alaska's sometimes harsh weather, or even proper manners," Mavis said and gave R.O. a look that would have killed a grizzly.

R.O. turned and walked toward B.A. and Heather without looking back.

"Well, what's the story?" Jack said and dropped his backpack on the floor and unzipped his down parka and dropped it on top of the pack.

"Nothing exciting. Just our son took flying lessons the last three months while we were in Italy and you were galavanting all over Europe attending one conference after the next," Mavis said with acid in her tone.

"Galavanting. Galavanting? I see. So if I had spent more time with Chris and the family, then he wouldn't have taken the opportunity to spend three months in a beautiful country, learn a new language, experience a possibly life-changing event like flying, and bond more with his father instead. Is that what you're saying?" Jack said and smiled and squinted his eyes at the same time.

"Well, if you put it that way. I really don't have much of an argument, do I? I'm glad the children can't hear me say this. Yes, I am very glad of that," she replied and pulled her hair over her right ear and away from her face.

"Mom is really ticked off," Heather said as she looked over at Mavis.

"I guess Chris let the cat out of the bag, so to speak," B.A. said and stood up.

"Heather, it's been good talking to you. Enjoy your stay in Alaska," B.A. said and walked away.

Heather stood up and watched her dream disappear. She let out a heavy sigh and walked over and plopped down on the end of the couch next to Roy, who was snoring.

"Males. I just don't get them," she said and pulled her sweater hood down over her face.

"Well, it's spilled milk. We must move forward and show Chris how much we are impressed with his courage and ingenuity. After all, honey, how many young men would have done the same thing? He did fly the helicopter away from a dangerous ambush in Egypt, didn't he?" Jack asked and gave Mavis another soft hug.

"You are such a soft touch, Jack MacGregor. It's a wonder our children aren't spoiled rotten to the core," Mavis said and kissed him on the cheek. "I concur. Chris is a courageous young man and we should be proud of him." Mavis then pushed back from Jack. "As long as he has his Chaucer assignment completed by Friday," Mavis said sternly and then gave Jack a big smile.

"I'll insist on it personally," Jack said.

As Jack and Mavis walked over to the four kids, Heather nudged Roy and he stopped snoring. She then got up and walked over and hugged her dad.

"Glad you're back, Dad," Heather said.

"Heard you had a close call with a wolf," Jack said.

"It wasn't too bad. I'm fine now," Heather replied.

"And we had a crash-landing in the forest too?" Jack said turning to Mavis.

Mavis turned quickly and looked at R.O., who was on his way up the stairs by the totem pole in a fast walk.

"Looks like we're back to normal again," Jack said and smiled.

9

Chocolate Mousse
and Caribou

The MacGregors had just wolfed down dinner without much discussion when the two Russian Orthodox priests walked into the dining room. R.O. was the first to finish and was playing with the remainder of his English peas and petit onions when he noticed the two men dressed in their robes. Mavis and Jack were talking about whether they would all make the trip to Barrow or whether they would split up again.

After the reaction that Jack had gotten from Mavis about Chris' flying lessons, he was leaning more toward everyone sticking together. He knew that in three days he had to meet Diann for a plane ride down the pipeline route and then the press conference. From a professional viewpoint, he had to have as many Alaskan experiences as possible if his opinion about the Arctic National Wildlife Refuge was going to have any credibility.

R.O. got out of his chair and wandered across the dining room among the crowd of tourists and people who had come for the conference. He eventually made it to the buffet line where he found a large bowl of chilled chocolate mousse. Even though he was full, he reached out and retrieved a bowl and was about to spoon out some of the chocolate dessert when a booming voice rang out behind him.

"May I be of some help, young man?" Father Fefelov asked.

"No, thanks," R.O. said and became wide-eyed when he turned and saw the tall man with long red beard and flowing robe. "I can just reach it."

"Very good then. I will wait to see if you leave me a portion. It is such a delightful dessert," Father Fefelov said and smiled.

R.O. noticed that his front teeth were crooked and then looked back at the large bowl and began scooping the dessert into his new bowl. When he turned around, he looked at the priest.

"I didn't see any churches around here. Are you here on vacation?" R.O. asked.

"Some would say so. But we're here to offer special blessings on this conference and be a visual reminder that God is watching and wants all men to live in harmony," the priest said and picked up the spoon in the chocolate mousse.

"Wow. My dad would say that's a pretty tall order," R.O. replied and leaned over and licked the top of the pile of chocolate mousse in his plate.

"It's always a tall order when God is involved, young man," Father Fefelov said and smiled. "It's been nice talking to you, uh, your name is?"

"R.O., that's short for Ryan O'Keef MacGregor," R.O. said.

"So you must be one of the three MacGregor children. Your father is quite the famous scientist. This conference is fortunate indeed to have his input. Mr. MacGregor, I will say a special prayer for your family so that you will have an enjoyable and safe journey while in Alaska. Good evening," Father Fefelov said and bowed.

R.O. noticed that the tip of his red beard slightly dipped into his bowl of chocolate mousse. He thought it best not to say anything.

"Good evening," R.O. replied and began to wander through the crowd of people back to the table.

When he arrived, everyone had finished eating, and Heather had already left to go up to her room. Roy was bowing out just as he walked up.

"Well, off to the bed. I'm pooped. Let me know if you want to go north tomorrow," Roy said to Jack.

"I will, Roy. Your father had already invited us before I left for ANWR yesterday. At the time, I didn't know the schedule that Northern Alaskan Oil had mapped out for me. Now I know I have a few days before the pipeline tour, and we might be able to swing it. Tell your dad I'll call him in the morning," Jack said.

"Sure thing, Dr. MacGregor. Later," Roy said and left.

"Later, dude," R.O. said and waved.

"Looks like you found a bowl of sugar, my little one," Mavis said and took a sip of coffee. She was finally beginning to relax.

"Yup. Been talking to a tall priest with a red beard," R.O. said and took a big bite. "He looked just like the picture at the bear cabin. Except the live one had a red beard. Remember that one, Chris?" R.O. said and took another bite.

Realizing that avoiding another issue was impossible, Chris decided to go along.

"Yes, I do. That was one of the saints," Chris said.

"How interesting," Mavis said. "And how were you both introduced to this wonderful saint in a bear cabin?" she asked, very slowly leaning back in her chair waiting for yet another major revelation from her boys.

"Well, Mom, we were driving through the forest at least fifty miles an hour on the dog sleds in the worst blizzard you've ever seen. It was so bad when suddenly through the storm we spotted this blue onion-shaped dome on an old cabin. You know, like a church steeple," R.O. began with chocolate mousse all over his mouth. "Then we ran up to the door and Chris pulled out the Colt Anaconda .44 magnum that Trader Jim gave him and blew the lock off the door with one shot. We ran the dogs inside so they wouldn't freeze 'cause the storm was getting worse. Heather started a big fire. I mean she could have burned the place down, when suddenly a giant, I mean a really humongous, mean, ugly grizzly, tears down the back wall and ran in just as we were running out the front door. He must have been twelve or fourteen feet tall, and Chris whipped out the big gun and shot him dead, or so we thought. Man this mousse is great," R.O. said and took another bite.

Mavis sipped her coffee again, trying to hide her amazement at R.O.'s intense and vivid imagination, which sometimes worried her. Jack leaned forward on the table and continued to listen intently.

"Well, we took off, I mean Heather and me, and left Chris with the bear. But we got down the path and heard Chris's cannon go off again and thought maybe he was dead or something, so Heather went back and there lay this giant bear on top of the dog sled. I mean the sled was crushed flatter than an armadillo on a Texas blacktop," R.O. said and took another bite.

"And so here you are today, all safe and sound," Mavis smiled and took another sip of coffee. "Now, Christopher. I would like for you to tell me and your father what really happened before I punish Ryan for telling such a big foolish story."

Chris fumbled around with the fork on his plate and set it down carefully.

"That's pretty much what happened," Chris said and looked his parents in the eyes.

"Son, the joke's over. We want to know what happened," Jack said in a very solemn voice.

"Dad, when did you ever know me to tell a lie? Sure, I haven't always shared every minute of my life with you . . ."

"No kidding," interrupted Mavis.

"But I don't lie. There was a bad storm. We hid in an old Orthodox church. I shot a huge bear that somehow survived because the bullet creased his skull and knocked him out but didn't kill him. He woke up and chased us down and I had to shoot him again. You might as well know the rest," Chris said.

"There's more," Mavis and Jack said in unison and looked at each other.

"Hon, I need more coffee," Mavis said and stood up, straightened her pants, and sat back down.

"Continue," she said in a businesslike tone.

Chris spent the next thirty minutes detailing everything from leaving Trader Jim's lodge, the bear chase, rescue at sea, and the flight to Anchorage. Mavis drank three cups of coffee and was now pretty wired.

"And you have a pilot's license from the Italian Aviation Administration," she finished. "I think that's it or something close."

"Civil Aviation Administration of Italy. Yes. But it's a dual license. It's for fixed wing and rotary wing aircraft," Chris replied.

"Airplanes and helicopters?" Jack asked.

"Yes, dad."

"Way cool, dude. Chris you're the best," R.O. said and grinned with chocolate all over his mouth.

"And when were you planning on sharing your secret life with us in detail, may I ask?" Mavis said, playing her British accent to the fullest, which she did from time to time. "And did you find any little Italian girls you want to tell us about?" Mavis added and raised her eyebrows.

"No, Mom," Chris frowned at her. "Natalie is my girl-friend. I was going to tell you, Mom. Really I was. I just knew that it was something I had to do, and I didn't think you would probably let me if I asked. I mean, Natalie and I nearly got killed at Asyut, and Jennifer January wouldn't have made it back with the photos of the sunken obelisk for Dr. Carpenter if I hadn't been aware enough about flying to save us all. I just thought I should know how to do it right. It was just too close of a call. Who knows what we're going to encounter for the rest of this year-long journey when I might need to know how to fly a helicopter or an airplane?"

"He's right, honey," Jack said and put his hand on Mavis's hand, which was tightly gripped around a spoon on the table. "Chris is a man now. He's survived hurricanes, elephant poachers, sandstorms . . ."

"Oh, my, don't bring up that silly mistake. I should have never driven a BMW into the desert on a picnic. How stupid of me," Mavis said and smiled sheepishly. "Alright. I forgive you. But I want your word, Christopher MacGregor, that if you have any further such impulses you will discuss them thoroughly with your father and me. In exchange, I promise I will be open-minded for the first ten minutes of the conversation before I say no."

"Ten minutes!" Chris said in astonishment.

"I got you on that one," Mavis said and smiled. "Let me say that I won't limit the time that I will be open-minded as long as you won't limit the things that you tell me."

"Good point, Mom," Chris said and got up and walked around the table and gave her a hug. Then he hugged his dad.

"Does this mean Chris and I get to go flying tomorrow?"

"No!" Jack and Mavis said in unison.

"O.K., O.K., I was just making a suggestion," R.O. said and wiped the chocolate off his mouth.

"I believe that a good night's rest is what we all need," Mavis said as they stood up and left the dining room.

Across the room, Father Fefelov felt the cell phone vibrating in the front pocket of his robe. He retrieved it and spoke softly.

"Hello," he said.

"Father, this is Dimitri," the voice said. "Have you any news?"

"We heard from Father Justin about a Vatican priest and the Polish archaeologist who are working their way across Alaska at a very high speed, as we speak," Father Fefelov replied and described the two men to him.

"Yes, Father. I saw them today. They were entering the Alaska State Library branch in Anchorage as I was leaving. They fit Father Justin's descriptions perfectly. I'm sure they have all the same information that we have now. And I'm also sure that they will get the same new information that I got today," Dimitri said.

"And what leads are those? We're getting so very close, Dimitri. But I am afraid we will be too late," Fefelov said.

"You've told me to always have faith, Father," the younger priest replied.

"Ah, yes. This is another one of my sermons coming back to haunt me. Thank you for reminding me. Father Kristov and I will review our plan tonight with the maps and the diary copies from the Vatican," Fefelov said.

"I can't get to Denali in time for you to follow this new trail. I need to stay in Anchorage and track some other sources that may be important if this doesn't pan out, to use a gold mining term, if I may. You and Father Kristov can check this one out. I discovered that the person with whom we need to speak is a Mrs. Natasha Novotski. She is a retired librarian and authority on our church and native Alaskans. I will fax it all to the lodge as soon as we hang up," Dimitri said.

"Very good, Dimitri. Thank you. Father Kristov and I will check this one out first thing in the morning," Father Fefelov said. "God be with you."

"And with you too, Father," Dimitri said and hung up.

Without speaking, the two older priests got up and left the dining hall and returned to their rooms on the third floor. As they opened their door, they noticed R.O. walking down the hall with an ice bucket in his hand.

"Hey, Father. Get enough of that mousse?" R.O. quipped as he walked by.

"Yes, son. I did, and it was just absolutely wonderful," Fefelov replied and smiled.

R.O. stopped at the doorway to the priest's room and glanced inside.

"Nice room but a lot smaller than our suite. We have three bedrooms and a great view," R.O. said.

"Father Kristov and I don't require much space. Just a place to lie down for a night's rest," Fefelov replied.

"No shower or television?" R.O. asked with a frown on his head.

"Absolutely a shower and a television. Even priests need a good hot bath and to watch international news and sports," Fefelov replied.

"Sports? Who's your team?" R.O. asked and smiled.

"Cubs, of course. Who could root against Sammy Sosa?" Fefelov replied.

"Cubs, huh. Well, the Cubs wouldn't have a chance to win a hot dog concession if the Rangers hadn't traded Sosa to Chicago. That was a bad deal. I'm a Texas Rangers and Dallas Cowboys fan, myself. We live just about a half-hour from where they both play."

"That would be fine with me. I don't care for hot dogs," Fefelov said seriously.

"What? Oh, I get it. You're pretty cool, Father. What's in that old bag there?" R.O. asked and pointed to the cracked and scarred leather bag about ten feet away.

"Just some old papers and things. I have to say good night, Mr. MacGregor. Maybe we shall see each other tomorrow," Fefelov said and closed the door.

R.O. continued down the hall to the stairway where he found a glass-enclosed room with an ice machine, pop machines, candy machines, and bill changer. After getting the ice, he pulled a dollar bill out of his pocket and bought a large Pay Day candy bar, which he promptly stuffed into his pocket so he could smuggle it back into the room without its being confiscated by his mother. In a few minutes, he was back into the room, and the Pay Day was safely positioned under his pillow for a midnight snack.

Two hundred miles to the north, Mickey sat in front of his radio and fine-tuned the correct frequency.

"Caribou calling White Fox, over," Mickey said and took a sip of coffee. The old shack was cold and airy.

"Caribou, White Fox here," the voice said over the speaker.

"Meeting with neighbors again tomorrow. Will discuss the fence project and see who gets to pay for what. Looks like we're on a three-to-five-day schedule to get the fence completed," Mickey said and clicked the receiver twice.

"Roger, Caribou. We'll have the telephone company check for underground cables. We wouldn't want any surprises," the voice said.

"Roger, White Fox. Caribou will be back in 22-18-8. Out," Mickey said and switched off the radio. He looked down at his old watch with the scratched crystal and noted that he would call again in twelve hours.

He got up from the desk and walked over to a metal wall panel and pulled it back. He retrieved a bag that had a metal zipper at the top. He unzipped it, reached inside, and pulled out a wad of $100 bills still banded together from the bank. Stuffing the money in the front pocket of his overalls, he walked toward the door and opened it slowly. He turned out the light before the door had opened an inch. Stepping outside, the cold blast hit him in the face and he shivered all over. He looked up at the beautiful night sky of the Arctic and slowly blew a breath in the air.

"What a beautiful place on earth," he said and walked away from the shack toward his old blue truck. For a second, as he looked at Molly he thought about her sister, an El Camino parked high on the cap-rock back home in Amarillo. He liked old trucks. They had personality. The shiny new ones just didn't fit.

"It would be a shame to let those people mess up all this beauty and keep all the money, too," he said out loud to the stars.

As he sat in the truck, he felt under the blanket in the front seat and received great comfort as he caressed the Ruger Super Redhawk .44 magnum revolver. Leaning over, he touched the Colt Python .357 magnum to be sure it was in place under the seat. "Guess we'll have to make some adjustments, won't we guys," he said and smiled. "But first, we'll get a good night's sleep. Take me to the cabin, Molly," he said to his old truck as it belched a cloud of gray smoke and pulled away from the shack headed for the hidden cabin near the Yukon River eleven miles away. A meteor entered the atmosphere over central Alaska, adding a new beam of light to an already Aurora-decorated sky. Mickey looked up and thought that this must be a sign or something. Then he shook his head.

"Well, maybe not," he muttered to himself and shifted

the gears on the truck. "I have all the omens I need," he said and touched the grips of the Beretta 9mm under his coat and smiled.

10

61°7′N, 146°16′W

———————◯———————

The sun rose over the southeastern mountains, straining to reach the gray shadowed surface of Denali, which it would not touch for several hours. The majestic summit loomed over the western slopes, leaving them in a dark shadow. At six o'clock in the morning, all the hangars on the small airstrip were busy getting aircraft refueled and warmed up for early flights across the long distances of Alaska. Without an early start, a pilot could fly for hours in darkness amidst quickly changing weather.

Mavis MacGregor was up first, as usual, and had all the clan packed and dressed and trudging down the stairs to the main lobby. There they found their Inupiat friend Roy Nageak happily eating a peach Danish roll that was set out among the fruit and pastries for the early risers before the restaurant opened.

"All right, kids," Mavis boomed as R.O. covered his ears.

"Mom, do you have to be so loud?" he complained.

She leaned down his direction and whispered.

"No, but I choose to be loud. However, in the future I'll seek your permission before I increase the decibel level of my voice. Will that please you, master MacGregor?" she asked and smiled.

"Sure, Mom. Just let me know," R.O. said and faked a smile.

"Eat up everyone. I want to see orange juice in everyone's hands, not just sweets. A glass of milk would also be suitable for our journey. Mr. Luff assured me this morning that there are no rest stops between here and Valdez, and there are no facilities on his aircraft," Mavis said.

"Valdez? I thought we were going to Point Barrow," Chris said as he took a bite of a cinnamon roll.

"Change of plans," replied Jack. "I talked to Northern Alaska Oil last night and two of the regional tribal representatives, and they felt that a look at the terminal down south would be more advantageous than more arctic tours. I agreed. We know the oil is there, we have the technology to go get it, so the most important part of the equation is the safety of the delivery system, the pipeline. We need to know if the increase in crude would strain the pipeline to capacity and require a second pipeline to be built, which means more environmental questions," Jack said in an almost professorial tone. Only Chris was listening as the rest of the group tuned him out and continued to feed on pastries and donuts.

"Suits me just fine. I'm getting tired of the cold weather. I mean, anything below 75 degrees is just not my thing," interjected Heather. "However, I don't want the extreme heat of Abu Simbel again either," Heather took a bite of a chocolate donut and chewed slowly, savoring the chocolate cream since pastries weren't in the normal fare for a MacGregor breakfast.

"Well, don't get your hopes up. The weather is always changing and with early winter projections still intact, I expect we'll get plenty of cold rain and some snow before we head off to China and their cold winter," Mavis said and sipped some coffee.

"Does my dad know we're not coming north?" Roy asked Jack.

"Yes, he said to ask you if you wanted to tag along. We

can get you back here to the lodge in about three days where he will meet up with you," Jack replied.

"Heck yeah! I love hanging out with you guys. I'm ready whenever you are," Roy replied.

"I also canceled the press conference and pushed back our flight to Beijing until Wednesday. There was just too much left to do," Jack said. "Well, then let's finish eating and get our gear out to the airstrip. I called B.A. late last night and asked if he was available to change his flight plan for a trip south and he said he would be happy to fly us anywhere in Alaska."

"Excellent," replied Chris as he picked up his backpack and parka.

"Our children are going to turn into donuts, Jack," Mavis warned. "We just haven't had enough time for a decent breakfast while we've been in Alaska. I guess I'll have to start serving jerky and boiled eggs in the mornings."

"Oh, puke. Mom, please," Heather said as she walked by.

Within twenty minutes, everyone was marching across the frosted ground toward the four hangars on the airstrip two hundred yards away.

B.A. taxied the big Cessna Caravan to a smooth stop and pulled some maps from the console beneath the side instrument panel.

"Valdez. Looks to be about two hundred miles. Mt. Baker is 13,176 feet, so we'll cruise at ten thousand feet and stay northeast by twenty miles. That'll take us over the Takeetna Mountains, so I'll turn south at, no. Let's go due south to Kenai, then due east across Prince William Sound. That'll avoid all the weather around Thompson Pass," he said out loud to himself. Programming the coordinates into the GPS device, he folded up the maps and put them back in the console. He noticed the MacGregors and Roy trudging his way and stepped out of his seat and walked back to the side door. Unlatching the door, he lowered the steps and got out.

"Good morning, folks. Looks like you followed my directions about luggage and backpacks. Overloading wouldn't be a good thing to do," B.A. smiled, and Heather was the first to smile back.

The seven-passenger Cessna Caravan would be filled to capacity, but the big single engine would be more than enough for this load. With decades of flying, this aircraft was a workhorse of the aviation industry from Alaska to Argentina and around the world. Fitted with an accessory luggage compartment and pontoons with retractable landing gear, the Caravan could take off from land and sea alike. As each MacGregor and Roy filed into the plane, seats were chosen quickly.

"I don't want to sit next to you," Heather said as R.O. plopped down next to her.

"Dr. MacGregor, do you want to ride co-pilot?" B.A. asked.

"No, let's have Chris do that. I'm sure he will want to watch you navigate this fine aircraft, " Jack said.

"Thanks, Dad," Chris said and stepped into the right front seat.

Jack sat behind him, with R.O. to his left. Heather and Roy filled the next two, with Mavis sitting in the back.

"Well, what a joy. I'll have a back seat to myself and I'll enjoy some quiet time," she said as she slipped off her parka.

B.A. radioed the control tower, which was the second floor of the airstrip maintenance building, where Kimberli Brownlee sat drinking her second pot of coffee, since she came to work at 3 A.M. that morning. At the young age of thirty, she was already a thirteen-year veteran of Alaskan aviation, having learned to fly with her father, who was a well-known hunting guide. As manager of Denali Field, she wore many hats, which included flying a mail route every third week, air taxi, med-evac flights, and generally keeping in line all the young bush pilots who were just as interested in landing a date with her as in taking her orders from the make-shift tower. And then, of course, there was her beau, a tall, handsome hunting and fishing guide from Mooseheart Mountain who flew a DeHavilland Twin Otter.

"Good morning, Kimberli," B.A. said into the radio headset.

"Who said it was?" Kimberli snapped back. "Hey, B.A., your flight plan needs to be in the office before you taxi the aircraft, not after. Regulation forms and large print. I can't read your writing and if you don't comply, I'll see if I can get someone in Fairbanks to ground your aircraft for a month. Get my drift?" she said and smiled, pretending to be grumpy.

"Roger that boss," B.A. said, hearing the same complaints she always made.

"And I'm not your boss," Kimberli shouted back into the microphone. "If you worked for me, you'd be sweeping the hangar every day instead of flying around pretending to be Chuck Yeager."

"I'd be honored to sweep your hangar anytime," B.A. said, trying to humor the young aviation veteran. "But today, I have paying customers, so I'll again have to pretend to be Chuck Yeager, Charles Lindbergh, or Wiley Post. I'll let you choose, Miss Brownlee," B.A. said with a big smile.

"Hey Kimberli. When are you going to dump that hairy Alaskan of yours and give a real gentleman a chance to sweep you off your feet?" B.A. said and squinted his eyes waiting for her reply.

"Well, if you think you're man enough, I might consider it. But B.A., I've got to tell you, I don't date boys. Flying Moose One cleared for takeoff," Kimberli Brownlee said and drank more coffee, adjusted her pink cap, and grinned at B.A.'s comment. "Be safe B.A. and come back in one piece . . . handsome. Who knows what could happen this winter? Denali Field out."

Kimberli Brownlee had become the best friend to many young aviators who were attracted to Alaska and her tall good looks, leaving friends, family, and Mom's fried chicken to seek the adventure of one of the last frontiers in the world. B.A. Luff was one of those whose family in Oklahoma missed him dearly but understood the desire that must be fulfilled in his flying. They were just glad it was Alaska and not Southeast Asia or Africa.

"O.K., everybody buckled up?" B.A. asked.

Within ten minutes the Cessna Caravan was warmed up and moving to the end of the runway for takeoff. It lifted smoothly into the gray morning sky. Mt. McKinley loomed in the distance, with the sun touching the peaks of the mountain. It would be several hours before the sun reached the slopes and valleys below.

Chris and B.A. discussed the flight plan and the operation of the aircraft while everyone else slept. The drone and the light vibration of the aircraft were perfect for putting everyone to sleep. The two-hour flight passed quickly with different MacGregors and Roy awakening, talking, and going back to sleep. It was nearly 10:30 when B.A. guided the Caravan in a wide arc across Prince William Sound and dropped to 2,000 feet.

"O.K., everybody. Time to wake up and take a peek at beautiful Prince William Sound," B.A. said into the intercom.

Slowly, everyone woke up. R.O. had to be nudged by Jack a few times before he wiped his eyes and looked out one of the side windows.

"Anchorage Center, this is Flying Moose two, Tango four two niner niner requesting clearance at 2,000 feet on a 90-degree heading toward Valdez," B.A. said into the radio.

"Flying Moose, once you make the turn, you've got traffic at twelve o'clock at 12,000 feet and three o'clock at 5,000. Maintain a due east heading until Valdez Narrows are sighted. Anchorage out."

"How do they know that?" Chris asked.

"It's all satellite. No way to build towers out here on these islands, so it's all satellite tracking. They can track nearly every aircraft in Alaska. The problem is radio communication. If a pilot isn't willing to talk to the air controllers, it's pretty tough to communicate to all the bush pilots who just take off and land on lakes or remote air strips," B.A. said.

"That's amazing. My parents used a GPS once to track Heather and me across the Serengeti in Tanzania a few months ago," Chris replied.

"Tanzania. I bet that was fun," B.A. said.

"Yea, loads of fun," Chris said and shook his head.

B.A. banked the aircraft a little to the right and then leveled out on his final approach to Valdez.

In a hangar, three hundred miles to the north, Marlena walked in front of the aircraft as three men and two women stood up. Yves walked beside her. She carried a black case and set it on a table next to a refrigerator. Next, she pulled a CZ75 9mm automatic pistol from a leather holster under her jacket and set it next to it. Looking around, she noticed all eyes were on her. Not one to miss a moment like this, she picked up the semi-automatic pistol and chambered a round. The smooth action of the gun was barely audible.

"My colleague has a few words to say," Yves said.

Marlena opened the case and dumped the contents on the table. Stacks of $100 bills fell into a nice pile.

"What you see is $200,000. There is another $200,000 waiting for you when you finish the job. It will be divided equally among you. That's $80,000 each," she said.

"But we don't do it for the money," one of the women said sternly.

Marlena looked her direction.

"Yes. I know that. But you wouldn't be opposed to taking the cash and giving it to your local environmental opposition group to fight the oil companies, would you?" Marlena said.

"No, I guess not," the female pilot said.

"Good. Even your righteous cause needs money to operate and stand firm against imperialist governments," Marlena replied, well-rehearsed in the rhetoric she once used as a core leader of the Red Army Faction, a remnant of the old Baader-Meinhof Gang. "Every day over the next three days, you'll fly the routes that you've been flying for the past two weeks," Marlena continued as the hangar doors began to open. A small Toyota truck drove in and stopped among the five airplanes. There were four Cessnas and one Beechcraft Bonanza. Two men got out of the truck and began unloading five black rectangular cases and one orange cylinder. They spoke to each other in German.

"What you see over there is the payload that you will drop on your designated targets. Each day you have been given new coordinates to fly so the authorities wouldn't be able to recognize a pattern. But today you will be given your final destination. You will not divert from your flight plan for any reason. Is that understood?" she said and glanced down at the money and the CZ75.

The pilots all agreed by nodding their heads.

"Good. The success of the mission is dependent upon your timing and your resolve to complete the mission," she said.

Marlena reached into the case and retrieved a brown envelope. A side door of the hangar creaked as Mickey walked inside dressed in hunting overalls that were a camouflage green. His heavy coat covered his Beretta 9mm pistol.

"Sorry, I'm late," Mickey said and smiled. Yves and Marlena didn't smile back. Mickey eyed the cash and the gun on the table and casually felt his own pistol inside the overalls. He slipped his hand inside his left pocket through the hole he had cut in the bottom and touched the Beretta. He casually pushed the safety off. He also noted the two men unloading the black cases next to the airplanes. Marlena walked over to him and handed him the folder. He opened it and stared at the map inside. He could see it was a detailed map of the Trans-Alaska pipeline, with nine red Xs marked from Point Barrow to Valdez.

"I see you took some of my suggestions," Mickey said to Yves and Marlena. He handed the map back to Yves.

"Yes, but only after we checked them with other sources for their value to the mission," Yves replied.

"Now you can narrow them down to the five most critical points on the pipeline, and be sure you number them in order of most damaging to least," Marlena said in a monotone voice and took the map from Yves and handed it back to Mickey.

Mickey looked at the map and took a pencil from the front of his overalls. After a minute of looking at the map, he started writing the numbers one through five next to red Xs. He looked back at Marlena and then at the map. All the pilots were still standing and staring at him.

"That should do it," Mickey said and handed the map back to Marlena.

She looked at it for one minute, studying it carefully, and then handed it to Yves. She then walked over to the pilots.

"Hold out your flight charts for me as I come by," she said sternly.

One by one she wrote on the charts, going from one pilot to the next. No one could see what she had written, and the pilots had no clue as to the destination of the other pilots. When she reached the last pilot, she quickly marked the female pilot's chart and then walked over to a steel tool bench where she laid the map down. She reached into her right pant pocket and retrieved a cigarette lighter. Igniting the butane lighter, she touched the flame to the map and it caught fire immediately.

"Commit your targets to memory and bring me your charts," she said. "You will not talk to each other about your destinations."

After looking at the maps, each pilot walked over and handed her the charts. Marlena then tossed them into the pile of flames and ashes. When the fifth and last pilot had concluded the drill, she walked back and stood next to the others.

Marlena turned away from the pile of ashes on the metal tool bench and walked over to the table where the money was stacked. She calmly picked up the CZ75 and clicked off the safety.

"It has come to my attention that one of you has been sharing information of this mission with people within your environmental movements. This is not allowed," she said.

Suddenly she raised the gun and pulled the trigger, firing off one round toward one of the female pilots. The bullet hit the pilot squarely in the chest and went through her heart, ricocheting off the hangar wall behind her. She fell to the floor dead. The other pilots stepped back with a look of horror on their faces.

"We must succeed in disabling the oil companies' advances in Alaska. Sacrifices have been made and no one person will cause us to fail. I am sure each of you can agree. Since we are now minus one pilot, I will fly her aircraft and successfully reach her target. That means that each of you will share her cut. You've just been given a $20,000 raise. I'm sure you'll find a good way to spend it," Marlena said with a wry smile.

Two of the men nodded and smiled while the other two pilots were still in a state of shock and fear.

"Proceed with your plan. Fly over your prescribed target zone every day for the next three days at twelve noon. My two men at the hangar will refuel your aircraft when you return. If on any of these days you find a red folder in the pilot's seat, you will know that is the day we attack. You are instructed to drop your payload over your target by one o'clock and follow the instructions in the folder toward the rendezvous site. I will have $100,000 waiting for each of you," she said. "Am I clear?"

All four remaining pilots nodded their head in agreement.

"You may proceed," Marlena said and turned around toward Yves.

The four pilots moved toward the airplanes, with the one remaining female pilot looking down at the dead pilot. She quickly glanced toward Marlena before walking briskly toward her aircraft. The noise of the four aircraft firing up was deafening in the hangar until all had taxied out to the airstrip and positioned for an orderly take off.

"To whom did she speak?" Yves asked and motioned toward the dead pilot whose body was being removed by the two men who had armed each aircraft.

"No one," replied Marlena coolly.

"No one," Yves replied incredulously.

"No one. She had to be sacrificed to be sure no one does talk. We are too close to success. As I told you yesterday, they are all walking dead anyway, and besides, I want to fly her route. It was her misfortune to draw that number. She would have had three more days of life," she replied and smiled as if she were discussing a raffle at the local community center.

"Marlena, *mon petit chou*. May I never be on your bad side," Yves said in his strong French accent and raised his eyebrows.

"I'm not your little cabbage, Yves. I told you that your French charm goes nowhere with me," she replied in her hard German accent and clicked the safety on the CZ75 9mm pistol. She then tucked it inside her belt under her fashionable black leather coat.

She noticed Mickey still standing by the tool bench and motioned for him to come over. She put the money back into the case and handed it to Mickey.

"This is your down payment. The remaining cash payment will be yours in three days. You can pick it up at the rendezvous site," she said.

"And how will I know where that is? Do I get a red folder too?" Mickey said and smiled.

"No, you will use this," Marlena said and pulled a cell phone from her coat pocket. "I will call you. Don't go anywhere without it. After I call, just drop it anywhere. It is what the American gangs call a 'throw away.'"

"You got it. It'll be my best friend until I hear from you. Is that it?" Mickey said.

"Das ist alle," Marlena replied in German.

"Sehr gut, und auf wiedersein," Mickey replied and walked away.

When he had left through the door, Marlena turned to Yves.

"Our Alaskan speaks a little German, I see. I detected a slight Bavarian accent. I find that interesting, Yves. Don't you?" she said as she stared toward the door where Mickey had left, as if trying to see through it.

"Maybe he has worked in Germany or was in the army as a young man, or maybe he had a good high school German teacher," Yves said.

Marlena turned toward him.

"My dear Yves. You are too gullible. That's why I planned this mission, why I carry a gun, and why I will fly one of the aircraft. If I left this to you and your friends in Quebec, we would still be walking a picket line outside

Northern Alaska Oil Company offices in Anchorage. I had
planned on letting our big Alaskan live so he could take the
rap for this mission when the FBI finds the money in his
possession, but maybe that's not a good idea. I've got three
days to make that decision. In the meantime, I'm starved.
Take me to breakfast and we'll talk about Paris and Berlin,"
Marlena said and smiled.

She put her arm through Yves' arm and began to walk
across the hangar. They both stepped around the pool of
blood that had settled on the cold hangar floor as if it were
an oil stain from the aircraft.

Mickey set the case full of money in the front floorboard
of his old truck and calmly walked around to the driver's
side. He quickly pulled the Beretta from under his jacket
and held it tightly, waiting for an ambush that never came,
as he stepped inside the truck.

"Molly, that German babe is one nasty . . . well, you
know what she is. But we'll be ready when the time
comes," he said and pulled the blanket off the Ruger
Redhawk and holstered his Beretta. "Yup, we'll be ready."

He put the old four-wheel drive pickup in gear and
drove slowly back to the road leading from the small
airstrip. He would be at the shack in about thirty minutes.

11

Port of Valdez

The Cessna Caravan leveled off at 500 feet as B.A. Luff positioned the aircraft to line up with the harbor at the Port of Valdez as he passed over the Valdez Narrows. He glanced out the left window and looked at the Anderson and Shoup Glaciers, always an impressive sight. The busy little town of 4,000 was already in the routine of a typical workday.

The winter sun, with an eight-hour day at 61° latitude, was a welcome sight. The six hours of daylight around Denali had begun to wear on the MacGregor clan while Roy was excited to be in any sunlight. His family's home, sitting on the rim of the Arctic Ocean, would be in virtual darkness for the next three months. The sun pierced the clouds to the southeast, casting a stream of light arrows down on the snow-covered mountains and brilliant blue ocean of Prince Edward Sound.

"Valdez Field, this is Caravan Amphibian tango four two niner niner," B.A. said.

"Go ahead, Caravan," Valdez field replied.

"Coming in for a sea approach into Valdez Harbor. What's the wind direction and do I have any company on my tail?" B.A. said.

"You have one aircraft ahead of you. Wind is 160° at 10," Valdez Field replied.

"Roger. Thanks, Caravan clear," B.A. said.

"Caravan?" Valdez Field said.

"Go ahead," B.A. said.

"Just noticed two more aircraft right behind you about five miles out, so once you're in the water continue straight into the dock," Valdez Center said.

"Roger, straight on in and out of the way. Caravan out," B.A. said.

"Busy little airport," Chris said.

"Yes, they have a lot of seaplane traffic plus the airstrip keeps them pretty backed up. It's especially bad in the middle of summer with tourists, hunters, fishing expeditions, and mountaineering. The oil terminal, of course, keeps them hopping all year around," B.A. said.

"Apparently," Chris replied.

B.A. began the descent. The Cessna Caravan settled into the approach for a landing. As the pontoons touched the water, everyone felt the gentle pull against the seat belts for just a second before the sleek aircraft leaned back on its pontoons and settled into the water for a nice smooth glide. B.A. began to reduce the speed until the Caravan had become a boat. The Pratt and Whitney engine hummed effortlessly, pulling the aircraft across the mildly choppy water of the harbor. B.A. revved up the RPMs of the engine to make the ride smoother and avoid a sudden onset of seasickness for his passengers. He wasn't aware of their seagoing skills and diving experience.

"Wow, that was awesome, " R.O. said. "That's our first water landing, Dad," R.O. said across the aisle.

"Yes, I guess it is, son," Jack replied.

Mavis and Heather were stretching and waking up as the aircraft reached the dock. B.A. turned the Caravan slightly to allow for drift with the waves. A young man in an orange parka ran to the end of the pier and picked up a tie-down rope. Still revving the motor to stay in control of the Caravan, B.A. moved in slowly in order to prevent the big three-bladed propeller from hitting the wooden dock. The young dockhand jumped over to the pontoon and tied the rope and began to pull the aircraft closer to the dock. B.A.

killed the engine and the propeller sputtered to a stop.

Within minutes, the Caravan was tied securely to the dock, and B.A. walked down the center aisle and opened the side door just in front of the stacked luggage. Chris was right behind him, followed by R.O., Roy, and Jack. As they unloaded the duffle bags and backpacks, Mavis leaned across the aisle and kissed Heather on the cheek.

"Here's where being a lady comes in handy," Mavis said. "Just remember to always let men be men," she said and gave a wink to Heather.

"I agree, Mom. I'm lucky to have you as my mother," Heather said and smiled warmly.

Taken off guard by the sudden return of affection, Mavis touched her right hand to her lips.

"You are just too sweet sometimes," Mavis said and blew her a kiss.

"Got it," Heather puckered in mid-air and smiled.

"Ladies, bundle up good. It's about 25 degrees out here and a nice breeze coming off the water from the glacier," Jack said as he stuck his head back into the warm cabin.

Heather and Mavis slipped on their down parkas and gloves, each tying a muffler around her neck. As Mavis stepped down to the pontoon and over to the dock, she stopped and turned toward the mountains to the north.

"My, my, what a beautiful view. The vista reminds me of the Scottish Highlands. Of course, the snowcapped peaks are an addition, but beautiful just the same," she said.

The drone of a small aircraft flying just overhead caused everyone to look up as a blue and white Cessna 310 made an approach to the airstrip for a dry landing. In the distance toward the narrows another seaplane could be heard dropping down to make a sea landing. It soon touched down and was cruising toward the dock.

Heather shivered as the cold air hit her before she zipped up her parka.

"Cold here, too. Everywhere we go in Alaska it's cold," she said and zipped up the parka.

Retrieving a yellow scrunchie from her jeans pockets, she pulled her blond hair back to fashion into a long ponytail. Mavis walked over to her.

"You O.K. honey?" she asked.

"Sure Mom. It's cold, but you're right. It's beautiful," Heather replied.

With the luggage all stacked on the dock, B.A. turned to the MacGregors.

"Well, folks, it's been fun. I'll be back in two days to pick you up for the flight to Anchorage. The marina office is right over there. You can get a cab to run you into town, or they might even take you if they have a free body to drive. I've got another job tomorrow out of Kenai with the trading company, so I'll be heading off," B.A. said and smiled.

Chris shook his hand and said a few words. Everyone did the same until it was Heather's turn. B.A. leaned down and gave Heather a hug. She blushed bright pink and let out a heavy sigh.

"See you later, Heather," B.A. said and turned toward the plane.

Heather only mouthed the words goodbye, too overwhelmed to speak.

"O.K., load up," Jack said.

Everyone found their duffle and backpack and started up the dock. Heather was still watching B.A. fire up the Cessna when R.O. walked up behind her.

"When are you getting married, Heather, or haven't you got that far in your fantasy yet?" R.O. said and laughed.

Heather gave a quick sidekick that landed her hiking boot on his left thigh.

"Hey, Mom!" R.O. yelled out.

Mavis had witnessed the event and turned toward them.

"I never advocate a violent response to an insult, but in this case, I'm going to pretend I didn't see that. Am I clear, Ryan O'Keef MacGregor?" Mavis said and threw her backpack over her shoulder and walked away.

Heather smiled at R.O. and hurried after Mavis.

Vitorio Luzano landed the Cessna 310 at busy Valdez Field. Seven other aircraft had already landed there that morning. The stop in Anchorage the day before had been fruitful and given them the name of a retired librarian, guide, and historian in Valdez. With the name came the possibility of more information about the early Russian settlements. The flight across Prince William Sound had been smooth and uneventful despite the fact that Vitorio was tiring of the endless tales and bragging of the Polish archaeologist.

"If it weren't for me, my fair Italian priest, the tenth dynasty of pharaohs would have never been discovered," he said and took a sip of whiskey from a silver flask he had taken from the inside pocket of his coat. "Those Brits had no clue about the hidden chamber in the tomb, and they had been studying it for fifty years. Idiots. It took my deciphering of the hieroglyphs to lead to the pivot stone that opened the hidden door. My museum now has a fine Egyptian collection because of it," he said and put the flask away.

"And I am sure they appreciate you greatly," Vitorio said in a condescending fashion.

"Look, priest, I have to put up with the insults from the morons at the museum, but I don't have to take them from you. Just remember our deal. You get the cross, I get whatever's left in the box," Januz said.

"And you've never said what you think is in the box," Vitorio said as he began to taxi the plane down the tarmac in front of the hangars. "Maybe I shouldn't agree to let you have it. Maybe we should split it fifty-fifty."

"Let's just say that your Pope would love to get his hands on it. But it will be my hands that open the box and it will belong to me, not the museum, not the Catholic Church, and not some billionaire collector of religious relics in New York, Tokyo, Rio, or Paris. It will be my ticket to the book that I'll write that will declare Januz Lemanski as the greatest archaeologist in the history of all of Europe and quite possibly the world. We have a deal, priest, and I would bet your life that the deal sticks," he said and gave a steely look to Vitorio.

"I see. I can only think of a few precious things that would lead to such greatness," Vitorio said, knowing that Lemanski had a ruthless reputation and couldn't be trusted. "The Ark of the Covenant, which hasn't been found, and would be too big to put in a small box. Noah's ark, which may sit on a mountaintop somewhere in Turkey, or so we suppose. We already have the Shroud of Turin and Veronica's Cloth, so I'm at a loss. I guess the robe of Christ would be a find that would make you immortal in archaeology and . . . ah, yes. Would it be the crown of thorns that Christ wore or the placard that hung over Jesus declaring him the King of Kings?" Vitorio asked and turned the aircraft toward a hangar marked for visitors.

"My dear Vitorio, you are a curious Roman priest, aren't you?" Januz said and unbuckled his safety belt. "Let's just say, you worry about the Cross of Charlemagne and I'll worry about the rest. Agreed?" Januz looked him firmly in the eyes and didn't blink.

"Look Lemanski. We've made our deal. Once is enough," Vitorio said and stopped the aircraft. "There is no guarantee that the Cross of Charlemagne made it to Alaska despite what other items of great value Catherine II sent with her priests. But we can only hope."

The vintage Grumman Goose glided to a smooth stop as the dock boy tied up the aircraft. Father Fefelov and Father Kristov stepped from the aircraft onto the pier, glancing up at the beautiful view. They were dressed in jeans and parkas, with only a purple sash draped around their necks and hanging from the bottom of the parkas to indicate their priestly status. Most people would think the sashes were only winter scarves.

"God's hand has painted another masterpiece, Father," Fefelov said and stroked his long red beard.

"He has indeed," Kristov replied.

"We'll proceed to the cabin before we call our retired librarian," Fefelov said.

"Good idea, Father," Kristov said. "I think your plan of jeans, flannel shirts, and parkas is a good idea. We must tuck in our sashes to prevent them from being noticed. This way, if we should encounter our Roman rivals, they won't recognize us for who we are. We could be just a couple of old miners, for that matter."

"Old miners? Well, I guess we could be that," Fefelov said as he took the old leather bag from the hands of the pilot and picked up his small suitcase.

The two priests walked up the dock in a spry step for men in their late sixties.

The MacGregors stepped from the red van in front of the Black Bear Hotel and Lodge on the main street in Valdez.

"Rustic but quaint," Mavis said.

"And still very cold," Heather complained again.

Within minutes, everyone had walked into the lobby, with R.O. making a beeline to a row of computers on one wall.

"Where are you headed?" Chris asked him quickly before Mavis or Jack noticed.

"Haven't e-mailed Drew since we've been in Alaska and this is my first chance," R.O. replied and dropped his backpack on the wooden floor under the table of laptops.

"I'll cover for you for a minute, but you better make it quick. You can always do this tomorrow," Chris advised.

"I better do it now or I'll get sidetracked and forget," R.O. said and quickly logged onto the hotel's website for visitors and typed in Drew's e-mail address.

Chris stood watch as his parents checked in and Roy and Heather walked over to the large stuffed black bear standing in the lobby next to a glass display case that held artifacts and a storyboard about the gold discovery of the last century.

"Dr. Jack MacGregor. The reservations were made by Northern Alaska Oil," Jack said to the clerk.

"Yes, I have it right here," the clerk replied. "Two suites, with an adjoining door. I also have a free rental certificate for a four-wheel-drive H2 and some free rental passes for snowmobiles."

"Jack, how nice of Miss McKasson," Mavis said. "You must have made quite an impression on her." Mavis smiled and winked at him.

Jack ignored her and signed the registry card, trying not to look at her because he knew he would blush. He always did when she acted this way.

"Thanks," Jack said to the clerk and turned away from the counter.

"O.K. Wrap it up. They're done," Chris said to R.O. who typed in a few last words and clicked on the send icon.

"You know, Chris. I can't believe I haven't seen Drew for five months. And it will be another seven months before we get back to Texas. I miss the dogs, the horses, my room, and my best friend, Drew," R.O. said with a sad look on his face.

Chris sat down on a leather stool at the table and looked at R.O.

"Yeah, I think about that, too. But we're getting to do what other kids only dream about all their lives. I mean the Cayman Islands, East Africa, Egypt, and now Alaska. By next week we'll be in China. Name one other family you know who would get to do something like this? You can't. It's just the five of us, you, me, Heather, Mom, and Dad. Sure, it hasn't been easy, and sometimes it gets pretty scary. But I'm sure the tough part is behind us and we'll have smooth sailing all the way through China, India, and on to your favorite place, Australia," Chris smiled.

"Australia, yeah, I can't wait. I want to ride a kangaroo and climb a tree to see a koala bear. And you know that big rock out in the outback?" R.O said.

"Ayers Rock?" Chris said.

"Yea, Ayers Rock. I want to climb that, too. That's where I'll try out my new radio," R.O. said.

"What radio?" Chris asked and frowned, knowing his brother's penchant for inventing things.

"Oh, it's nothing. Just something I started in Italy," R.O. said as Mavis and Jack walked over.

"And what did you start in Italy that we should know about?" Mavis asked.

"Nothing important," R.O. replied and was cut off by Heather.

"Did you know that this hotel wasn't even here in 1964? In fact, the whole village of Old Valdez was wiped out by a tsunami," she said.

"Tsunami, a large wave caused by a sudden shift of the ocean floor," R.O. recited quickly.

"Nobody asked you," Heather said quickly.

"Good job, though," Mavis praised. "Wish you could remember your history lessons as quickly."

"Math and science are more fun, Mom," R.O. replied.

"So they had to rebuild the whole city. Isn't that amazing?" Heather said.

"And they have bottles of gold over in that case from the streams around here," Roy added. "Isn't it about time to eat lunch?"

"Well, I guess it is," Jack said. "Let's take our gear up to the rooms and then we'll go on a food hike around town and find a place to eat."

Vitorio Luzano and Januz Lemanski walked into the hotel lobby and right by the MacGregors. Soon they were checked in for two separate rooms and were stepping into the elevators as the MacGregors walked into their suites two floors above them.

Four hundred miles north, Marlena drove the black jeep to the airstrip and parked to the side of the hangar after dropping Yves at the inn. Her excuse to leave was that there were more loose ends to take care of. He understood perfectly. One of her men met her at the door and let her in. He quickly lowered the Polish-made Onyks 89 assault rifle from her face.

"I am glad to see that you're ready and waiting for the unforeseen," she said.

"I'm always ready, *fraulein,*" the man said in German.

"Good. Is the Bonanza fueled and loaded?" she asked.

"Yes, it is," he replied.

"Fritz, here are the red folders. Tomorrow, put them on the seats of the other four planes," Marlena said.

"But, *fraulein,* I thought it was a go in three days," Fritz said.

"Good. Everyone else will think so, too. It is always best to do the unexpected, Fritz. That way, even Yves wouldn't know enough to betray us. We are too close to trust anyone. When the pilots drop their payloads, they will go to the alternate landing strip thirty miles down the Yukon River. As they arrive one by one, you will let them get out of the aircraft and go into the hangar, where you will eliminate them. According to the schedule, they will arrive thirty minutes apart. After the last one has arrived and has been killed, load the bodies into the Jeep and drive to the lodge and park it. Yves will think I have returned and will be waiting for me there. Someone will notice the bodies and connect them to Yves and then to the bombings. I will call the big Alaskan and arrange to take care of him. If he shows up here again, kill him," she said. "Do you understand?"

"Yes *fraulein,*" Fritz said.

"Good," Marlena said and reached into her flight bag and pulled out a roll of hundred dollar bills, a plane ticket, and passport. "After everyone has been eliminated, then you need to leave as quickly as possible. Take one of the airplanes and fly to Fairbanks. Use this ticket and passport and fly to Seattle. Then you are on your own to get back to Berlin. This is a good passport. One million dollars will be put into your account in Zurich as soon as I get back to Europe," she said.

"I trust you. We have done many jobs together. This is but one more," Fritz said and smiled.

"Is my cargo safe?" Marlena asked, looking over at the bright orange cylinder attached to the underbelly of the Beechcraft Bonanza.

"It's safe. There was only minor leakage that I discovered with my meter but that is repaired now. It was a small seal. No detection devices will notice it wherever you land. The plutonium and cesium are in a box designed like the black box on a jetliner. A craftsman in Hamburg built it for me. It can explode only when you push the detonator I mounted on the instrument console of the Bonanza. Nothing else can detonate it. Not even a surface-to-air missile. It would have to be a direct hit, or it would simply break apart and fall free to the ground," Fritz said.

"You are truly efficient, my dear Fritz. German efficiency is in our genes. We must carry on the tradition of not allowing other nations to control us," Marlena said and stepped closer to him. As she softly touched his left cheek with her right hand, she smiled. "You have always taken care of Marlena, my sweet Fritz. We shall meet in Berlin in one week. And don't forget to get rid of your helper," Marlena said.

"He is already enjoying a new adventure in the Alaskan wilderness," Fritz replied.

"You're always ahead of me. Goodbye," Marlena said and walked toward the Beechcraft Bonanza.

As she fired up the engine, Fritz pushed the hangar doors open. A cold blast of air rushed in and gave him a chill. Within a few minutes, Marlena had taxied to the end of the runway and prepared to take off. She thought how good it would be to see the sun again for more than four hours a day.

12

White Fox

———————————⬭———————————

Mickey opened the door to his old shack and checked the security camera that was mounted through a peephole on the tin siding through twelve inches of insulation. Closing the door quickly, he opened the black case and dumped the money on the table and counted the banded $100 bills. There was $200,000 exactly.

He laid the Ruger Redhawk .44 magnum next to it. He pulled out his Beretta and popped the clip and laid it down. He reached inside the middle front pocket of his overalls and retrieved his thick wallet. Rifling through it, he shuffled through credit cards, ID, and pictures of his family, looking for his fuel card, when suddenly he stopped.

He pulled the ID from the stack and held it up in the light of the single light bulb of the shed. There was a red dot glowing next to his face on the front of the driver's license. A cold chill went down his back. He quickly walked over to the wall and pulled out the tin panel revealing the radio, satellite telephone, and GPS tracking system. After turning on the radio, he quickly switched to a secure channel that he knew would raise someone on the other end.

"White Fox, this is Caribou, over," Mickey said.

There was no reply.

"White Fox, this is Caribou, over," Mickey said again.

Again, there was no reply. He knew he was not on the right schedule to communicate and expected no response but was hoping to get one. Mickey walked over to a four-drawer file cabinet and opened it. There were rows of files that to the untrained eye would seem normal for any citizen of Alaska who lived in the great outdoors and had worked for an oil company. He quickly reached for the file that read Honda Motors and Compressors. Retrieving an owner's manual, he turned to page 99 and returned to the radio.

"White Fox, Honda compressor number J as in Jerry, two two niner, T as in Tom, four one niner. Over," Mickey said with a little sweat now appearing on his forehead and running down his cheeks.

"Caribou, this is White Fox. We have a repair situation on our hands, please confirm, over," the voice said.

"White Fox, the red service light is glowing, I repeat the red light is glowing," Mickey said taking a deep breath and sitting down.

"Caribou, please confirm," the voice said.

"White Fox, the red service light is glowing. We have a repair situation on hand. I repeat, we have a repair situation on hand. Caribou over," Mickey said.

"Please stand by, Caribou," the voice said, and static gushed through the radio receiver for nearly five minutes.

Mickey got up and checked the clip for the Beretta and shoved it back in and chambered a round, leaving the safety off. He opened another panel in the wall, revealing several automatic weapons, shotguns, and explosives. A crackling noise was heard on the radio and then a clear voice.

"Caribou, this is White Fox, are you there?" the voice said.

"That's affirmative, White Fox," Mickey replied.

"Caribou, a repair team has been activated and will be on its way in twenty-one minutes. I repeat. A repair team has been activated and will be on its way in twenty-one minutes. Use an alternate compressor until they arrive. ETA will be ninety minutes. Do you have coordinates, Caribou?"

"That's affirmative, White Fox. Yukon 66. Yukon 66," Mickey said and clicked the receiver.

"Yukon 66, White Fox over and out."

Mickey clicked off the radio and the shack was now subdued by the silence. Only the wind blowing through the tin could be heard. He pulled a red handkerchief from his pocket, took off his hat, and wiped the sweat off his face. He calmly walked over to a large trunk and took out a small meter and laid it on the table. He turned it on and slid his ID into the opening on the side. The needle on the Geiger counter moved a little to the right but didn't enter the red zone. He let out a sigh of relief. Then his heart began to race again.

"I don't know what nerd designed this little jewel but I'd like to kiss him right now," Mickey said and looked at the red dot on his ID photo. "A microchip that detects radioactivity. I never thought I would ever see this one light up. Not here in Alaska."

He pulled down one of the Colt AR15 rifles and quickly popped in a clip. He then retrieved seven loaded clips for the rifle. Then he loaded his Beretta 390 Silver Mallard 12-gauge shotgun with five magnum slugs and retrieved a block of C4 explosive. He put the guns and clips in a sleeping bag and carried them out to his truck. He returned and put the C4 inside the case with the money and picked up the case and walked out. Locking the shack, he got in the truck and drove about a mile away to a stand of trees and left the motor running. With his reserve tank, he could sit and idle for a couple of hours. The repair team would be there by then.

Staring up into the sky, he looked at the beautiful landscape all around him.

"Molly, I think we've got something on our hands besides a bunch of crazy eco-terrorists. It scares me to think of just what," Mickey said. His right hand was on the trigger of the AR15. He thought for a few minutes and remembered the black cases in the hangar. "Oh my goodness," he said to himself. "I think there is more there than just a little TNT." He looked down at the satellite telephone lying next to the Colt AR15. He would wait eighty-two more minutes. If the repair team hadn't arrived by then, he would break procedure and call Washington. With the information he had supplied the terrorists and the possibility of a radioactive weapon, he couldn't afford to wait. The security of the United States might be at stake.

With the window slightly cracked on the driver's side of the truck, Mickey breathed in the fresh air to be sure that the old truck didn't leak carbon monoxide into the cab and put him to sleep permanently. Time passed quickly. For a second, he wished he had grabbed a cold root beer. He looked at his old watch, as he had been doing every few minutes, and noticed that eighty-eight minutes had passed since he had been given the ninety-minute countdown.

He grabbed the Globalstar satellite telephone from the seat and turned it on. After a few seconds, the digital readout cleared him to dial his number. Just as he had begun to dial, he heard the distant noise of a helicopter. Then there was another. Soon he could see a squadron of three Black Hawks and one larger Sikorsky HH-60G PAVE Hawk skimming across tree-top level and crossing the Yukon River.

Within a minute, all four helicopters were hovering over his shack. He had already put Molly in gear and was driving out of the cover of the trees toward the shack. By the time he reached the shack, the PAVE Hawk had landed and five armed soldiers had surrounded the cabin. Two men in officer's uniforms and another in a civilian suit and tie climbed out and stood waiting for him as he drove up and stopped. The three Black Hawks circled overhead in a wide arc.

Mickey got out of the truck as the five men trained their Colt M15 rifles on him. He raised his hands high in the air.

"Mickey Banister, FBI," he said.

"Lower your weapons," one of the officers said.

"Mickey, what's cookin', man?" said Chuck Smith, chief of the Fairbanks field office of the FBI. At six feet, three inches and two hundred and fifty pounds, he was a formidable sight and had managed to keep in shape after his linebacker career ended with the Chicago Bears.

"Let's go inside, Chuck," Mickey replied and unlocked the shed. One of the armed men jumped forward and pushed Mickey to the side and swung open the door and trained the rifle inside ready to fire. He carefully stepped in and turned on the light and walked around followed by a second armed man.

"All secure, sir," the soldier said and stepped out.

Mickey went in and was followed by the two officers and Special Agent Smith.

"Mickey, this is Brig. Gen. Casey Cooper and Col. Luke Haney. General Cooper is the commander of the 3rd Wing, which is home to the 19th, 54th, and 90th fighter squadrons at Elmendorf. Colonel Haney is the 3rd operations group commander whom I've been working with the past year concerning your operation and what federal and military implications it may bring. They just happened to be nearby at Eielson Air Force Base when I got your call, so we picked them up on the way over. Rather, they picked me up and brought the hardware you saw outside," Chuck said.

"It's always good to get off base, Banister," General Cooper said.

"The Bureau felt that we might need their airpower if something big developed on this case, and with Alaska possessing great expanses of territory, our resources at the bureau might be limited and force a delayed response, which could be catastrophic. It's been the same kind of relationship that we have with the DEA and the Coast Guard in checking the flow of illegal drugs from Colombia," Agent Smith said.

"General, colonel. I'd like to spend more time learning about the relationship, but we've got a potentially grave situation. Chuck, we need to cut the crap and get down to business," Mickey said and closed the door. The armed men stationed themselves around the rusting shack as the Black Hawks circled like giant wasps ready to pounce on a spider.

"Here's my ID," Mickey said and handed it to Chuck.

"Well, that's a positive reading for sure," he said and slid it into the meter again. The needle moved slightly and then settled back to zero when he took it out. "Have you been around any oil equipment or drilling equipment or pipeline X-ray machines that might have triggered the microchip?"

Chuck said and sat down on a bench. The two Air Force officers just listened quietly.

"Not a thing. I had just left the rendezvous hangar where the pipeline assault was going to be staged," he said and was interrupted by the general.

"Pipeline assault! You said nothing about a pipeline assault. What's going on here," the general yelled at Chuck.

"General, I was going to notify you as soon as Washington said I could. It was only this week that we learned that eco-terrorists had decided to hit the pipeline and use several small planes to do it," Chuck replied.

"I'll have to notify the Pentagon immediately. This is a national security issue, not just a regional FBI operation," the general barked back.

"I understand. That's why I called you less than two hours ago and said that it was imperative that you and Colonel Haney come with me on this run. I didn't know if it was a legitimate call, but I have never known Special Agent Banister to make a bad call in the thirty years since we were at Quantico together. I knew there would be a 90 percent chance that Mickey had encountered a nuclear device, and I wanted the chief military officer in the region by my side to evaluate the crisis," Chuck said. He took out a cigar, bit off the end, and stuck it in his jaw.

"Very well. What's your take on this, Agent Banister?" the general asked.

"Two hours ago, I witnessed an eco-terrorist, a German national I suspect, and I believe from the Red Army faction, from the conversations that I have had the last three days, murder a female pilot in front of four other pilots. She fits the profile perfectly, and I don't think the environment has anything to do with this. Have a seat, general," Mickey said and pulled out a dusty folding chair. "Can I offer you something to drink, general?" Mickey asked as he leaned back and opened the old Frigidaire.

"No, thanks. Go ahead, Banister," the general said.

Mickey grabbed a brown bottle of root beer and unscrewed the cap, took a drink, and continued.

"I had just arrived at the hangar and was asked to mark

on a map the most probable points of attack if they were going to destroy the Trans-Alaska Pipeline. Special Agent Smith and I had discussed this scenario several times. We didn't know if they would go for the pipeline, a holding facility, an offshore drilling site, or whatever. But I knew that whatever information they trusted me to supply had to be as close as legitimate as possible or my cover would be blown. There were plenty of other oil people who would sell their soul for the $200,000 in this case," Mickey said and dumped the money on the table.

"That's right, general," Chuck said. "We've kept Washington informed all the way, and you were informed of a possible threat over a year ago. Today, we are telling you what the actual threat is because we have just found it out."

"As of yesterday, the attack is planned to go in three days. That's the day after tomorrow," Mickey said. "I couldn't stop the murder because it happened in seconds and it would have blown my cover and exposed us to the attack. The targets I suggested to Marlena, the leader of the group, were sections of the pipeline that had automatic shutoff valves and could be repaired in a few days. However, that is to say, if we didn't stop them in time with a ground assault forces or air interception by your people," Mickey said.

"That's right, general," Special Agent Smith said. "As you and I have discussed in planning sessions, if an assault on any target ever got airborne, your F-15 Eagles from Elmendorf or the F-16 Falcons from Eielson could take them down quickly. But we had planned to use our ground assault team to stop them at the hangar once we found out who the major players were. We couldn't go too soon or we wouldn't discover the money trail, how they got the explosives into Alaska, or who the international leaders of these eco-terrorists could be. We needed to know if there were similar criminal assaults planned elsewhere on United States soil or internationally against any of our allies," Chuck said.

"Agent Banister, what's your assessment of the success

of a ground assault?" Colonel Haney asked and picked up a Colt AR15 rifle from the wall panel.

"My plan was to radio in the time of the assault to take place tonight so that when the pilots arrived in the morning, our team would be waiting for them. We could then go into Steven's Village and take the three other players into custody. That would end the operation once our clean-up team came in and dismantled and confiscated the explosives and the aircraft.

"It would have been a nice, clean ending to a two-year operation with top leadership behind bars and much of their network penetrated throughout the northwest United States and Canada. This is only one of fifteen eco-terrorist cells we have identified. These suspects are at the top of the food chain. But we didn't foresee the red dot showing up on my face," Mickey said and tapped the ID lying on the table. "I was never closer than 100 feet to the explosive containers. Whatever is in one of those boxes, and now on a airplane, is one big chunk of nuclear material."

"Describe the containers," the colonel said and laid the rifle down.

"About three feet long. One man lifted them out of the truck and handed them to another man," Mickey replied.

"That's a relief," the general said.

"The smallest nuclear bomb that can be assembled can be no smaller than about 180 pounds and four to five feet long. Just too much hardware to get into the size of container you just described, Banister," the colonel said.

"That's right, colonel. But don't forget that a dirty bomb could easily fit into a case of that size, and if it's dropped and detonated at a critical point in the pipeline, then it would be virtually impossible to repair," Chuck said.

Mickey stood up and pulled a map of Alaska off the shed wall, leaving two taped corners that tore from the map attached to the tin. He moved the meter and raked the money onto the floor as Chuck and the general stood up and leaned over. Mickey then took a marker off the tool table and began to trace the Trans-Alaska Pipeline, beginning at Point Barrow on the Beaufort Sea. Every few seconds he would stop, think about the location the marker was sitting on, and then continue his tracing. He finally reached the oil terminal at Valdez and looked up.

"I can see several places that would take months to repair where teams couldn't get in because of radioactive contamination. But the worse case scenario of all would be these two locations," he said and made two big circles. "Isabel Pass southeast of Fairbanks and Thompson Pass just northeast of Valdez. If a dirty bomb were detonated at either of these two points, the entire pipeline might have to be rerouted around the respective mountain ranges." Mickey laid the marker on the table.

"In your last report, you said there were four Cessna 185 small aircraft and one Beechcraft Bonanza. Right?" Chuck said.

"That's right," Mickey replied.

"Any fuel tanks added on for extended range?" Chuck asked.

"No, I didn't see any. The Bonanza had an unusual addition on the fuselage that the Cessnas didn't have. I couldn't tell what it was, but it was an orange cylinder about four feet by two feet and was mounted next to the black case that I assume carried the TNT. All of the aircraft had seen better days. Most were probably vintage 1970s, and the Bonanza may have been older than that. They probably picked them up at different auctions across the state over the last year in order to avoid suspicion, and if they were going to walk away from them, they didn't want a million dollars tied up in the airplanes," Mickey said and took a sip of the root beer to try to relax.

"Well, general, my team will move tonight to take them out and eliminate the threat. I'll need your best HAZMAT crew available to take possession of the nuclear device," Chuck said. "Colonel, you have expertise in that area. What's your take?"

"Probably a cesium product of some kind, maybe plutonium. There was just too much plutonium floating around Turkmenistan after the Soviets left power. Any half-baked nuclear scientist could cook up a good dirty bomb. It would take a lot of explosive to detonate from impact so they were probably, if this is right, planning to drop it, clear the area, and then detonate by remote control."

"O.K. I'll inform the Pentagon that you will take out the threat tonight, Agent Banister," the general said.

"Yes, sir," Mickey replied and looked him in the eye.

"Which of these passes do you think they were going to target?" the general asked.

Mickey rubbed his gray beard and tilted his fur cap back on his head. Adjusting his glasses, he looked back at the map.

"Valdez. I would go for Thompson Pass. It's the only ice-free port available and more critical than Isabel Pass. To reroute the pipeline around the mountains and find another port would be an unbelievable challenge," Mickey said.

"I disagree, Agent Banister," Colonel Haney said. "These are eco-terrorists who want to stop oil drilling in Alaska. They want to make a major statement, but don't forget, they love the environment and an assault on Isabel Pass would make their point without the extensive environmental damage of Thompson Pass and Prince Edward Sound. The Exxon Valdez was bad enough. I wouldn't expect them to risk doing it again. But that's just my view. The civilian side of this, you guys, have to make the call. We can only assist."

"If it's my call then its Isabel Pass," Special Agent Chuck Smith said.

"Sounds logical to me. Colonel, have a squadron of F-15s on standby for Isabel Pass as the primary target. Keep in mind, we may have to pull your F-16 Falcons off of air sovereignty alert patrol for NORAD if this all moves to the south. But I think that we'll be covered with the Thompson Pass scenario," the general said. "O.K., proceed and keep me informed. All hours of the day, doesn't matter. The colonel can reach me on a moment's notice. I want this all wrapped up by midnight tonight."

"Thanks, general," Smith said and stood up.

The general stood up and walked toward the door and stopped.

"Looks like we dodged a major bullet this time gentlemen. Good work, Banister," the General said and stepped out into the cold breeze. The armed men came to attention and accompanied him back to the big helicopter.

"Chuck, I want it on the record that I disagree. I think it's Valdez. Do you want me to meet you at the hangar?" Mickey said to Chuck as he walked by.

"No, we'll take over from here on out. You're done, big guy. Turn in the money tomorrow in Fairbanks and then take a month off. Don't you have family in Amarillo you haven't seen in a while?" Chuck said.

"Sure, but I won't feel easy until this is wrapped up. I watched that German babe murder someone in cold blood. She's a dangerous person to have on the loose," Mickey said.

"We'll get her tomorrow. Don't worry," Chuck said and spit tobacco on the ground and walked toward the helicopter.

Mickey watched the big helicopters rise into the air and gradually disappear into the oncoming darkness. He closed the door to the shack and locked it. Walking around the table, he slowly picked up the $200,000 and placed it in the black case. Putting the contents of his wallet together, he held up the ID one more time and stared at the red dot. Taking a deep breath, he slid the ID back into his wallet and began to unload the automatic rifles.

After about an hour of housekeeping and packing some of his personal belongings, he looked around the shack and felt rather sullen, which was unusual for him. He knew that when he walked out the door, he wouldn't be back. The shack had been his second home for nearly a year as he had worked to infiltrate the militant environmental groups of Alaska. He glanced around the shack at the tools he had never used but that had been mere stage props, like place settings of silverware on a dining table in a furniture showroom. He opened the wall panel to the radio and turned off the main power switch. A cell phone suddenly rang. He reached down to the cell phone sitting next to the radio and realized it was not ringing. By the time he had heard the third ring, he remembered the cell phone that Marlena had given him, and he felt in his coat and found it. He quickly hit the green button.

"Hello," he said. Every muscle in his body was tense.

"Mickey. I told you to keep the phone next to you," Marlena yelled into the phone.

"I'm here now," Mickey said. "What's up?" he tried to sound as casual as possible.

"There's been a change in plans. I want you to go to the hangar in the morning and pick up the other $100,000," she said.

"Are we going tomorrow?" Mickey said.

"No, not for two more days. But you have done such a good job, I thought you might want to get out of the area early before the, well, you know, it all hits the fan," she said.

Mickey stood listening carefully. He could hear a noise in the background he couldn't identify.

"Hey, thanks. That's awfully hospitable of you. Guess we won't be seeing each other again. Good luck," Mickey said.

"No, we won't. You take care of yourself, Mickey. Yves and I can always use a good man like you. We'll be in touch maybe for another job in the future. Goodbye," Marlena said and the connection went dead. She knew Fritz would be there to greet him with his Onyks 89 assault rifle.

Mickey looked down at the screen on the cell phone. It read "call ended." He set in on the table and leaned back against the tool bench, rubbing his beard and talking to himself.

"Go in tomorrow. It's a trap for me, I wager," he said to himself.

He picked up the Ruger Redhawk and checked the rounds, pulled back the hammer, and let it down carefully.

"What was that noise?" he said again. "It's all been moved up early. She shot one of the pilots and took her place with the aircraft with the longest range."

He looked back down at the map on the table. He reached over to the tool bench and found a tape measure.

He quickly ran a line from Steven's Village to Valdez. Four hundred fifty miles and an easy flight in a Bonanza, he thought. Talking aloud, he said, "She could set down anywhere tonight, probably Fairbanks or Anchorage. Then fly on tomorrow to Valdez. Drop the bomb there, and fly back to Anchorage by two o'clock, or she could refuel at Valdez, make the drop, and head southeast along the coast and into Canada."

He sat down and dialed his cell phone and laid Marlena's on the table.

"This is Chuck. What's up, Mickey?" Chuck said over the cabin noise of the PAVE Hawk helicopter.

"I just heard from the German woman, Marlena. She told me to go in tomorrow and pick up the rest of my payment," Mickey said.

"Good, she doesn't suspect you. Just relax. They'll all be in chains by noon tomorrow," Chuck said.

"Chuck, I think she was in an aircraft when she called me," Mickey said.

"Are you sure?" Chuck replied.

"That's affirmative. It sure sounded like an airplane engine to me," Mickey said.

"Hang on," Chuck said.

A long minute passed before Chuck came back on.

"I told the general and he said not to worry about it. Our team will be at the hangar in a few hours. He'll have his F-15s over Isabel Pass in less than an hour. They'll station a tanker up there to refuel every two hours. If she tries to move early, we'll get her. Isabel Pass will be covered," Chuck said.

"What about Valdez?" Mickey asked.

"We discussed that again after we left. No way Valdez can be their target, Mickey. Isabel Pass has the higher altitude pumping station and would be an easier target for a small aircraft. So quit worrying and go home and get some rest," Chuck said.

"But Chuck . . ." Mickey started.

"Special Agent Banister, you are off this case. Got it?" Chuck said.

Mickey paused and then answered.

"I got it, Chuck," he said.

He heard silence as Chuck cleared the connection on the other end. Mickey sat in the chair just staring around the shack for a good fifteen minutes. Finally he got up and walked over to the radio panel and turned off all the equipment. He then pulled a duffle bag out from under the tool bench and opened it on the table. He put the case with the $200,000 in the wall panel and closed it. It looked like a normal wall with tools hanging on it. He reached up into the gun rack and picked up four boxes of 9mm shells and two boxes of .44 magnum shells. He checked his pocket and found he still had the roll of $100 bills from the day before. Sliding the wall over the weapons, he walked to the door and turned out the light before he opened it. Securing the lock, he walked to the truck and got in the front seat.

"O.K., Miss Molly, we've got some work to do so take me to the village," he said as the old truck headed down the road toward Stevens Village just five miles away. The airstrip was on the other side of town.

When Mickey arrived, he got out of the truck and walked into the small building that had posted a sign reading Stevens Village Field. As he walked in, he couldn't see anyone but could hear country music playing from the back room. Stepping around the counter, he saw a man sprawled out on a cot with salt-stained lizard-skin cowboy boots hanging off one end and a newspaper covering the face.

"Hey, cowboy," he said.

The body didn't move. Mickey walked over and nudged one of the boots.

"Anybody here?" Mickey asked again.

Slowly one hand pulled down the paper to reveal two sleepy eyes.

"Yup. Sorry. Been takin' a nap it's been so slow around here this evening," the man said.

"Got any charter pilots around?" Mickey said.

"In a town of just fifty-three families, everyone who's got a plane is a potential charter pilot. But they're all home enjoying a nice fire, hot stew, and warm hugs. I am the only idiot still around Stevens Village Field," the man said.

"Don't suppose you would be interested in taking on a paying fare?" Mickey asked.

"Sure, what time tomorrow do you want to leave?" the sleepy-eyed cowboy asked and began to sit up slowly.

"I want to go tonight," Mickey said and counted out five $100 bills. "Here's the down payment. When I get there, you'll get two more."

"Seven hundred cash. Where to, big guy?" the cowboy asked and sat up.

"Valdez. Do you have an IFR rating?" Mickey asked, not wanting to commit suicide.

"I have every rating you can think of. Two tours of flying for Uncle Sam gets you qualified for just about everything," the cowboy said and stood up. "Smith's the name, Slick Smith," he said.

"Mickey. Not related to Chuck Smith in Fairbanks are you?" Mickey said and offered his hand.

"Probably, and every other Smith or Smythe on the planet. Valdez it is as soon as I get a weather report. I'll fire up the Piper. No, I better take the amphibian Caravan since we'll approach Valdez from the Sound tonight. In an emergency, the pontoons might come in handy. Can't be too careful where you can land. I'll file a flight plan through Fairbanks and Anchorage just for safety purposes to allow for weather changes. It'll take a couple of hours longer, but I can guarantee you I'll get you there tonight," Slick said.

"Sounds good to me," Mickey said. "Say, by the way, do I detect a West Texas accent in there somewhere?"

"Lubbock, Texas, U.S.A.," Slick said and smiled.

"I grew up in Amarillo and my family still lives there," Mickey said. "Looks like we'll have a lot to talk about on the way down."

"What's the reason for your visit on such short notice, Mickey?" Slick asked as he filled out some pre-flight papers.

"I'm going hunting," Mickey said with a serious look on his face.

"Hunting. I've learned never to ask for what, when I hear that one," Slick said.

"Good idea," Mickey said and walked back out to the truck to get his duffle bag.

As he closed the door on the old pickup, he spoke out loud.

"Be back in a few days, old girl. Just take it easy until you see me," he said and slung the duffle over his shoulder and walked across the tarmac to the hangar.

13

Czarina Catherine II

"There's a restaurant," Heather said and pointed to the log cabin up the hill from Hazelet and Galena streets.

"I'm starved," Roy said.

"Well, let's try it. Looks interesting," Mavis said and led the way up the thirty-two steps to the rustic building with the blue metal roof.

Huffing and puffing, they reached the steps with Chris bringing up the rear. He stopped and looked across the Port of Valdez and the beautiful blue ocean with the perfect mountain vistas.

Mavis came over to him.

"Time to go in, honey. What are you thinking about?" she said and gave him a quick hug with one arm.

"Just thinking about Natalie, that's all," Chris said and smiled. "Just wondering what's she doing today."

"Probably sitting in a lecture hall, taking an exam, or hanging out with friends. I'm sure she misses you, too. I'm glad she got to stay with us in Italy for a couple of weeks before going back to Oklahoma. And just think, we'll spend Thanksgiving in China, and she's supposed to fly over for the week, isn't she?" Mavis said trying to cheer him up.

"Yes. That'll be here in a couple of weeks. Yeah, I'm O.K. Thanks, Mom," Chris said remembering the pep talk he had just given to R.O. in the hotel lobby which had put him in this melancholy mood in the first place.

As the group sat down at some long benches and began to order, R.O. walked over to the window to watch another seaplane land. He looked down at the street and saw two old men walking along, one with a long red beard. He watched them for a minute then headed for the front door.

"Hey, mister. Where do you think you're going?" Mavis said from ten feet away.

"I'm going to say hi to Father Fefelov," R.O. said and broke through the door in a run.

"No, you're . . . shoot, why does he always do this to me?" Mavis said under her breath as she bounded out the door behind him and down the steps toward the street.

R.O. was taking three steps at a time and reached the street in a few seconds.

"Father Fefelov. Father Fefelov," he yelled at the men down the street about a hundred yards.

Father Kristov started to turn around.

"Don't respond, Father. It's the young man from the hotel," Fefelov said.

R.O. kept running after them until he was just a few feet away.

"Father, are priests hard of hearing, too?" R.O. said and stopped.

Fefelov and Kristov stopped and turned around.

"Oh, my young Mr. MacGregor. Is that you? My heavens, what are you doing in Valdez, so far from Denali?" he asked.

"Well, Father," R.O. said and took a deep breath. "I should ask you the same question. I mean, I call your name and you don't stop. And you don't even have your robes on."

"You are very observant, young man," Fefelov said.

"Father, I'm twelve, not blind," R.O. said, showing his exasperation.

"I see that you are, not blind I mean," Fefelov said as Mavis reached them.

"Ryan, could you explain why you are pestering these gentlemen?" Mavis said and stepped next to him and turned him toward her with a jerk.

"Madam, may I address this question?" Fefelov said.

"Why certainly, sir, and I do apologize for my son," Mavis said.

"He's a father, Mom, not a sir," R.O. said.

Mavis squinted her steel blue eyes at him.

"He's quite correct, madam," Fefelov started but was interrupted by R.O.

"And she's a doctor, not a madam," R.O. said.

"Ryan, if you don't clam it up right now . . ." Mavis said leaning down in his face.

"Dr. MacGregor, I am Father Fefelov and this is my friend and associate Father Kristov. We met young Ryan in Denali this past week, and I suppose he spotted us walking along the street and decided to come and pay his regards. Am I right, Mr. MacGregor?" Fefelov said.

"Yes, and my friends call me R.O.," he said.

"Ryan," Mavis said loudly.

"Very good, R.O. Father Kristov and I will do the same," Fefelov said.

"We are very sorry to bother you," Mavis said just as Jack ran up out of breath.

"Father Fefelov," Jack said and offered his hand. "I wouldn't have recognized you if I hadn't just heard Father Kristov's name. Are you on vacation?" Jack said, thus bombarding the two Russian Orthodox priests with another round of questions.

"No, not exactly," Fefelov said.

"Father, I think an alliance would be a good idea considering that our cover, as you call it, has been blown," Father Kristov said and looked from Mavis to Jack to Fefelov. "Some younger and fresher legs might be advantageous to us since our rivals are getting so close."

"Perhaps, that would be a good idea," Fefelov said and looked up at the restaurant. "Would the MacGregors mind if we joined you for a bite of lunch?" Fefelov asked.

"No, Father. We would be honored," Mavis said.

"Good, Father Kristov and I will follow you back up the steps to the restaurant. We have something to share with you. Go ahead. It will take a couple of old men a few minutes to catch up with you, so order me some hot tea. Anything for you, Father Kristov?" Fefelov asked.

"Hot tea sounds very good right now," Kristov replied.

Within a few minutes all the MacGregors were back at the table with two more chairs being pulled up for Fefelov and Kristov. Right afterward, the two old priests walked through the doors, lightly winded but in a good humor. Their decision to ask others to help them had given them some extra strength and a new resolve until Father Dimitri could arrive.

The entire group ate fresh salmon, clam chowder, crab cakes, potatoes, green beans, and a big apple pie for dessert. Mavis was drinking a hot cup of coffee, long ago having broken her English tea habit, as the kids drank sodas and ate the last of the pie crumbs.

"Well, Father, what is it you wanted to share? I flew up to the Arctic National Wildlife Refuge two days ago for a fly-over, courtesy of Northern Alaska Oil. Is it about the conference or the drilling negotiations?" Jack asked.

"Dr. MacGregor, I wish it was something so simple as to measure a need against a resource and make a logical decision. That's all the tribes and the government need to do about ANWR and then work to protect God's creation while they meet the need," Fefelov said.

"But it is more difficult. Father Fefelov, Father Dimitri, and I are on a quest to find a religious artifact that was lost many centuries ago," Kristov said.

"We believe the artifact may be in Alaska," Fefelov said.

"Is it lost treasure?" R.O. chimed in as he licked his fork.

"Yes, you could say it is lost treasure. But it is treasure of a different kind. To some men, it would be valuable because it's made of gold and jewels. To other men, it would be valuable because of its place in history. But to us, it's valuable because it represents the faith of a great man during a time of darkness among all men," Fefelov said and sipped his tea.

"He must have been a great man," Chris said.

"He was a great man," Kristov said. "He was Charlemange, the Holy Roman Emperor, and it's his cross that we are seeking."

The chatter around the table fell silent. Everyone, including R.O. became still.

"And how will you find his cross?" Heather asked softly.

"It's a long story, my child. But if you'll order me another pot of tea, I'll be happy to tell you," Fefelov said.

"The story begins," Father Kristov said, "when Charlemagne was fighting his way across northern Europe trying to Christianize the barbarian and pagan tribes that had ruled there for centuries. It was about four hundred years after the Roman Empire had fallen. He was known for his wisdom, his tough leadership, and for being unmerciful to those who would deny his authority. But it's recorded that he always had a priest travel with him, and with each village he conquered he sent a priest to evangelize the area. Each priest would stand before him and hold and kiss the cross that hung around his neck.

"Over time, Charlemagne became more powerful, and then there are other stories about his life and his death, but the cross was lost in time. We have always been fascinated with lost relics of the Church. Then last year, we received a special invitation to the Vatican. This is rare, since we are Russian Orthodox priests. However, we are also well known for our efforts in finding and retrieving artifacts that share an importance with both the Roman, Greek, and Russian arms of Christianity. So we traveled to Rome and were treated with warm hospitality," Kristov said.

"There we met a young priest by the name of Vitorio Luzano. He is a curator with the Vatican collection of European artifacts and gave us a thorough tour of everything. We were even allowed to spend some time in the great Vatican Library, with the exception of the lower vault area. It's there we found a reference to the lost cross of Charlemagne. It mentioned the Great Emperor of Christ of the North.

"It is a rare title for Charlemagne. It has been used only

twice, according to my research. Then I found a document that recorded the testimony of priests visiting the Holy Church in Sophia, Bulgaria. It referenced a shrine to a cross that had many jewels and was from the Great Emperor of Christ of the North.

"The hidden reference led to yet another document that told of the efforts to hide precious artifacts from the Ottoman Empire as it expanded north into what is now modern day Turkey and Eastern Europe. I was able to find more pieces that fit together where the Orthodox Church of Eastern Europe grew closely tied to the church in Russia. We found a connection between the priestly order in Bulgaria and priests in the court of Catherine II of Russia," Fefelov said and sipped his tea.

"It was Catherine II who commissioned priests to come to Alaska in 1795, just one year before she died. There was an eleven-year period of exploration in which the Russians tried to start settlements all the way from Kodiak to Sitka," Kristov said.

"I read that Natasha Shelikov was the first woman from Russia to come to Alaska," Heather said.

"That's correct," Fefelov said. "Then there was Irina Baronof Yanovskii and many other great women who helped settle this rugged country and bring priests to the new Russian colonies. But it was Catherine who had a penchant for sharing her wealth and guaranteeing one's loyalty by giving emissaries and governors objects of wealth and art. It was Catherine who we believe sent two priests with the Cross of Charlemagne to Alaska."

"Or the priests smuggled it out of Russia to find a new home where it would be more greatly appreciated," Kristov added. "Nonetheless, all the evidence from Greece, Eastern Europe, and Russia follow a trail to Alaska of the religious order who last had possession of the cross of the Great Emperor of Christ of the North, the Cross of Charlemagne."

"And since I have returned from Rome and most recently Greece, we have been hot on the trail, as you would say, from Sitka to Kayak Island to Anchorage to Valdez," Fefelov said.

"We believe we're very close, because our rivals have been seen visiting every lead we've visited," Kristov added. "Father Dimitri has been shadowing them, as a detective would say."

"And who are your rivals?" Mavis asked.

"One is the young archaeologist and Roman Catholic priest whom we met at the Vatican last year, Vitorio Luzano. The other is Dr. Januz Lemanski, a well-known Polish archaeologist. They have been seen in several places across Alaska in the last few days collecting many of the same clues we have," Fefelov said. "Obviously, I left too big a trail in the Vatican last summer."

"And that's why we have decided we need your help," Father Kristov interjected. "We believe they'll be in Valdez in the next two or three days, so time is running out. We need fresh legs in finding the last person on our list who might lead us to the final resting place of the cross, if it still exists at all."

"Who's your last contact, Father?" Jack asked.

"She's a retired librarian and historian who worked for the Alaska State Library but is also a member of the Russian Orthodox faith. Her grandmother was a member of the Alutiq tribe. She has written for several publications about the history of Alaska, and just yesterday we discovered that she retired to Valdez about ten years ago and has an unlisted telephone number. We just arrived in Valdez and haven't had time to locate her, but Father Dimitri learned that she is still alive and lives alone here in Valdez," Fefelov said.

"That shouldn't be too hard. This is a very small town. We can help you find her," Mavis said. "This should be fun."

"Thank you very much," Fefelov said.

"Do we get to keep the cross if we find it?" R.O. asked.

"No," Jack and Mavis said in unison.

"Good grief, I was just kidding. Don't forget who found the lost treasure of Devils Grotto," R.O. said.

"How could we be so lucky to forget? You constantly remind us," Heather said.

"Where do we start?" Roy said. "This sounds like a lot more fun than being home in the dark. I could get used to this warm weather." He smiled and licked his fork.

"Oh, Roy, you need to see Texas to get really warm," Heather said. "I mean, if you live in Texas, then you learn how to sweat properly and in a dignified fashion."

"That's right. It took me quite a while to get accustomed to the heat after leaving England," Mavis interjected.

"Let me drink my last sip of tea and then we shall begin," Fefelov said.

14

Natasha Novotski

Father Fefelov led the way as the troupe of Texans and one Alaskan marched down the steps from the restaurant to the flat sea-level streets of Valdez.

"Dr. MacGregor, if you'll go to the Chamber of Commerce, Mrs. MacGregor, rather the other Dr. MacGregor, if you'll go to City Hall and check for utility records, Father Kristov and I will go to the Valdez Historical Society. We'll meet back at your lodge in two hours," Father Fefelov said.

"I'm going with Mom," Heather said.

"Chris, stay with your Mother, and Roy you stay with Chris," Jack said.

"Can I go with Father Fefelov and Father Kristov?" R.O. asked and looked at Jack.

Father Fefelov's eyes widened a bit before he heard Jack say, "If it's O.K. with them."

"Yes, it's fine," Kristov said and got a grim look from Fefelov.

"Remember, her name is Natasha Novotski," Fefelov said.

"You didn't mention she was also of Russian heritage," Mavis said politely.

"It slipped an old man's memory," Fefelov said.

"Natasha Novotski. Got it," Jack said and walked away on his way to find the Chamber of Commerce.

Mavis, Heather, Chris, and Roy were walking briskly away when R.O. turned to face Father Fefelov and Father Kristov.

"We'll make a great team, fathers," R.O. said.

"I'm sure we will," Father Kristov said. Father Fefelov remained silent and proceeded in the direction of the historical society and museum.

Heather and Mavis window-shopped at the many shops along the streets while Roy explained which pieces of jewelry were not carved from bone, which clothing items were genuine Alaskan, and which were made in India. Chris just walked along enjoying the view of the mountains. Soon they reached City Hall and went in. After Mavis told the young clerk what she needed, she grimaced when she heard that because of privacy laws she wouldn't be getting an address. Thanking the young woman, they left the small building.

"Looks like we've got more than an hour to kill, so that means more shopping," Heather said and smiled.

"That's fine with me. I never get to do anything like this," Roy said.

A few blocks away, Jack entered the Chamber of Commerce.

"Hello, my name is Jack MacGregor, and I'm looking for an address for a Valdez citizen," he said.

"I'm sorry, sir, but I can't give out names and addresses of members or residences because of privacy restrictions, unless they are listed in the telephone book or our approved directory," the young lady said.

"Are you Dr. Jack MacGregor?" another young lady said.

"Yes. I am," Jack replied.

"Wait, right here," she said and walked into another room.

In less than a minute, a middle-aged man walked out of the adjoining room. He was tall and balding, with a blond beard and was wearing a red flannel shirt and jeans.

"Dr. MacGregor, I'm Steve Funk, director of the Chamber of Valdez. I've been reading with interest in the Anchorage paper about your visit to Alaska, but I didn't know you were coming to Valdez," Funk said.

"It was a sudden change of plans. I wanted to check out the oil terminal before I went back to the ANWR conference. But that's not why I'm here. I'm helping a friend locate a retired historian/librarian who lives in Valdez. Her name is Natasha Novotski," Jack said.

"Mrs. Novotski, I know her well. She is quite a colorful lady. Her ancestors were both Russian and Native Alaskan. She lives in a big house up on Porcupine Drive overlooking Valdez. You just go up Hazelet to Robe River Drive and take a right. Porcupine is the only street that turns left as you go from Hazelet," Funk said.

"You've been a great help, Mr. Funk," Jack said.

"Call me Steve, and if I can be of any further help while you're in Valdez, just call me," Funk said and handed him his card.

Jack said goodbye and started back to the hotel when he saw Mavis, Heather, Chris, and Roy walk into a store just a block away. He headed that direction.

"Father if you want me to run ahead, I can ask about the Russian lady," R.O. offered, already tiring of the slow pace of the priests.

"No, I don't think your parents would like for me to do that," Fefelov said.

"I agree," Kristov added.

"We will be there soon enough, and if we aren't, then we'll find something else of importance to do," Fefelov said.

"What do you mean?" R. O. said, trying to understand the statement.

"I mean that life is always full of opportunities if the one we are working on at the moment turns out not to be to our liking," Fefelov said.

"I see, I think," R.O. replied.

After another twenty minutes of walking, they were a block away from the Valdez Historical Society when they saw Jack, Mavis, Heather, Chris, and Roy walking toward them. R.O. looked for cars and took off in a run after a black Toyota Land Cruiser drove by.

"Hey parents, Roy, and beloved siblings. Am I glad you all happened along," R.O. shouted.

"You are so full of crap," Heather said, quickly regretting it as soon as it came out of her mouth.

"I suppose you want to stay at the lodge and read more Chinese history while the rest of us go snowmobiling tomorrow?" Mavis said to Heather.

"Sorry, Mom," Heather said and faked a big grin.

We haven't made it to the museum yet. I mean, they are slower than a . . . well," R.O. began to say and was interrupted.

"Be polite. You must respect men of such age and wisdom," Mavis said.

In a few minutes, the group was together, and Jack was sharing the directions to Natasha Novotski's house on Porcupine Drive.

"I think I should use the certificate for a vehicle. I'll go ahead to the lodge and arrange for the H2 while you all walk that direction," Jack said and took off in a brisk walk. Chris went right behind him.

"I'm going, too," R.O. said but Mavis reached out and grabbed the hood on his parka and jerked him back.

"I think I need your presence with me for a while," Mavis said. "We haven't bonded for a few days."

R.O. just looked at her and rolled his eyes. Father Fefelov smiled.

About the time the group had reached the lodge, Jack and Chris drove up in a white H2.

"Cool, Dad," R.O. said.

Heather, Roy, and R.O. climbed into the third seat that popped up from the cargo bed while Mavis and the two priests got in the second seat. Chris was driving while Jack was riding shotgun. Small talk continued until Chris steered the H2 up the steep incline on Porcupine Drive and stopped at a big house nestled among some tall pines at the end of the street.

"Everyone stay in the H2, while I go with Father Fefelov and Father Kristov. We don't want to frighten her," Jack said.

In a few minutes, Jack was back at the H2.

"O.K., come on in. She's very nice and wants to meet all of you. Ryan, don't touch a thing. Got it?" Jack said.

"Got it, Dad," R.O. replied.

As they walked into the big front room, they were impressed that it looked just like a miniature hunting lodge, with furs tacked to the walls and animal heads scattered around. The large log crossbeams gave it a spacious appearance, and a fire was going in the fireplace.

"What a pleasure to have so many guests in my home at one time," the short, grey-haired woman said.

"You must be Mrs. MacGregor," she said and shook her hand. "You have such handsome children, and this one is nearly all grown." She reached out and patted Chris on the arm.

"And you must be from one of the northern tribes," she said to Roy.

"Inupiat," Roy replied.

"I was going to guess that. You have such a strong face. I know your people well," she said.

"Madam, shall we sit? I have some questions for you," Fefelov said.

"Oh, please, sit, sit," Natasha Novotski said.

"Father Kristov and I have been searching for answers for some time to an interesting puzzle and we were told in Anchorage that you might be of help," Fefelov said.

After a few minutes of going back through the story of Charlemange, Catherine II, and the Russian priests coming to Alaska, Father Fefelov was ready to pose his first question.

"Father, I think I know what you are going to ask. Do I know anything about the Cross of Charlemagne? I am sorry to disappoint you, but the answer is no, at least I don't think so. There was a small church in early Valdez that helped the gold miners as they tried to travel across Valdez Glacier to the Copper River Canyon and on to McCarthy for the first gold strikes, which some say were just a big fraud. But that's another story all by itself. By the way, can I get anyone some tea?" she asked.

"No, we're fine. We just ate about an hour ago," Mavis said for everyone.

"Good. But I have to tell you that you aren't the first to ask such a question. There was a priest, about thirty years ago, who came by my office in Anchorage and asked me extensively about any Christian artifacts that I might have heard legends or lore about. He mentioned a cross of some kind, but that was a long time ago.

"There were many stories that circulated among the believers within the tribes about such things that were brought from Russia to this exciting new world of ours in Alaska. So many, that I have forgotten most of them. You see, my mother was a direct descendent of the tribe that helped settle some of the early priests, and my father was a fourth-generation Russian-Alaskan. Both of them told the stories that were passed down about the church, the Russian priests that would come and how they would struggle to reach out to the Indians and miners.

"I only heard mention of some things that were brought over from Russia, but I can't remember if one was a cross," the gentle old lady said and adjusted her position in the wooden rocking chair. "But I do remember something that I think will interest you."

"Father Fefelov, Father Kristov, what I'm going to tell you I haven't told anyone. I am eighty-nine years old and I have been an Alaskan all my life. I am very proud of this land, her people, our culture, and our rich heritage. There is no better place on God's earth to be. But it's time I shared my secret with someone before it's too late and the story is lost. I don't know if it's true, but the story needs to be shared, and you can do with it as you will," Natasha Novotski said.

Everyone in the room was quiet, and all eyes were glued on Natasha as she adjusted the hand-knitted shawl around her shoulders.

"My mother was a young woman and had only been married to my father for a year when a priest arrived in Valdez from Sitka. He was very ill from a fever and said that he carried something of great value that needed to be hidden until he got better. He was afraid that it would be stolen or in his illness he would lose it.

"While he was sleeping, she looked in the leather suitcase that he carried. She was a rather nosey young thing. She saw a black velvet pouch and knew something inside must be of great value. When he awakened and she fed him, she asked him what it was. He knew he had to tell her and gain her confidence because he was afraid that she might take it while he was weak. He didn't know my mother. She had a heart of gold that was purer than any nugget Alaska has ever given up. So he told her the truth.

"He said it was a black pearl set in gold with diamonds and rubies and had been commissioned by Catherine the Great to be sent to the Russian Orthodox Church in Alaska. It was the size of a twenty-dollar gold coin and was of immaculate beauty. He told her it had been named by Catherine as the Czar of Alaska," she said and leaned back in her easy chair as if a great weight had left her shoulders.

"The Czar of Alaska," Kristov said. "It's no wonder Luzano and Lemanski have been racing so close behind us. We were looking for a great religious artifact that belonged to a great man of faith. They were looking for treasure, for something to turn into dollars. How disgusting."

"Did you say Lemanski?" Natasha said and adjusted her thick spectacles. "A man with that name called me this morning around eleven and said he would be by later today or tomorrow to see me. I wondered how he got my number. I had it unlisted years ago so history buffs and tourists would let me retire in peace. He seemed like a very pleasant man."

"That is Dr. Januz Lemanski," Father Fefelov said. "He is an archaeologist from Warsaw, Poland. We knew he was close but not this close. He's well-known for looting great sites and selling what he finds on the black market to private collectors."

"This sounds serious," Jack interrupted. "I'm glad we're all here together for your safety, Mrs. Novotski."

"Thank you, Dr. MacGregor. I am, too. But the sheriff is a close friend and if I need him, he'll be here in a few minutes," Natasha said.

"I insist that we call him and he be here, or one of his deputies come before we leave," Jack said.

"I'll be just fine. There is no need to bring in the sheriff. I have a double-barrel shotgun right there by the door if I need it," Natasha said.

"Now let me get back to the Czar of Alaska," she continued. "My mother helped nurse the priest for over a month until he had strength enough to travel back to Sitka. But he left the leather case with her to keep until he came back through. He said he wanted to take it to a safer place in the West for the church to keep for future generations. So after he left, my mother gave the case to my uncle to take to his cabin near Thompson Pass.

"He had been a fur trapper and small-time gold miner. He had a worthless little mine where he used to store salted beef and other foods for miners on their way to McCarthy, and it would be a place that no one would look for treasure. It was a very lucrative business for him for many years. Didn't make a penny in gold nuggets, just gold coins. But he was killed in the thirties during an avalanche, and only one of my nephews has been back up there to check on it. He said he found the remains of the cabin and the entrance to the mine under the cabin floor. He didn't have time to stay, and he didn't know about the black pearl, so he came back here and flew home to Portland," she said.

"Why didn't you tell him about the Czar of Alaska?" Mavis asked.

"Well, I have seen so many bad things happen to people who find sudden wealth. Some of these miners were poor and kind one day and rich and mean the next day. I was afraid he wouldn't give it back to the church but keep it and try to sell it. So I thought I would wait for the right time. Frankly, I hadn't thought about it in years until today. I mean, it just hasn't been important to my life," she said.

"It's not something we were seeking either," Father Fefelov said and looked around the room. "I thought we were on the verge of finding the cross of one of the great men of faith of all time, and now we are faced with making a decision as to whether we move forward to look for an object of material wealth."

"I can understand your dilemma, Father," Jack said. "But the Czar of Alaska is a great artifact that should fall into the hands of the right person. Obviously, the trail that led to Mrs. Novotski was purely coincidental because of the heritage she shares with Alaska and her knowledge of the Russian Orthodox Church. Unfortunately, she was singled out from several sources with the government, the Church, and the Native Alaskans with having the most important information in all of Alaska and now we know why."

"Jack is right. The Czar of Alaska must be recovered and placed in the hands of the Russian Orthodox Church here in Alaska," Mavis said.

"And how would we find this cabin?" Father Fefelov asked and looked at Natasha. There was a gleam in her eyes.

"I have a map. I keep it in a safe place," Natasha said and leaned over and picked up a pair of scissors from her knitting basket. She gingerly got out of her chair and walked across the room to a beautiful quilt of a map of Alaska. The patchwork and embroidered picture of Alaska was hanging on the wall next to a picture of her mother. Everyone was spellbound as she took the scissors and began cutting the seam along the edge next to the Aleutian Islands. After she had cut for about ten inches she reached up inside the quilt and pulled out an old yellow piece of paper.

"I told you I was good at finding treasure," R.O. said. "And here we are. What can I say?"

Heather mouthed the words "shut up" to him across the room. He just smiled back.

"Here it is," Natasha said and unfolded it as she walked across the room. The old paper began to tear, so Chris jumped up and helped her unfold it. She walked over to the big wooden table next to her spacious kitchen and laid it out. Everyone gathered around under a big moose-horn chandelier.

"The old miner's trail was first set to go across the Valdez Glacier. But the trek was so treacherous that it would take up to two months to carry in a year's worth of food and equipment. When Thompson Pass was discovered, it was a safer journey, and pack teams could be used with sleds carrying more weight. You'll need to get a four-wheel-drive vehicle," she said. "Thompson Pass gets a lot of snow and it may already be closed. The Richardson Highway runs through it, so I imagine they keep it open. You better check. Just as you come to the pass, you'll see Wortmanns. It's just a burg, but good people live there.

"See this line here," she said. "I can just barely see it. That's the road out of Wortmanns to the cabin. It's only two miles, but it's rough country. I imagine you'll need a snowmobile. I used to ride those. They're a lot of fun," she said and chuckled. "The map says, 2.1 miles, I think. On the left of the road you'll see the ruins to the log cabin. The mine entrance is under the floor in the back room. My uncle wasn't very trusting in those days. Couldn't afford to be. Don't know the shape of the mine, so be careful, especially if you take these two old codgers with you," she said and laughed.

"Madam, we may be aged, but we are not old," Fefelov said and smiled back.

"O.K., there's our Alaskan adventure kids," Jack said. "I'll get four snowmobiles hitched up to the H2 and we'll leave at 6 A.M. sharp."

"What's with this 6 A.M. stuff, Dad? I'm so tired of getting up early. I would give anything to be back in Italy," Heather said.

Mavis walked over to her because everyone had ignored her.

"Sweets, I haven't heard you complain like this since Africa. I mean in Egypt you were a real champ. But ever since we left Italy, it's been one complaint after another," Mavis said.

"I know. I'm just not sleeping well and I'm cold all the time. Can I just stay at the lodge tomorrow?" Heather asked.

"You know how your father feels about that. He wants us all to experience this year-long adventure together," Mavis replied.

"O.K., but I'm wearing three layers of clothes, and I'm buying a pair of electric socks I saw in the gift shop at the lodge," Heather said.

"Good," Mavis said and rejoined the group.

As everyone was standing next to the front door, the diminutive octogenarian got a little teary-eyed.

"I haven't had this much fun in years. This is just so exciting. I don't expect you'll find anything but an old log cabin with a big hole in the floor. But to think that someone actually went there and looked would make my mother so pleased. I can't thank you enough," she said.

"It's our pleasure and our duty, madam," Father Fefelov said and held her hand.

Everyone said good-bye and walked out to the H2 with hopes of seeing the Czar of Alaska within the next twenty-four hours. Father Fefelov had other hopes on his mind.

15

Thompson Pass
Elevation 2,771 Feet

———————————⬭———————————

"Are you sure you've got to get to Valdez tonight?" Slick Smith asked Special Agent Mickey Banister through the headset.

"Yup, as sure as a West Texas twister, and we've both seen plenty of those," Mickey replied.

"Well, we've got good weather all the way. All the Arctic and Siberian fronts are holding up north for a couple of more days. I'm going to vector us to the south and go east until I get past the glaciers. Valdez Field has a lot of good equipment because of the oil terminal being there. Aircraft fly in there 24/7. Since there are no amphibious landings at night, the airstrip has good radar, lights, the whole works, but I always fly an amphibian along the coast for safety measures. It's easier to ditch in the ocean if you've got pontoons," Slick said.

"That's comforting, I'm sure," Mickey said and pulled his seat belt tighter.

"So once I make the turn at Valdez Narrows, it's just a matter of letting them beam me in, like a tractor beam on a spaceship," Slick said and smiled.

"You've had experience with spaceships?" Mickey asked and smiled.

"Oh yeah, they beam me up from time to time. But I never know it. It's a time warp thing. Don't tell anybody I told you, though. Everyone thinks I'm kind of nuts anyway," Slick replied.

"There are days when I wish they would beam me up," Mickey said and looked out the side window of the aircraft. "Right now would be a good time," he muttered.

The first leg of the flight took only two hours and forty minutes before Colonel Richard Smith, U.S. Air Force (ret.), banked the Cessna Caravan sharply to the east. In ten minutes, he made another course correction back to the northeast.

"Time to wake up, Mickey. We're lining up with the Narrows. The oil terminal is quite a sight at night. There she is," Slick said as the Caravan entered the large horseshoe bay at 1,000 feet.

"She looks like Las Vegas on a slow night," Mickey said.

"Yup, quite a sight for these parts. Alaskan pilots adapt to IFR conditions flying for hours without seeing lights at all except for Fairbanks and Anchorage," Slick said and began talking to Valdez Field.

Mickey noticed four seaplanes tied up at the lighted dock as they flew over and decreased altitude for a slow approach to the landing strip. The runway lights were dead ahead with a beam of lights on both sides of the runway that flashed like a neon sign saying *land on me.* Slick touched down without so much as a skid or bump.

"Impressive," Mickey said.

"Compliments of twenty-two years with Uncle Sam and learning how to land C-47s in a landing zone under hostile fire. Quick in and quick out." Slick smiled and turned the aircraft onto the tarmac toward the visitor's hangar.

Mickey reached into his pocket and pulled out two more $100 bills.

"Here's the rest of the money. I really appreciate it," Mickey said and put his billfold back in the front pocket of his overalls.

"Glad to be of service to my country," Slick said. "You don't fit the mold of most of the Feds that go through here. Only FBI and ATF pay cash. Everybody else wants to use a credit card, and since your duffle has an AR-15 stuffed in it and several rounds of ammo, I figure you're undercover FBI."

Mickey smiled.

"You know the drill, if I told you . . . "

"You'd have to kill me," Slick laughed. "Good luck and be safe," he said as Mickey walked to the back of the Cessna Caravan and opened the door and stepped down. A cool breeze hit him in the face, but it was still 40 degrees warmer than his nights on the Yukon River. He turned and secured the door to the Caravan.

Slick Smith taxied up to the hangar and figured he would bunk in the plane that night in a nice warm hangar before flying back over to Anchorage tomorrow. Then he would fly back to Stevens Village the next day. He thought there was no need to hurry with $700 cash in his pocket.

Mickey walked across the tarmac with his duffle slung over his shoulder and entered the airstrip office. A sleepy old man sat searching the Internet and turned around to talk to him.

"What can I do for you?" he asked.

"Which direction is the hotel or hotels?" Mickey said.

"We've got several but since it's the winter season only a couple are open. The most likely one to have a vacancy is the lodge in the middle of town. Do you want me to call them to come pick you up?" the old man asked.

"Yes, thanks," Mickey said and walked back outside to get some fresh air.

Within a few minutes, a red Jeep Wrangler pulled up to the small building and the driver motioned for Mickey to get in. In five more minutes, the jeep was pulling up in front of the lodge without much said. Mickey offered a tip but the young man refused.

"The lodge pays me a good salary to do all kinds of stuff during the night shift. If you order room service, I do that, too. Thanks anyway," the young man said and drove away.

After Mickey checked in and paid cash for two nights, he

took the elevator to the third floor to locate his room. As he entered, he locked the door and laid the duffle on the bed. He picked up the telephone and ordered two plain hamburgers on white bread. No lettuce, no pickles, no ketchup, no mustard, just plain. While he waited, he took off his coat and unsnapped the leather holster that kept the Ruger Redhawk .44 magnum in place. He pulled up his right pant leg and pulled the Beretta 9mm out of a leg holster.

He leaned the duffle bag up against the side table next to the bed with the Colt AR-15 fully concealed. He turned on the cable TV to a news channel and sat down on the bed and took off his old oil-stained, leather hunting boots. Thirty minutes passed as he watched the world news. He heard a tap at the door. He picked up the Beretta and held it behind him. As he opened the door, he recognized the same young man who had dropped him at the front door of the lodge.

"See, I told you I do the room service deliveries, too," he said and smiled.

"Thanks," Mickey said and gave him a $5 bill. "Will you take this?"

"Sure will. I always take the room service tips. Just not the taxi tips," he said and put the money in his jeans pocket. "Have a good stay," he said and walked away.

Mickey took the tray with his right hand, his left hand still holding the Beretta behind his back. He walked over to the table, set down the tray, and returned and locked the door. He placed the Beretta on the table. He thought he didn't have much of an appetite with so much to think about and the fact he didn't really like to fly all that much. But he hadn't eaten since breakfast, and he needed to eat and get a good eight hours of sleep.

He downed the hamburgers faster than he had thought he would and drank the root beer. He thought how it just didn't hit the spot like Henry Weinhard's Root Beer, and a little Tascosa Hot Sauce on the burger would have been good, too. But he knew he needed the food. The next day could be the most challenging day in his thirty years with the FBI.

Before long, he was standing in a steaming hot shower, thinking about just what he was doing in Valdez and what it was he thought he could prevent. But for Mickey Banister, FBI, it was always a matter of gut feelings and faith that good could win over evil, if given the chance. Too tired to think, he toweled off and decided not to put on clothes he had been wearing for three days and crawled into bed with only his boxers and the Ruger Redhawk to wear. He decided he would buy some new clothes tomorrow on his way to Thompson Pass. Before he had finished the thought, he was fast asleep.

The three black MD Explorer helicopters landed next to the hangar ten miles from Stevens Village. Fifteen heavily armed FBI special agents ran quickly to the side door and kicked it in and raced into the hanger ready to fire. Startled from his sleep, Fritz sat up on the cot next to the tool bench and reached for the Onyks 89 assault rifle that was leaning against the hangar wall. Before he could touch it, three silenced shots popped off like an air rifle and he fell dead. Special Agent Chuck Smith walked over to him and felt for a pulse.

"I told you I wanted him alive," he said angrily to the two men who had shot him.

"He was going for the weapon, sir," one of them said.

"That's why you shoot low and not to kill," Chuck said and stood up. The other squad members had fanned out and reported that no other subjects were to be found and that there appeared to be no booby-trapped explosives. Then a frown appeared on the agent's face.

"Bardequez, bring me a secure radio. We've got a problem here. Agent Jolly," he said to one of the three female members of the team, "turn on the detection equipment and do a scan of the hangar. I need one as quickly as possible," he barked at the two special agents in black jumpsuits with black face paint and automatic weapons.

Bardequez arrived with the radio in less than two minutes.

Chuck punched in some numbers and heard a series of beeps and buzzes.

"Colonel Haney," Haney said into the radio.

"Colonel, this is Special Agent Chuck Smith on a secure frequency. We've got a problem. We've just secured the hangar but there are only four aircraft, I repeat, four aircraft, present," the FBI special agent said.

Agent Carrie Jolly hurried over to him.

"Sir, take a look at this," she said and held up the Geiger counter so he could read the dial.

"What are you telling me?" Chuck said and looked at the young female agent.

"The meter is telling us that a nuclear device leaking gamma radiation was recently in this hangar. We found a container that had a lead lining to it and was painted with black lead paint," Jolly replied. "It set off the meter like a fire alarm."

"Chuck," the voice on the radio said.

"Sorry. One second, Colonel," Chuck said and turned back to the agent. "Would Cesium 136 put off that kind of reading?" Chuck said.

"It could, sir, but there would have to be a lot of it. The typical dirty bomb we were briefed about would only emit about a third of this reading or maybe even a fourth. Looks like to me a more standard reading for a plutonium product, most likely plutonium 238. We discovered that the four Cessnas have devices that can release the bombs from inside the cockpit and remotely detonate them. Just a lot of TNT in those, sir," Jolly said.

"Plutonium," Chuck said. "Colonel, we've got a situation here," he said into the radio.

"Spell it out, Agent Smith," the colonel replied.

"We have taken custody of four aircraft, fully loaded with lots of TNT and with remote detonators. But, Colonel, my bomb expert says we are getting readings for a very big dirty bomb plus some nuclear material that might be plutonium," Chuck said.

"Plutonium?" Colonel Haney asked again.

"That's correct, sir," Chuck said.

"I'll notify General Cooper that the cat's out of the bag and it's a meaner cat than we thought. When did the fifth aircraft leave the hangar?" the colonel asked.

"I don't know, sir. Maybe four or five hours ago," Chuck said.

"That's not much help, Smith. You should have had better surveillance on that hangar. I'll check on this end. We should have it on satellite. I already have two F-15s over Isabel Pass at 30,000 feet. If your eco-freaks had already made an attempt, then we would have heard by now. Looks like it might be at first daylight. Our pilots will be waiting in ambush when she shows up. Stay in touch, Smith. We screw this up and we'll both be seeing duty in the Middle East," the colonel said.

Chuck watched as his men bagged up Fritz's body and began to secure the hangar from different positions to arrest the pilots as they arrived the next morning. He thought about calling Special Agent Banister at the Yukon shack but decided to wait until the pilots were in custody. He felt confident the F-15s could knock down the small plane with whatever device was on board before it was detonated at Isabel Pass, but he hated that he had miscalculated the attack by two days and had not stopped the first plane from leaving. He knew Washington would have his neck for that mistake. He found a small coffee pot next to a refrigerator and plugged it in, planning for a long night.

Marlena listened to the live band in the club in downtown Anchorage, lounging in a big red leather chair. It closely matched the leather pants she was wearing under her white parka. Having enjoyed a quiet evening of eating alone, she felt she needed a little excitement and had ventured to a club that had been recommended by the hotel. With the Beechcraft Bonanza securely locked in a private hangar she had reserved over a week ago, she felt confident enough to relax for a few hours before getting a good night's rest.

Yves had never suspected her plan or her motives. She would leave promptly the next morning by ten o'clock, fly over Thompson Pass by noon, drop the load and proceed to Sitka by evening. It was a foolproof plan. The Bonanza had plenty of range to do the job with gallons of aviation fuel to spare. Weather reports were good and would hold for forty-eight hours. It couldn't be more perfect, she thought. Within a day, she could be in Montreal and on a flight to Berlin. She would follow the same route into Canada that she had used before over Devils Paw Mountain just north of Juneau, where there are literally dozens of aircraft in the air at the same time. It would make it easy to slip over into Canada.

She sipped her drink and smiled at what she knew would be the result of a nuclear device exploding over the Trans-Alaska Pipeline in Thompson Pass. The American stock market would be in shambles, and the Arab oil states would be in a prime position for blackmailing the Western nations and maybe even NATO. Japan could be brought to her knees because of the loss of Alaskan imports, and the Pacific Rim nations would tremble in sheer terror. Too much American oil was being sold to Asia. Gasoline prices would increase sharply, and she laughed at how Americans would react when they finally had to pay the same as Europeans had been paying for years.

"And Yves thought we were just going to hug a few trees a little harder," she said and chuckled as the band ended a tune. "Sorry, *mon petit chou,* or whatever your little cabbage means," she said and motioned for the waitress. "I've always hated French, but times have changed and if one doesn't change, my dear Yves, then one gets replaced, or eliminated." She smiled as the band began playing.

16

Grover Cleveland #2
Wortmanns, Alaska

Heather had convinced everyone that six in the morning was beginning to cramp her style, so Mavis let the brood sleep in until nearly seven-thirty. Shortly thereafter, everyone was loaded into the H2 with four blue metallic Polaris Frontier Classic snowmobiles perched neatly on a trailer behind. There wasn't much conversation except for R.O., who was picking out which snowmobile he was going to drive because everyone was sleepy-eyed and cold.

Mavis opened a large white box and turned to face everyone. Father Fefelov was sitting in the second seat with Heather in the middle next to Mavis. Chris drove with Jack up front. Roy and R.O. were sitting in the cargo area partly stretched out on top of four duffle bags of gear that Jack and Chris put together the night before. Father Kristov had decided to stay in Valdez and contact Father Dimitri to let him know of the new developments.

"O.K. I hate doing this to you. You should be eating a wholesome breakfast, but anyone for a chocolate Long John?" Mavis asked.

"Me, me," said R.O. first.

"I have a cinnamon roll for Chris, one for Dad. Father, what can I get for you?"

"I think I'll have the sugar donut. That's my weakness," he said and smiled through his red beard and moustache.

"Mom, I want a chocolate donut," Heather said.

Soon the donuts were passed around with plenty more to spare in the large box for second helpings. Mavis opened a sack on the floor between her feet and started passing around small bottles of orange juice. After she had completed her motherly duty, she reached down into the sack and found a thermos of coffee. Unscrewing the lid, she poured the steaming black java into a cup and inhaled its aroma.

"Ah, coffee. I don't think I could make it a day without a cup," she said in her British accent as if she was performing a television commercial for her favorite coffee blend.

"You mean, five cups a day, don't you, Mom," Heather added and took a bite of a chocolate donut.

"Shhh. Let me savor the moment," Mavis said.

Within minutes, the H2 was out on Richardson Highway and entering scenic Keystone Canyon. There was plenty of snow on the mountain and shoulder from the early winter storms, but the road was clear and dry. Chris was glad for this, but he knew Jack would take over at a moment's notice if it got too hazardous.

The H2 made it along at a steady 40 miles per hour as the road began a gradual climb to Thompson Pass. The farther up the pass they drove, the deeper the snow on the side of the road became, with patches of snow and ice on the black-top that caused Chris to slow to 15 m.p.h. With the H2 running all four wheels on studded tires and with studded tires on the small trailer, the journey to the top was without incident. On the right, there was a sign that read Wortmanns 5 Miles.

Mickey Banister, FBI, had dressed in his old camouflage coveralls and walked downstairs to the lobby.

"Where's the nearest store with hunting equipment and outdoor gear, and I need to rent a four-wheel drive vehicle, too," he said to the clerk.

"I can take care of the vehicle right here, sir, and Valdez Hunting and Fishing is just next door," the clerk replied.

After a few minutes, Special Agent Banister had rented a Jeep Wrangler and was walking next door to the sporting goods store. Once inside, he grabbed a red basket and started pushing it around. Tossing in insulated coveralls, heavy boots and socks, and three thermal shirts and pants and boxers, he made the rounds through the store to the gun counter.

"What can I help you with?" the man behind the counter asked.

"I need a big gun that shoots a big bullet," Mickey said and smiled.

"I've got several of those, but the cream of the crop would be this Weatherby Mark V Magnum. It shoots a .378 caliber magnum that can reach out there and knock down about anything on the planet. Alaska, New Zealand, Africa, it's the rifle to carry," the man said.

"What's the ticket on one of those?" Mickey said.

"Well, it's been kind of slow lately. It sells for about $1,400 but I'll let you have it for $1,200," the man said and smiled.

"I'll take it. And I want that Zeiss scope, too. The one marked $499," Mickey said and reached into his pocket and pulled out his billfold. He produced his personal credit card and laid his FBI identification next to it.

"FBI. Nice to have you in Valdez," the man smiled. "That'll make the paperwork faster and easier since you guys already have all those gun permits. Probably just about five minutes for a check. I'll be right back."

Within fifteen minutes Mickey was carrying the new gun, a shopping bag loaded with his new clothes, another bag full of winter survival gear, and a backpack holding a box of shells for the Weatherby to the hotel next door. The clerk barely glanced at him as he walked through the lobby.

Once back in his room, he redressed into the new clothes and boots and repacked the backpack, loading the survival gear into his duffle with the AR-15 rifle. He checked the block of C-4 explosive to be sure it was clean and safe. He picked up the telephone and dialed a number in Amarillo, Texas. It rang four times before it was answered.

"Hello," said the female voice on the other end.

"Hi, babe," Mickey said to his wife, Jane.

"Oh, hi, honey, it's been over a week. I was getting worried," Jane said.

"Just checking in. By the way, I'm coming home in a few days," Mickey said.

"Good, I'll call all the kids and tell them to pack the grandkids in the cars and come to town," Jane said. "It's been two months since you came home for a week off."

"No, don't bother. There'll be plenty of time to see them. I've decided that when this case is over, I'm retiring," Mickey said with a lump in his throat.

There was a silence on the other end.

"Jane, honey. You O.K.?" Mickey asked.

"I'm fine," Jane said between the silent tears.

"I know it's been hard the last two years, but it's been a very important case. It's the kind of case you retire on when it's done," Mickey said.

"When will you be home?" Jane asked.

"Probably in four or five days. I have to arrange for my truck to be shipped back, but other than that, I'm traveling pretty light these days," Mickey said.

"Can't leave Molly in that icebox, can you?" Jane said.

"Nope. Gotta go," Mickey said. "Love you."

"Be careful. See you soon. Love you, too," Jane said and hung up.

Special Agent Banister laid all of his weapons on the bed. The Ruger Redhawk .44 magnum and 100 rounds of ammunition, the 9mm Beretta with five loaded 14-shot clips, the Colt AR-15 rifle with four loaded clips, and the new Weatherby Mark V with the Zeiss scope and fifty rounds of ammunition. He looked at the arsenal and knew that what he was going to attempt to do had a thousand to one odds against success. But he knew it would only take one good shot to do it and not the dozens of rounds he was used to carrying on a mission and shooting at the scum of the world.

Looking at his watch, he calculated he had about two

hours to get to Thompson Pass and get ready if this was the day. He thought that tomorrow might be the day, but he didn't want to take any chances. He knew these people were ruthless and unpredictable. He also figured that Marlena probably wouldn't be flying over until noon, allowing for flying time from the Yukon River and optimal daylight for her escape. He had time to drive the twenty-five miles and set up over ground zero where the pipeline begins to worm through the pass at Pumping Station 12. That would give him an hour to spare. He would wait until dark and then if nothing happened, he would come back to Valdez and do it all over again tomorrow.

As he packed the guns and ammunition into the duffle, he thought about Jane, the kids, and the grandkids and knew he might never see them again if he failed. He stood up, stroked his beard, and adjusted his glasses.

"I'm not going to let that happen," he said out loud. "They are not going to win."

He chambered a round in the Beretta and holstered it under his left shoulder. He holstered the Redhawk under the other shoulder. He then threw the backpack full of gear over his shoulder and picked up the heavy duffle and the new Weatherby rifle case. He turned and looked back at the room. He suddenly had a gut feeling, knowing Marlena, that this was the day. He walked out of the room and shut the door, his old clothes and boots lying on the floor. He had a feeling he wouldn't be back, one way or the other.

"Wow, look at that waterfall," R.O. said. "It's frozen solid. That is way cool."

"It's beautiful," Mavis said. "There are so many wonders in Alaska."

"More ice ahead, Dad," Chris said and slowed down.

Another road sign read Wortmanns 1 Mile.

"Well, we're almost there, so take it easy, son," Jack said and put on his sunglasses to block the glare.

"O.K., everyone, sunscreen on your faces," Mavis said annoyingly. Everyone ignored her as she attempted to pass around the tube.

"Well, I choose not to be old and wrinkled," she said.

"I beg your pardon," Father Fefelov said and smiled.

"Oh, I'm sorry, Father, I was just talking to the kids," Mavis said slightly blushing.

Chris drove carefully on the slick surface and noticed a gas station and convenience store just inside the Wortmanns village limits sign.

"We'll stop here for a bathroom break. Everybody go," Jack said.

Once inside, everybody lined up at the door to the two bathrooms and also bought soda and chips. Jack bought some packages of meat and bread just to be on the safe side, even though they would be only a couple of miles from the main highway. The clerk tossed it in a bag as the last person cleared the bathrooms, that being Father Fefelov, who was wearing a blue flannel shirt under a red parka that nearly matched his long flowing beard.

"The clerk said the road we're looking for is about a hundred yards up the hill on the left. So we're going to leave the H2 here. Chris let's get the snowmobiles down. They're all fueled up and we've got fifty gallons in the spare tanks on the trailer," Jack said.

"All right kids, put your snow gear on over your clothes. It's going to get wet. Father, I picked up an extra set for you," Mavis said and handed him the navy blue jacket and pants.

"You are too kind," the gentlemanly priest said and leaned up against the H2 to slip on the pants.

It took about thirty minutes for everyone to get dressed and the snowmobiles to be unloaded. The exhaust fumes filled the air as Jack and Chris tested each vehicle.

"That really stinks," Heather complained again.

"Smells like fun to me," R.O. said to Roy, who quickly agreed.

"O.K., listen up," Jack said.

"Mom and Heather on one. Father Fefelov will ride with me. Chris will ride one alone. And Roy I want you to drive the fourth one with R.O. behind. I bet you've had a little experience with these," Jack said and smiled.

"Since I was five," Roy said.

"Chris, we'll tie down the gear bag behind you. Everybody ready?" Jack said.

"Yes," they said in a chorus of voices as a truck passed by on the highway.

"Goggles down and on tight," Jack yelled to everyone over the noise. "Let's go."

He quickly moved forward on the snow-packed parking lot. Mavis was second in line, followed by Roy, then Chris. The caravan of snowmobiles covered the quarter-mile in a few seconds, and Jack pointed to the road that was covered in about a foot of snow. He turned and the tracks of the snowmobile dug in and started kicking up the snow as Jack plunged forward into the beautiful forest. Going slowly but deliberately, everyone enjoyed the magnificent beauty of Thompson Pass with an occasional peak through the trees at the valley beyond.

The road turned and twisted, but the drivers made each curve as if they had been driving in this country all their lives. Roy had, except his home had no trees. The two miles were covered in about fifteen minutes at a safe speed. Jack wasn't sure whether there would be logs or debris hidden beneath the snow. After a quarter of a mile, he reasoned that the road was a camping or hunting trail during the summer months and was kept clean and clear.

At the estimated two-mile mark, Jack started pointing to the left to get everyone to start watching for the remains of the cabin. Within a minute, he spotted a stack of old logs about fifty feet off the snow-packed road and slowed to a stop, signaling everyone behind. Mavis didn't slow quickly enough and passed by about a hundred feet and slid sideways. Heather slid off the back into a bank of snow.

"Mom!" she shouted, lying flat on her back in two feet of snow.

Mavis stopped the snowmobile and killed the engine. She hopped off and trudged through the snow over to Heather, who was glaring at her.

"Sorry, honey. Guess I'm not a good driver. I'll let you drive back," Mavis said and offered a hand.

"Too late. Now I'm really cold. Thanks a lot," Heather said with a disgusted look on her face as she stood up and dusted off the snow.

"Are you all right?" Chris asked as he walked up.

"We're fine," Mavis said ending the discussion.

Jack and Father Fefelov had already trudged through the snow toward the stacks of logs.

"This was too easy to find," Jack said.

"Yes, but the mine entrance will be more difficult. I am sure hundreds of hikers and campers have had their pictures taken all over these old logs," Father Fefelov said.

"But they didn't know they were standing over an old mine," Chris said as he walked up.

R.O. and Roy were already climbing on the remains of one wall and standing on a widow sill that was over a hundred years old.

"Be careful. Those logs might be slick and icy," Mavis said.

Chris wandered through the ruins looking at where the logs had fallen, trying to visualize the original floor plan. Jack and Father Fefelov were doing the same.

"This was the front door," Jack said standing on a log.

"And this is the back of the cabin. Then to my right is one room, and to the left is the other room," Chris said thinking out loud, trying to visualize the rooms through the maze of logs.

"Covered with ice, snow, and old logs. This challenge gets greater by the moment," Father Fefelov said, trying to stroke his beard with his gloves on.

"Hey, Dad, look at this," yelled R.O. from atop the only standing wall.

"Ryan O'Keef MacGregor. Get down from there right now, mister. You'll be sent back to Texas at the next airport if I see you pull another stunt like that," Mavis said with her sternest voice.

"No, Ryan. Do it again," Heather said under her breath.

"O.K.," R.O. said and stepped across the top of where the window had been.

As he made the small leap, his foot landed on a piece of ice and he lost his balance.

"Oh," he yelled as he began to fall, his arms flailing in the air. He reached out and grabbed a low branch of a pine tree that quickly bent nearly two feet before it stopped. He was kicking out with his feet when suddenly the top log began to move. It was perfectly balanced in the center, and it pivoted 90 degrees until it straddled the wall. Roy leapt to the ground into a mound of snow. Another log started to move, then a third.

"Oh no," Heather said loudly.

Chris ducked out of the way as a log swung two feet over his head. Another one tumbled off to the side. Father Fefelov stood still, knowing he couldn't move fast enough and hoped it wouldn't come his way. Jack rushed over and grabbed R.O.'s legs and pulled him down.

"Let go of the branch, I've got you," he yelled at R.O.

R.O. let go and Jack caught him and dropped him on his feet.

Then the log began to move again. Jack turned and grabbed Father Fefelov and pulled him backward a few feet. Mavis put her hands over her mouth in silence. The massive log began to roll and then tilted inward toward the inside of the cabin until one end dipped, and it fell with such a force it drove one end deep into the remains of the old floor. It kept piercing into the pile of logs until it was totally gone. The pile of logs rolled to the side and everything became still and quiet.

Chris was the first to the massive hole in the middle of the cabin floor. He looked up at everyone.

"I think R.O. found the entrance to the mine," he said and smiled.

"Blessed be the saints," Father Fefelov said and smiled.

"Dumb luck, R.O.," Heather said and shook her head.

It took a few minutes for Mavis to cool down and everyone to get collected after the near-tragedy. Chris and Roy brought over the two packs of survival gear and broke out the climbing ropes, flashlights, and safety belts.

"Did Mrs. Novotski say there was a name for the mine?" Mavis asked to everyone.

"No, I didn't hear one, Mom," Heather said.

"I didn't hear one," Chris said.

Jack and Father Fefelov just shook their heads.

"Me either," Roy said.

"Jack, honey. You remember that mine your cousin has been paying the taxes on for thirty years on your side of the family? The one in Colorado," she said.

"Sure, the Grover Cleveland Silver Mine in Bonanza, Colorado," Jack said. "I hadn't thought about it in years."

"I hereby christen this mine the Grover Cleveland Number Two, Wortmanns, Alaska," she said and sprinkled some snow over the gaping hole in the floor of the cabin.

"Oh, Mom," Heather said. "You get so soapy sometimes."

"That's my privilege, dear," Mavis replied.

"I think it is a marvelous idea, madam," Father Fefelov said.

"Time to go down," Chris said with the gear and ropes all tied together. Jack was right behind him. They had tied their ropes to a solid pine tree ten feet away.

As he stepped to the edge of the old log floor, he leaned back against another log for balance and began to walk down the angled log that had fallen from the wall penetrating the floors. He slipped on the ice a couple of times but soon had dropped out of sight. The lantern hanging from his belt lit the room underneath the cabin floor.

"How is it?" Jack asked as he stepped out to the edge and followed Chris into the hole.

"The log is stuck into the floor. Looks like mud, silt, something," Chris said. "It's solid."

Soon Jack was down in the hole with him.

"Reminds me of the temple at Abydos, Dad," Chris said.

"Yes, but if you remember, it was about a hundred degrees warmer," Jack replied.

"How can I ever forget that?" Chris asked.

They pointed the lights around and discovered they were in an old cellar. There were racks and shelves everywhere. Old barrels that were scattered around had rotted in place over the last century, with only their metal bands left sitting on a heap of debris. On one shelf were neatly stacked tin cans. The labels were long since gone but the cans were still intact.

"We've stepped into a time warp of an old mining camp, Dad," Chris said.

"I'll say. The Valdez Museum will love to get their hands on this," Jack replied.

"You O.K.?" Mavis shouted down through the hole.

"Just fine, hon," Jack replied.

"Look, Dad," Chris said as he pulled hard on the handle of a door.

"Swollen shut from years of nonuse," Jack said and began to look around the cellar.

He quickly located a miner's pick and brought it over and started wedging the door open. Within a few minutes, he and Chris had their fingers around the edge and were pulling vigorously.

"The hinges are rusted, but it's moving," Chris said.

Suddenly they heard a snap as the metal broke and the door swung free. They caught it and laid it down carefully so as not to kick up any dust. They pointed their light beams through the door and could tell it was the entrance to the old mine.

"Jackpot," Chris said.

"Couldn't have said it better," Jack said.

He walked back over to the hole and looked up.

"We found the entrance to the mine. Anybody want to come down?" Jack said.

"Yes," R.O. yelled back.

After Chris and Jack climbed back to the surface, they rigged a rope system and began lowering each person one at a time into the hole as they walked down the fallen log. Father Fefelov insisted that he go down. He took his time and made it without a hitch. Soon, the whole party was in the cellar, and with seven lanterns it looked like daylight.

Jack and Chris were the first to venture into the mine. It had been well cut and braced and since it had been lost for over seventy years, there hadn't been any activity that would have destabilized it, except for the occasional earthquake. The old logs that braced the walls seemed to be dry and strong.

As Chris forged ahead, he found a side tunnel that suddenly stopped about twenty feet in. Dozens of old wooden crates were stacked against the dead-end wall.

Chris called out for Jack and turned back to the crates. He noticed they were in pristine condition as if untouched by human hands for decades.

"What did you find, son?" Jack asked as he walked up.

"It's not the tomb of Seti I, but it does look interesting," Chris replied and disappeared into the darkness.

17

Alaska Gold

Special Agent Mickey Banister left Valdez about a hundred yards behind a black Toyota Land Cruiser. He thought he would just stay far enough behind to let the Land Cruiser knock any loose ice off the highway at this time of the morning. He flipped through the radio dial of the Jeep Wrangler and found a country station from somewhere. One thing he had learned in Alaska was that radio stations were a luxury, and one depended on tapes and CDs or the lucky bounce of radio waves if music was desired. The weather was beautiful and that concerned him now that Marlena might be ready to fly. He instinctively looked over at the case of the new Weatherby and took a deep breath. His satellite phone rang.

"Hello," he said.

"Mickey, this is Chuck. We hit the hangar last night and found only four aircraft. The Bonanza is gone," Chuck said.

"Not good news," Mickey replied.

"You're telling me. Agent Jolly also came up with more bad news," he said.

"She's your weapons expert, isn't she?" Mickey asked.

"That's right. She says the radioactivity was gamma radiation and was from either the biggest possible dirty bomb or another radioactive source, most likely plutonium," Chuck said.

"You aren't making my day, Chuck," Mickey said.

"I want you to get back to the shack and call me when you get there. We may need to brief the general about all the subversives you met in this cell of eco-terrorists. This has gotten out of hand. But we have an ace up our sleeve. General Cooper sent four F-15s to cover Isabel Pass last night. Jolly says the weapon is remotely detonated so if we shoot down the aircraft without exploding the weapon, it will crash harmlessly to the ground. Should contaminate no more than just a few square feet that any good HAZMAT crew from Elmendorf can handle," Chuck said.

"I still think Thompson Pass is the target, Chuck," Mickey said again.

"Well, I don't and neither does General Cooper, and so that's the end of it. Head back to the shack and call me," Chuck said and disconnected the line.

"Yeah, I'll call you, Chuck. From Amarillo in three days," Mickey said and put the satellite phone back into his pocket as he heard a low battery chirp. "Should have charged you up last night," he said to the phone.

He noticed the Land Cruiser pulling over at a convenience store just inside the village limits of Wortmanns and decided he needed a pit stop as well. Another cup of coffee and a muffin wouldn't hurt either. He noticed two men get out and walk inside.

Mickey stopped the Wrangler next to a white H2 with an empty trailer, thinking that some family must be enjoying the wilderness of Alaska on this mild winter day before the pass was shut down by severe weather. As he walked into the convenience store, he heard one of the men from the Land Cruiser talking to the clerk and pointing to a crude map drawn on a table napkin.

"You say this road is just a couple of hundred feet up on the left," the man said.

Mickey guessed it was a Polish or Czech accent. As a

trained agent, he watched the other man with long black hair stroll around the convenience store. He thought it was suspicious that he wasn't touching any of the food items, pouring coffee, or heading to the bathroom. When the man stopped in front of the magazine rack and quickly grabbed a magazine, it was a dead give away that he was stalling for time and trying not to be noticed.

Mickey walked over to the counter and paid for the tall cup of coffee and the blueberry muffin in a cellophane package. He quickly left the store and went out to his jeep and pulled down the road a little ways and stopped. He couldn't figure out if he was watching a convenience store robbery in the middle of nowhere or two anxious men. He checked his watch. It was only ten o'clock, and the sun was just beginning to peek over the mountains into the valley to the northeast. He had one hour to set up but that would take but just a minute.

From his map, the pipeline and pumping station were just on the other side of Wortmanns. He had calculated that Marlena would fly down Keystone Canyon surveying the pipeline, and after two or three passes she would notice the pumping station where the pipeline was visible from the air. The snow was melted around the pipeline. That should be her target. With luck, he could put her in his sights on the second run and disable her engine before she could drop the weapon.

He looked in his rear-view mirror and noticed the men had not come out of the store yet. Worried, he drove back to the store. As he stepped from the Jeep, he pulled both guns from inside his parka, first with his left hand on the Redhawk and second with his right hand on the Beretta. He clicked off the safety on the Beretta and cocked the hammer on the .44 magnum revolver.

Casually, he walked up to the store with both guns down to his side, the Beretta for close combat and the Redhawk to shoot through walls. When he stepped in, he couldn't see anyone but suddenly heard the noise of a snowmobile as it raced from behind the store toward the road. The two men were on it. He quickly turned and rushed through the store expecting to find a body when the young clerk stepped through a doorway from the back room.

"Don't shoot," she screamed and raised her hands as Mickey brought the Ruger up to eye level.

He immediately lowered the gun.

"Don't shoot. I'll give you the money. Don't kill me," the young girl began to cry.

Mickey set both guns on the counter and quickly pulled out his FBI identification card.

"I'm sorry, honey. I'm FBI and I thought those two guys were robbing you," he said.

"Oh, my gosh. You scared me to death," she said trying to calm down. "Oh, my gosh."

"Mickey Banister, FBI," Mickey said, thinking that the stress of this case was getting to him. "What did they want?" he asked, helping the young girl to a chair behind the counter.

"They wanted to know about the H2 and the people who were through here about two hours ago. Asked for directions to the same road with this crude map. I gave it to them. Didn't have any reason not to," she said and looked up through tear-filled eyes.

"You did O.K. Where did they get the snowmobile?" Mickey asked.

"They asked me if we rented snowmobiles and I said yes, but there weren't any available. Then they offered me $500 to find one fast, so I let them take one of my boss's. He won't be back until tomorrow, and they left their SUV here with the keys for collateral, so I thought what the heck. I could make a fast $500. There's nothing wrong with that." she said. "I'm just a clerk."

"Do you have another one?" Mickey asked.

"Another what?" she said still flustered.

"Snowmobile," Mickey replied.

"He has one more out back, just like the one they took. For you, it's free," she said and smiled.

"Thanks, young lady," Mickey said and started to leave. "You all right?" he said to her.

"I'm calming down," she said.

Mickey walked back over to her and gave her a card.

"Here's my card. It has a Fairbanks address and telephone number. In case you need to do some explaining, I'll help you out," Mickey said.

She looked at the card.

"Thanks, Mr. Banister," she said and waved goodbye as Mickey walked out the door.

Mickey walked around the store and found the small building where the other snowmobile was sitting. Checking to see if the gas tank was full, he straddled the snowmobile and fired it up quickly. He drove it around to the front, where he got his large duffle and tied it down across the second seat. He took the Weatherby out of its case and loosened the leather sling and swung it across his chest. As he stepped back on the snowmobile, he zipped up his parka and pulled the knit cap tight around his face.

"I am getting too old for this, Jane," he said. "And I guess I'll have to call you Molly Junior for a couple of hours," he said to the snowmobile and pulled away from the convenience store following the tracks of the five snowmobiles.

The snow was already pretty torn up and packed down so the ride was fairly smooth. He cruised along quickly. A mile ahead, Vitorio Luzano and Janus Lemanski were also cruising along with ease. The Polish archaeologist had a broad smile across his face. Vitorio was anxious and sad all at the same time. His motives were totally different from those of the greedy treasure hunter. As they rushed through the forest, Vitorio noticed its beauty and was awed. Lemanski noticed nothing other than signs of the MacGregor's snowmobiles.

"We better shut down and walk the last quarter-mile," Lemanski shouted to Vitorio over the noise of the motor.

"I agree," Vitorio said and began slowing down to a crawl. He stopped and leaned around to Lemanski and could smell the alcohol on his breath. "I estimate that we are about a quarter of a mile away right now. We can try it and if not, we'll walk back and move the snowmobile closer."

"Sounds good to me," Lemanski said and got off the back.

Jack turned around and walked up to the side tunnel where Chris was standing.

"Dead end?" he asked.

"I don't know, Dad. If you look close, it looks like mud has been packed on the wall. See here," Chris said and pointed up close where he was shining his light.

"That's cool, Chris," R.O. said from behind them.

"Wow! I've never been in a mine before," Roy said.

"How did you get past your Mother?" Jack asked.

"She was busy talking to Father Fefelov," R.O. replied.

"Well, stand behind us for a moment. In fact, Ryan, go get the miner's pick lying beside the door in the cellar," Jack said.

"Roger, Dad," R.O. said and hurried back to the entrance, swirling his lantern around and creating a psychedelic effect on the mine walls.

He was back in a minute. Chris took the pick and handed his lantern to Jack.

"Take an easy swing, son. We wouldn't want to jar the ceiling loose," Jack said.

"Gotcha, Dad," Chris said and swung the pick.

It sank into the dirt wall and a chunk of dried mud fell to the floor. Chris looked at Jack and saw him nod his head yes. He took two more swings, and more chunks of mud fell to the floor. On the third swing, he hit something solid.

"That was solid, but it didn't feel like rock. I'll do it again," Chris said.

On the next swing, another big chunk fell free.

"Stop," Jack said and stepped forward.

Jack retrieved the hunting knife he had attached to his belt and scraped at the hard surface.

"Not good for the blade, but it'll have to do," he mumbled.

"Do you see the pattern, Dad?" Chris said.

"That I do. Old bricks, but it's not cement mortar. Just mud. Looks like we found a hidden room down another tunnel," Jack said and smiled. "Let's get these crates back to the cellar and check them out first before we try to break through. We might save ourselves a lot of work."

Jack, Chris, R.O., and Roy started carrying the century-old wooden crates to the cellar. Suddenly, a screeching noise filled the mine and everyone stopped in their tracks. Mavis stepped into the mine.

"What on earth? Jack are you all right?" she shouted down the tunnel.

"The noise came from over here," Chris said and looked at R.O.

Jack walked over and looked down at him. He was still holding a wooden crate that was pretty heavy. Jack took the crate and set it on the floor of the tunnel.

"Sorry, Dad. My radio went off," R.O. said.

"What radio?" Jack asked.

"This one," R.O. said. He reached into his pocket and produced a radio about the size of his hand.

"Explain and make it quick," Jack said.

"I built it in Italy from an old CB radio I found in the basement of the house where we stayed. It took me nearly two months. It's really cool. I can pick up radio stations from four continents, and see this," he said pointing to part of the radio. "It works like a transmitter. I took it off a walky-talky I found in another box in the basement. I once talked to a guy in Sicily. He couldn't speak much English but we had fun anyway. It's powered by four lithium batteries but only weighs about six ounces. Pretty cool, huh?" R.O. said.

"Yes, it's pretty cool," Jack said and touched his knit cap. "Let's get back to work before the girls get cold."

After about three trips each, they had the crates neatly stacked in the center of the floor next to the log that appeared like a giant spear protruding from the cabin above. Jack and Chris found some old tools and carefully removed the nails from the lids while Mavis and Father Fefelov pulled off the tops.

"Two more to go, and so far all we've found are clothes, boots, salt, some old records, and possibly a diary or two," Mavis said, pulling her hair away from her face where it had fallen from under her knit cap.

As the lid came off the last crate, Jack announced that they would have to tear down the wall.

"O.K. team, let's go," R.O. said and picked up a second miner's pick.

"I think this will work better," Chris said and stepped forward with a very old sledgehammer. "Must weigh ten pounds. The handle must be solid walnut. It's hard as stone."

Soon, they were all back in the mine and had walked back to the junction with the other tunnel. Standing around quietly, they watched as Chris struck the first blow, shattering the old brick that had been exposed.

"Wow, that was easier than I thought," Chris said. "But we'll have to take off some more mud."

Jack and Chris took turns chipping away at the mud until they had a circle of exposed old brick three feet in diameter. Chris pulled his goggles back over his eyes and swung the massive sledgehammer at the cracked brick. He put a hole in the wall about five inches across. After about ten swings, he was breathing heavily. He handed the hammer to Jack, who took about ten swings and stopped. Their light revealed a hole about two feet in diameter. Mavis walked over and peered inside with her lantern next to her face.

"Looks like some old furniture stacked around. A few more boxes and some barrels filled with something," she said and stepped back.

Chris took a few more swings until the hole was three feet across and big enough for anyone to crawl through without effort.

"Who's first?" he said and stepped back.

"I think I'll take that honor," said someone's voice behind them.

Everyone turned around and quickly shined their lights toward Vitorio Luzano and Januz Lemanski.

"Please lower your lights from our eyes. I find it rather rude," Lemanski said.

"Who are you?" Jack said and stepped forward with the miner's pick in his hand.

"No need to hold the pick like a weapon, Dr. MacGregor. We're your allies in this endeavor," Lemanski said.

"I'm Vitorio Luzano and this is my colleague, Dr. Januz Lemanski," Vitorio said.

"They are the treasure hunters I warned you about," Father Fefelov said and stepped forward in front of Jack.

"Fefelov, my old nemesis. I see you beat me to the location this time. Most of the time, you're either in second or third place and I'm already back in Warsaw," Lemanski said and laughed. His deep voice boomed down the mineshaft.

"How did you find us? Did you harm Mrs. Novotski?" Mavis said with concern in her voice.

"Mrs. Novotski is fine. We were waiting for you to leave yesterday and recognized Fefelov. So we knew we were on the right trail to find the cross. When we went back there this morning, our new friend Natasha was more than happy to share the story of her uncle with us after a little persuasion," Lemanski said and pulled a Walther PPK .380mm pistol from his coat pocket.

"What did you do to her?" Mavis said.

"Nothing really. You did it for me. Your children made quite an impression on her. All I had to do was tell her I would shoot your children, and she became very cooperative. In fact, she's waiting for us back at the convenience store neatly tied and gagged and covered in a warm down blanket in the back seat. The last thing I want is a murder charge to follow me around the world," Lemanski said. "Unless it's your kids, of course."

"You animal," Mavis said and stepped forward. Jack grabbed her arm.

"Hold it, babe. He's got the gun, not me," Jack said quietly.

"If you didn't have that gun, my dad would make you eat dirt, scumbag," R.O. shouted.

"We'll see," Lemanski said.

"Enough of these theatrics, Lemanski," Vitorio said. "Let's have a look inside the blocked tunnel."

Vitorio took R.O.'s lantern and stepped through the hole.

"Hand me two more lanterns and the pick," he said.

"And do it real slow," Lemanski said and pointed the Walther at Heather's face.

Mavis stepped in front of her to block his view.

Chris gave him his lantern and Roy's and took the pick from Jack.

Special Agent Mickey Banister drove up to the abandoned snowmobile and kept on going around it. In a hundred yards, he found the four metallic blue Polaris snowmobiles and checked his watch. It was 10:30. He had thirty minutes to get into position. He was guessing that Marlena could arrive between eleven and noon.

Marlena flew the Beechcraft Bonanza south southeast from Anchorage before making a 90-degree turn across Prince William Sound. She estimated she was thirty minutes to an hour away from her target because of her reduced speed and altitude. She visualized she would need several flyovers to find the pipeline in the snow and that would add another thirty minutes to an hour. With her full load of fuel, she would still have plenty to reach Sitka before dark. She had been warned by Anchorage Center to keep at a steady altitude and eyes open because of a lot of small aircraft in the area today.

She hummed an old German folk song as she looked out at the beautiful patchwork of islands and ocean, constantly checking her instruments. She had flown small aircraft for twenty years and was accustomed to virtually all kinds of flying, having been trained in the extremely bad winters of East Germany. She adjusted her radio to the frequency for Valdez Field and sang the chorus of the song. It always made her smile.

18

The Fighting Bat
November 15, 1999

A squadron of F-15s had been trading places on patrol for eleven hours. Brig. Gen. Casey Cooper had ordered Col. Luke Haney to scramble another two flights of F-15s, four aircraft in all. The F-16 Falcons from Eielson were on stand-by for NORAD and weren't figured into the equation. The F-15s had orders to secure the airspace over Isabel Pass and to shoot down any Beechcraft Bonanza that refused to divert from the pass or the Trans-Alaska Pipeline. They were ordered to give the pilot only one opportunity to comply and then take the shot.

The F-15 pilots streaked along at 30,000 feet and chatted about their assignment, not knowing what to make of it, but following orders as they had been so meticulously trained and were committed to do. The flight from Elmendorf Air Force Base to Isabel Pass took only a few minutes, and the fighters had been on patrol since midnight, breaking off to refuel every couple of hours. A tanker was sent aloft to be on station with them. An AWACS command aircraft from Tinker Air Force Base in Oklahoma City had been diverted from a routine patrol to coordinate the operation.

As they had many times during the early morning of November 15, 1999, they again made radio contact with the AWACS that was also coordinating an exercise with a B-1 bomber out of Dyess Air Force Base in Abilene, Texas. With four F-15s and a B-1 bomber on a weapons test flight over central Alaska, all the pilots were double checking their communications cards with the legitimate call signs for the day so there would be absolutely no confusion and everything worked perfectly. With each aircraft, except the AWACS, carrying sufficient ordnance to destroy large targets and multiple threats to the security of the United States of America, there was no room for error.

"Wolfman 16 . . . Hammer 34," the pilot of the B-1 radioed to the AWACS.

"Go ahead, Hammer 34."

"Wolfman, Hammer 34 is commencing a weapons test exercise. We're at 20,000, running Mach .72, with a heading of three two zero degrees, requesting clearance into the Yukon Test Range," Brig. Gen. Jeff Mager said from the pilot's seat.

Strapped in tighter than a NASCAR driver to allow only slight arm, leg, and neck movements, the general ran a check of all systems. The computer screen on the console between the pilot and copilot flashed a series of codes as he entered the required mission data. The fluffy clouds of the Alaska sky wisped by like ghosts trying to penetrate the airplane in a horror movie. The sun was sitting on the southern horizon, shining intensely on the cold winter day that Alaskans so enjoyed.

"Hammer 34, maintain flight level of two zero and turn to a heading of three five zero degrees, cleared 450 knots true airspeed. Commence test exercise at 1900 Zulu time," the AWACS colonel said.

Switching the radio to the B-1 intercom system, the general glanced over at his copilot as he addressed the crew of the B-1 with the black bat painted on its tail.

"O.K., everybody. Run the checklist one more time. We're approaching the Yukon Test Range over the ice pack in twenty-nine minutes. The two munitions on board are too expensive to screw up on this test run. It was hinted that we're carrying a cool ten million in each one. But if we have a successful first test, then we're looking at a new theater weapon in less than five years that will enhance the war capabilities of this bird. You've heard me say all that before. I want to thank your commander, Col. Virgil Trout, for inviting me to pilot *The Fighting Bat* and to sit as my copilot today. The star of the show, if everything works, is our offensive systems officer, Major Hare. Eileen, are you ready?" General Mager said.

"Yes, sir," the major snapped back and smiled as she glanced out the tiny window on her right, her hand gripped tightly around the track handle mounted on the console to her right. She thought for a second how the Alaskan terrain was much more appealing than the canyon walls of the Rio Grande River at 600 miles an hour and a few hundred feet off the water, typical of a training run out of Abilene. Her eyes were glued to the nine-inch computer screen in front her as she re-checked the target coordinates. To her left sat the defense systems officer, or DSO. Behind her was the compartment that housed the two test weapons. The midbay carried four JDAMS. *The Fighting Bat* rarely went anywhere unprepared, always ready to fly and attack in defense of the United States at the president's first command.

"Good. People, we can make a difference today that may save thousands of lives sometime down the road. Sit back and relax, and in roughly twenty-five minutes the show begins," General Mager said and flipped the intercom on the control stick.

"General," the DSO said.

"Yes, 'D'," General Mager replied.

"I've been picking up some radio traffic from a couple of F-15s on patrol straight ahead 100 miles. We'll fly right under them in exactly ten minutes. Correction, there are four aircraft, sir. Just listened to the flight lead Bullet 22 talking to Wolfman 16 about an intruder target," the captain said.

"Thanks, 'D'," General Mager said and turned the dial on the radio to the AWACS frequency.

"Wolfman 16 . . . Hammer 34."

"Wolfman 16, go ahead, Hammer 34," the AWACS radio-officer replied.

"Put me through to the colonel," the general said.

"Go ahead, Hammer 34, this is Wolfman 16 Commander," the colonel said.

"Colonel, I wasn't briefed about F-15s in our flight path," General Mager said.

"Hammer 34, we're on alert for an intruder into restricted airspace."

"Roger Wolfman. I didn't know there was restricted airspace in this part of Alaska," the general replied.

"Hammer 34, it's a national security alert, beginning at zero hundred hours. There're four aircraft and a tanker on station. It's being coordinated with the FBI. The threat is to the Trans-Alaska Pipeline pumping station at Isabel Pass."

"Roger, Wolfman. Vector us around the traffic and rolex our entry into the Yukon Test Range three zero minutes. 'D', contact the range and let 'em know we'll be thirty minutes late," the general said replying to both the AWACS and his DSO.

"Roger, Hammer 34. Maintain flight level two zero and turn to a heading of zero four five degrees for four minutes. Then cleared on course," the AWACS commander said.

"Roger and thanks, Wolfman," General Mager said and looked over at Colonel Trout and shook his head.

"Looks like they've got some wacko in a small plane on their hands, Virgil," Mager said. "Probably some irate oil field worker wanting revenge for getting laid off or something."

"We've seen it all, Jeff," Colonel Trout replied.

"That we have. That we have," Mager replied.

Special Agent Mickey Banister walked up to the old crumbling cabin and noticed the bright orange climbing ropes tied to the trees and descending down the hole. The clerk had told him that they were one big family with four kids and a grandfather with a red beard. He checked his watch. There was still time to get to a location before

Marlena would fly over, if this were the day. He walked over to the hole and could hear voices deep inside, but they seemed far away.

He slung the Weatherby over his head and leaned it against two old logs from the cabin, jamming the butt of the rifle firmly into the snow. He carefully grabbed one of the ropes and stepped out to the log that was sticking into the hole at a 45-degree angle. He lowered himself to a crouching position and started to slide carefully down the log on his seat. He heard a rip in his new parka and kept going without blinking an eye.

As he reached the bottom of the log, he could see he was in an old cellar of some kind. He quickly let go of the rope and pulled the glove off his right hand. Reaching inside his coat, he found the Beretta 9mm and pulled it out and released the safety. He then pulled a small flashlight from the front of his coveralls and walked toward the voices. He kept the light off.

"General Cooper," Colonel Haney said and walked into his office. "We need you in the command post, sir. NORAD has picked up a North Korean 747 Airliner that left Paris seven hours ago and is now approaching the Beaufort Sea. They are flying outside of the international flight corridor and are off course by nearly 800 miles. NORAD command wants F-16s scrambled to meet the airliner 400 miles from Point Barrow and escort it toward Russian territory into the flight corridor across the Bering Sea. They want the F-15s sent to the Bering Sea as a deterrent to any intruders, a full scale air sovereignty alert."

The general jumped up from his desk and hurried into the command post. In front of him were the various satellite monitors with nearly twenty people at work trying to avert a crisis.

"We can't pull the fighters off Isabel Pass. Not until 1500 hours," he said. "Any word on the Bonanza?"

"Negative, sir. There hasn't been any traffic around the Yukon River hangar all day except two that were identified as charters. The FBI informed me that they have four pilots in custody and are questioning them right now. Fairbanks

Center hasn't followed any traffic near Isabel Pass since midnight last night, and all that traffic went to Anchorage and Kodiak. It looks perfectly clear, sir. I would say the attack won't happen until tomorrow," the colonel said.

"What's Agent Smith's take?" General Cooper asked. "They have to make the call on this. We can't, colonel."

"He concurs, sir," Haney replied.

"Good. Order one flight of F-15s to the Beaufort Sea and turn them over to NORAD with the Falcons. Have the second flight patrol over the Bering Sea to the west to be sure the North Koreans don't have something up their sleeve and try to come back in after we escort them across the Arctic for a couple of hours," the general said. He leaned on the console next to the satellite monitor. "And, colonel, have another flight ready to go at Elmendorf just in case."

"That's affirmative, sir," the colonel said and walked over to the communications room to send the orders to the AWACS and the four F-15s, while at the same time bringing in another refueling tanker for support over the Bering Sea.

As Colonel Haney radioed the AWACS, the big B-1 bomber was listening.

"General, you should listen to this," the DSO said.

General Mager and Colonel Trout raised their eyebrows at almost the same time.

"Did you hear that, Virgil?" General Mager asked.

"Sure did. That's strange. Two escorts and shoot down orders in one day in Alaska. Haven't heard that since the U.S.S.R. collapsed," Colonel Trout replied.

"Hammer 34 . . . Wolfman 16," the AWACS commander said.

"Hammer 34, go ahead," the general said.

"General, we've got a situation, well to be exact, two situations going on right now. NORAD is requesting that you postpone the weapons test for several hours and for your aircraft to reverse course to the Alaska coast and to begin approach for the test at 2400 Zulu," the AWACs commander said.

"Wolfman, Hammer 34 has been airborne for five hours. If we don't commence the test by 2400 Zulu, we'll be forced to abort and return to Texas," Mager said.

"Roger. We'll do what we can, but with a national security

alert in two places of Alaska at the same time, our hands are tied. Thanks, Hammer 34," the AWACS commander said.

"Well, Virgil, guess we'll turn it around and head back to Texas," Mager said as Major Hare typed in the coordinates and the autopilot made the correction. "We should be over Juneau by 2300, with time to turn it around and run the test if we get the clearance," General Mager said.

Within thirty minutes, the Air Force fighters were cruising over the dark blue water of the Beaufort Sea, waiting for the lumbering North Korean 747 as it crossed the pole in a presumed faulty vector that would send it on a collision course with the United States. General Mager turned his B-1 around and was now crossing the Arctic Circle with the computers set on a course to Abilene, Texas, at 24,000 feet. Thanks to the jet stream and the 110-m.p.h. tailwind blowing from the Arctic, *The Fighting Bat* would arrive in West Texas in three hours and thirty minutes, 4:30 P.M. Texas time.

Colonel Haney ran back into the command post and stopped quickly, almost crashing into General Cooper.

"General, FBI Special Agent Chuck Smith is on the phone, sir. You should talk to him," he said.

The general turned around and picked up a blue phone and pushed the flashing light.

"Yes, Agent Smith," the general said.

"We just got one of the pilots to talk. She was the only other female pilot and was pretty shaken when the German murdered the other female pilot. She can speak fluent German, grew up in Strasburg, Austria, and said she overheard the German leader of the group talking to one of the hangar hands in German. We've been grilling her for two hours, and she said she remembered the leader telling the helper to be sure the Bonanza had enough fuel to reach the coast," Chuck said anxiously.

"Yes, but that could mean after the attack, and she would fly to the coast to escape by boat. The Bonanza has that kind of range," the general said confidently.

"Yes, general, but she said she specifically heard Valdez," Chuck said.

There was silence on the other end.

"That's Thompson Pass, Special Agent Banister was right. I've got a national crisis on my hands with a North Korean Airliner about to invade our airspace. It could be carrying an atomic weapon, so protocol says we escort it from the region or shoot it down. We don't suspect the pipeline attack will occur until tomorrow. Hold on a minute," the general said. He thought briefly. "Thanks for the information, Agent Smith," he said and slammed down the telephone.

"I want to talk to the AWACS commander right now," the general said

In thirty seconds, the general had walked over to a console and put on a headset.

"Wolfman 16, this is Cowboy Control, Alaskan Command. Do you have any assets in the sky over south central or southeast Alaska?"

"Yes sir, Cowboy Control. I have a B-1 out of Dyess at 24,000 feet and headed back home. She's just now over the Wrangell Mountains," the AWACS colonel replied.

"Wolfman 16, I want her diverted to the Port of Valdez and be alerted to a small aircraft. We've got a new target. This is a national security priority. Pass it on to Tinker and NORAD and tell them to contact me immediately," the general said.

"Cowboy Control, what can Hammer 34 do with a small aircraft intruder?" the AWACS commander asked, raising his eyebrows. "*The Fighting Bat* is on a test flight for a new weapon."

"Wolfman, we'll just have to hope he's carrying something that neither of us know about but just might solve this problem. Tell Hammer 34 to go to our radio frequency so that he can be in direct contact with my command post," General Cooper said.

"Roger, Cowboy Control," the AWACS commander replied.

"Hammer 34 . . . Wolfman 16," the AWACS commander said.

"Wolfman 16, we copy," Mager said and sipped on a tiny cup of coffee as the B-1 cruised smoothly through the Alaskan sky headed to the coast and then on to Texas.

"Hammer 34, you've got new orders, and it's not a war game," the AWACS commander said. "This is command security code niner seven two zero. Do you copy?" General Mager downed the last drop of coffee and disposed of the cup.

"Go ahead, Wolfman. We copy," Mager said.

"Cowboy Control requests that you come to a heading of one niner zero degrees southwest of your current position and to hold in an orbit pattern over the Port of Valdez. It seems they have an intruder alert, and they want you down there to make them feel better. Restricted airspace is now over Thompson Pass."

"Wolfman, what can we do about a small aircraft?" Mager said.

"Cowboy Control didn't say. Those are the orders. Good luck. Wolfman 16 out," the AWACS commander said.

"O.K., team, you heard the man," General Mager said to his crew. "We're going to Valdez. 'D', check that security code. I hope they get all the traffic along the coast out of the way when we come blazing through. ETA for Valdez is 1931 Zulu."

"The security code checks out, sir," said the DSO.

"Virgil, looks like I picked a fine day to visit Alaska," Mager said to his copilot.

Trout just smiled and nodded as he did his part in flying the bomber.

Marlena flew the Bonanza through the middle of the Straits of Valdez and could see the way to Thompson Pass across the Bay. She ignored the radio call from the controller at Valdez Field and made the course adjustment to fly east through Keystone Canyon. She checked the release switches. The green one was for the TNT bomb that would puncture the pipeline, the red one was for the nuclear weapon, plutonium-enhanced Cesium 136.

It was enough nuclear material to make the highway impassable and contaminate the pumping station for decades. With a little luck, the gravity flow of oil in the pipeline down Thompson Pass would carry the radioactivity all the way to Valdez. Once inside the pipeline, it couldn't be stopped. She smiled as she lowered her altitude below the surrounding peaks and began to focus on her final approach. As she flew over the oil terminal, she could see a couple of cars below on the Richardson Highway. The twenty-five mile trip to Thompson Pass lasted only six minutes, and she was soon looking at the beautiful sunlit valley on the other side. She banked the aircraft to the north and spotted the pumping station and the 200 feet of exposed pipeline. She smiled, knowing that she was just minutes away from making the drop.

But then she decided at the last minute that two or three more passes were needed to gauge the wind blowing through the canyon and practice the timing of pressing the release button followed by remote detonation. She had only one shot at the American imperialists, and she didn't want to blow it. She banked the Bonanza into a turn and headed back up Keystone Canyon toward Valdez.

Mickey looked up toward the hole in the cabin floor as he heard an aircraft overhead. He hoped it was someone else and not Marlena. He was betting the life of this family it was someone else, and stepped into the mine. He could see several lights up ahead and walked slowly until he was just twenty-five feet away. He heard a voice from a side tunnel.

"Januz, I found something that will make you very happy," Vitorio said and tossed a sackcloth bag through the hole into the main tunnel. It made a funny noise when it hit the rock floor.

"Pick it up," Lemanski said and motioned with the Walther toward Mavis.

Mavis walked over and picked it up and untied the string around the top. She poured part of the contents into her hand, and the light reflected off gold coins, filling the mine with an eerie light show.

"My dear, Vitorio. I believe we have struck it rich. Hand it to me," Lemanski said and motioned with his gun.

Mavis handed him the sack, and he awkwardly held

onto the gun and rummaged around in the sac.

"Gold coins. Not as good as a priceless cross, but they will do," Lemanski said as Vitorio entered the main tunnel through the hole with four more bags of coins.

"Looks like you can buy your cross, Dr. Lemanski," Father Fefelov said. "Or maybe I should say that these coins will weigh your cross down someday."

"Shut up, priest. I'm tired of dealing with you religious freaks who think you're so much better than the rest of us. If it weren't for us, there wouldn't be any of you," Lemanski said and laughed.

"I get your point exactly," Father Fefelov said.

"And so do I," Mickey said and stepped into the glow of the many lanterns.

Lemanski turned quickly and pointed the gun toward Mickey and fired. The bullet plucked a goose feather out of the right sleeve of Mickey's parka and ricocheted three times off the rock walls of the mine. Mickey fired back instantly and hit Lemanski in the chest causing him to fall backward to the cold floor of the mine. He dropped the Walther. Chris was the closest and picked it up and pointed it at Vitorio. He held up his hands.

"Relax folks, I'm Mickey Banister, FBI. You're safe now," Mickey said.

"Father Fefelov," R.O. said, and everyone looked across the tunnel and saw Father Fefelov kneeling on the floor of the mine.

Mavis rushed over and helped him to the floor and laid him back. Blood was seeping through the front of his parka. She unzipped it quickly as Special Agent Banister checked Lemanski.

"He's still alive," Mickey said.

"Father Fefelov has been shot. Must have been the ricochet from Lemanski's gun," Mavis said and tucked her gloves inside his shirt and pressed on the wound. We've got to get him to Valdez soon."

"I'll go back and get the H2. I bet I can get it up here since the road is in such good shape," Chris said.

"O.K., son. Go get it. Roy, go with Chris and stay at the

convenience store and call the hospital in Valdez. Stay there," Jack shouted as they ran toward the cellar.

Mickey walked over to Vitorio and pressed the Beretta up against his cheek.

"I don't know who you guys are, but when this is over, you're going to forever regret crossing my path in Alaska. Sir, take this, I've got some unfinished business topside. I'll be right back," Mickey said and pulled the Ruger Redhawk from his other inside holster and handed it to Jack. "If he misbehaves, just pull the trigger. We'll mop up later," Mickey said and hurried toward the mine opening following Chris, Roy, and R.O. to the surface.

Just as Mickey stepped into the snow his satellite telephone rang. He quickly unzipped the inside pocket, retrieved the phone, and pushed the receive button.

"Banister here," he said knowing that only a few people had the number.

"Mickey, this is Chuck. I want you to go to the rendezvous hangar on the Yukon River and wait there in case Marlena flies in to refuel. We don't know where she's going, maybe even to Valdez like you suggested. Sorry I didn't listen to you, old man," Chuck said.

"Don't be sorry, Chuck. I think I just heard her flying in," Mickey said.

"You're already at the hangar?" Chuck said.

"Nope, not on the Yukon River. I'm in Valdez, and I think Marlena is lining up with the target right now. Better go, Chuck, my phone batteries are chirping. Always forget to keep them charged," Mickey said and hung up. He looked down at the phone and saw that it just went dead. He set it on one of the fallen logs.

Colonel Haney handed the telephone to General Cooper, whose flying handle had been Cowboy 31.

"It's Agent Smith," he said.

"Look, Smith, I don't have time to deal with you anymore," General Cooper said into the phone. "You guys had your chance to make the call. Now it's out of your hands."

"Wait, general. Agent Banister is on the ground in Thompson Pass," Smith said.

"Does he have a communication device? Radio, satellite telephone, anything?" the general asked.

"Yes, sir," Smith said.

"Good, I'll let our asset over Thompson Pass know about him and give him the numbers. Here's Colonel Haney. He'll take care of it," the general said.

"Where're you going little feller," Mickey said to R.O. as he stepped from the log to the snow. Mickey picked up the Weatherby Mark V rifle.

"I'm going to radio Valdez and tell them to call the hospital," R.O. said and pulled his radio from his pocket and turned it on.

About that moment, Marlena made her second pass, and Mickey looked up and could see it was a Beechcraft Bonanza. He had a weak feeling in his stomach. He was hoping she had one more run to go. He looked down at R.O.

"Come on, you're going with me," he said and ran toward a snowmobile.

"Cool," R.O. said and ran behind him.

Mickey swung the rifle sling over his head and hopped on the snowmobile and fired up the machine. R.O. jumped on behind. Chris and Roy had already disappeared down the road toward the highway.

"I bet this road goes higher. At least, I hope it does," Mickey said and turned into the fresh powder.

"Wolfman 16 . . . Hammer 34," General Mager said. "We're over Valdez and making a slow turn back to the north."

"Roger, Hammer 34. Here's the new information. You're scouting for a Beechcraft Bonanza that is targeting the pipeline pumping station at Thompson Pass. I also just spoke to Cowboy Command and they have an FBI agent on the ground. Be alert to civilian radio frequencies for possible contact,"

"Roger, Wolfman 16. A Beechcraft Bonanza, is that correct?"

"Roger, Hammer 34. A Beechcraft Bonanza. It's a suspected terrorist operation with a dirty bomb on board. The proposed target is the Trans-Alaska Pipeline," the AWACS commander said. "We have F-16s coming your way so be alert. Wolfman 16 out."

"Roger, Wolfman 16. Is it an active weapon or it is a compression bomb? What are we dealing with here? I need to know right now," Mager said and put the communication on the intercom for his crew to listen, too. Col. Virgil Trout was already shaking his head as Major Hare keyed information into the onboard weapons systems computer.

"Hammer 34, all we know is what Cowboy Control has told us. The FBI has been working the case and it went sour, and this Bonanza got out of the bag. Now it's in your sky, and you are the closest asset of the United States Air Force. This is totally out of the books, Hammer 34," the AWACS commander said.

"Wolfman, thanks," Mager said, returning to official decorum. "What's the order if we spot it?"

"Hammer 34, you are ordered to bring it down any way you can," the AWACS commander said.

"Thanks, Wolfman. That's an affirmative. My crew has been on the line as my witness. Just wanted you to know," Mager said.

"Hammer 34, Wolfman would do the same. Good luck. We'll be watching."

"Roger, Hammer 34 out," Mager said.

Mickey and R.O. climbed higher on the side of the mountain on the snowmobile until finally Mickey could see a break in the trees and the sun shown in brightly. As he got closer, he realized he had a bird's-eye view of the pumping station and the exposed pipeline down the mountain about a quarter-mile away. He stopped the snowmobile and felt a rumbling noise. The trees began to shake as a B-1 bomber flew by at 600 m.p.h., maneuvering like an agile hawk above the canyon and avoiding the 7,000-foot mountain peaks all around. R.O. put his hands on his ears.

"Wow, gee-ma-nee. What a plane!" R.O. shouted.

Mickey raised the Weatherby and sighted on the opposite side of the canyon. He adjusted the Zeiss scope, trying to estimate the distance that Marlena would be from him and the pumping station. He watched the grey smoke of the B-1 as the aircraft trailed off, making a wide bank towards Valdez.

"You don't suppose they finally believed me, little feller," he said and wiped the condensation off his glasses with one finger. "What other reason would that big warplane be cruising over a canyon in southern Alaska? Man, I wish I could talk to her. How far does your walky-talky work?" he asked R.O.

"I once talked to a guy in Sicily while we were staying north of Rome. That was 800 miles, I think," R.O. said.

"You think you could talk to that big jet?" Mickey said, hoping for a miracle.

"Sure, I talk to airline pilots all the time. Don't tell my folks. They would get really mad. I once talked . . ." R.O. started and was broken off.

"Try to reach him now," Mickey said seriously and looked at R.O.

R.O. turned on the radio and flipped some switches.

"It's got the best microchips made," R.O. said and started spinning the dial slowly.

"Valdez Field, did you see that B-1 zoom by?" a small Cessna radioed as it came through the Narrows and blared through R.O.'s receiver.

R.O. made another adjustment, and Mickey looked up and saw Marlena make another flyover. He trained the rifle on her, but he was too late. He held his breath until she accelerated in the turn and disappeared back down the canyon. He knew he would have to be waiting and not move, and then he would have only five seconds to make the shot. The odds got bigger and he began to sweat. He positioned himself across the saddle of the snowmobile and turned his hat backwards to look into the scope, trying to estimate the Bonanza's flying time down the canyon and back. He figured he had about three to five minutes.

"Jane, I'm getting too old for this," Mickey said under his breath. The thought of his wife made his heart beat even faster, knowing the odds of surviving this were getting slimmer by the second.

"Wolfman 16 . . . Hammer 34," Gen. Jeff Mager said.

"I've got something," R.O. said. "I think it's the B-1 talking to another airplane."

"Go ahead, Hammer 34," the AWACS commander said.

"Wolfman, we've got two small aircraft in the region. One is just taking off from Valdez, and another is flying northeast through Keystone Canyon," Mager said.

"Hammer 34, it's probably the one going through the Canyon. The pipeline terminal is at the southwest end. This could be the drop run or the final run through. Your call, Hammer 34," the AWACS commander said.

"Roger," Mager said. "Wolfman, vector us to intercept aircraft."

"Roger, Hammer 34. Come to a heading one nine three. Bogey at twenty miles," the AWACS commander said.

"Remember our weapons test, Wolfman? We're getting ready to run it. Keep your eyes wide open," General Mager said.

"What's the plan, sir?" airborne command on the AWACS asked.

"Don't worry, we've got it all figured out," Mager said and looked over at Colonel Trout, who raised his eyebrows.

"Roger, Hammer 34. Good luck. Wolfman 16 out."

As Mager keyed off the radio, he flipped the switch on the intercom and said,"O.K., crew, any ideas . . . fast?"

"Give me that radio," Mickey said to R.O.

R.O. handed it to him.

"How do I send?" Mickey asked, trying to stay cool.

"Just push the red button," R.O. said.

"B-1 bomber, I mean Hammer 34, do you read me? Do you read me? Hammer 34. Do you copy? This is the FBI at Thompson Pass," Mickey said.

"General, I think I have your FBI agent on the ground. He's using a UHF frequency, and he's got our call sign," the DSO said.

"B-1 bomber, this is Mickey Banister, FBI. I repeat FBI," Mickey said.

"Go ahead, FBI. This is Hammer 34, B-1 at Thompson Pass," General Mager said.

"Yes," R.O. shouted and jumped up and down.

"This is the FBI. The Beechcraft Bonanza flying up the canyon is loaded with a nuclear device. It must be destroyed before it is detonated. It must be destroyed," Mickey yelled into the radio.

"Roger, FBI. The aircraft is flying too low for me to knock out. We've got some tall peaks to avoid, and we don't carry traditional air-to-air missiles, and our bombs would take out the pipeline. But we've got something that might work," Mager replied. "We need your help to get the aircraft up higher to us. Can you do that?"

Mickey thought for a second and then put the radio back to his mouth.

"Hammer 34, when she makes her next run down the canyon I'll force her up to you. I'm a dead shot with a deer rifle. Be ready. FBI Special Agent Mickey Banister over and out."

"Did you hear that, Jeff?" Colonel Trout said.

"I did. Don't ask me how he's going to get the plane higher up to us, but let's get ready. Major Hare, run the checklist for our test weapons. Make it quick. You've got the aircraft on the radar flying down the pass about 200 feet above the highway. When she makes her turn over the Valdez oil terminal, she'll be in the canyon before we can turn around," Mager said.

"Sir, she's already there. She entered the canyon two minutes ago and will be over target in about ninety seconds," Major Hare said.

"Making the turn over Prince Edward Sound now. Major Hare, on my mark you have *The Fighting Bat,* three, two, one, mark. She's all yours, Eileen," General Mager said as he turned over aircraft steering to the offensive systems officer.

"Accelerate to Mach 1.2. Target intercept in 85 seconds at 3,400 feet, sir," Major Hare said, staging the battle and working the computer. "Test weapon device is set to deploy on command," Major Hare said.

Major Hare gripped the track handle on her console

delicately and watched the computer monitor directly in front of her. As OSO of *The Flying Bat,* she was now steering the B-1 at Mach 1.2 to overtake the Beech Bonanza.

"I hope our guy on the ground knows what he's doing," Colonel Trout said. "No way we can engage the target if it is still below the rim. We're still going to have to stand on our tail to get out these mountains."

"I agree. Did you copy, major?" General Mager replied.

"That's affirmative, sir. We're up and out after deployment of the weapon," Major Hare replied.

Mickey could hear the Bonanza as it flew up the canyon to Thompson Pass on what he figured was Marlena's final run. He knew she would have to bank the aircraft to get a final approach on the pumping station. He handed the radio back to R.O. and felt lucky she hadn't already dropped the weapon.

"Time to pray, little guy," Mickey said and wrapped the rifle sling tight around his arm and held steady on the back of the snowmobile.

R.O. slowly knelt beside him and watched in the sky as the Beechcraft Bonanza suddenly appeared from the canyon and slowly banked to the north, exposing the top of the aircraft.

Mickey took steady aim and fired. He missed. He chambered quickly and fired a second time. Still no hit. Then, as the Bonanza began to straighten out, dipping the right wing slightly, Mickey looked through the Zeiss scope and pulled the trigger. At over 2,200 feet per second, the bullet ripped through the windshield and side door and left a hole in the left wing big enough to put a fist through.

Marlena, startled by the cracking glass and thud of the big slug, immediately pulled back on the controls to gain more altitude. The mountainside was closing in fast. Climbing still higher, she had yet to get her composure when she reached 3,400 hundred feet altitude. Wiping blood from her cheek cut by glass from the windshield, she saw with every blink of her eyes a terrifying sight, a B-1 bomber dead ahead and closing.

Maj. Eileen Hare opened the forward bomb-bay doors and depressed the manual release button. A hailstorm of marble-sized shrapnel blasted from the underbelly of the B-1 and hit the Bonanza like a cloud of angry African bees. Marlena blinked only once before the thousands of explosions ripped through the cockpit, tearing her into little pieces and shredding the Bonanza. Mickey and R.O. were still in their crouched position as the remnants of Marlena and the Bonanza plowed into the mountainside full of snow. For a second, as he watched through the Zeiss scope, Mickey thought he saw the orange case tumble free into the side of the mountain, but it could have been a hopeful illusion. But there was no explosion, and he finally took a breath.

Mickey leaned back on his heels and wiped the sweat off his forehead as he watched the mighty warplane become a dot on the horizon. Within seconds, four F-16 fighters rocked the canyon walls with their sonic blasts. He set the rifle down and turned and saw a look of shock on R.O.'s face. He leaned over and pulled him close and held him like he did his own grandchildren.

"That's all right, little buddy," he said. "You did good."

Ryan put his arms around him and hugged him tight.

"What did you say your name was?" Mickey asked.

"Ryan O'Keef MacGregor, but everyone calls me R.O.," he said and leaned back.

"You wouldn't need a good hunting rifle, would you? I've got one of these back home in Amarillo and I can't use two of them," Mickey asked.

"I'm from around Dallas. I've got a Weatherby 7mm, but I don't have a Mark V. If my dad will let me keep it, sure!" R.O. said. "Do you ever hunt mule deer in the Big Bend Country?" R.O. asked, still shaken by the explosion.

"Sure do. Maybe we'll meet down there sometime and go hunting," Mickey said.

"I'd like that," R.O. replied.

"We better get down the mountain and check on the priest, the Father. What's his name?"

"Fefelov. He's Russian Orthodox," Ryan said.

"I guess that makes you Russian Orthodox doesn't it? R.O.," Mickey said and they both laughed.

"One more thing," Mickey said and picked up the radio and clicked the transmit button twice. "Hammer 34, you still on line?"

"That's affirmative," Jeff Mager said. "Good shooting, FBI. You forced it up just enough."

"Thanks, Hammer 34, pretty darn good shooting yourselves. If you're ever up in Amarillo from Abilene, look me up. I'll be Mickey Banister, FBI, retired in three more days," Mickey said.

"Nice to cross your path, Agent Banister. From now on your call sign is Deadshot 44. Good luck to you. The crew of *The Fighting Bat* salutes you, sir," Mager said.

"Hammer 34, that's a big 10-4, buddy. Thank you. Deadshot 44 over and out," Mickey said and slowly handed the radio to R.O. He let out a heavy sigh.

"Colonel, that's one for the annals," General Mager said to Colonel Trout.

"The never-to-be-published-or-revealed annals, I'm sure," the colonel replied.

"Let's go home. Weapons test successfully completed. We've still got that tailwind, so we'll be in Abilene in time for a late dinner. Anybody up for a big ribeye steak from Joe Allen's?" Mager said. "I'll buy."

"My favorite place for a steak," Colonel Trout replied. Everyone agreed as the big warbird climbed to 24,000 feet and headed home to Texas.

Mickey and R.O. drove back down the road just in time to see a sheriff's deputy drive up in a jeep.

"FBI," he said as he flashed his ID to the deputy. "Where is everyone?"

"The two gunshot victims were taken into Valdez. Unfortunately, one of them died," the deputy said.

R.O. froze in his tracks.

"Which one?" Mickey asked and put his arm around R.O.

"The one with the chest wound. They identified him as Lemanski," the deputy said.

"I guess I killed that one. I'll stick around for the investigation to clear and do the paperwork. I'm going to warn you, son, this is a national security issue and you need to bring your sheriff into it today. He needs to call Elmendorf, too. Get my drift?" Mickey said.

"I understand, sir," the deputy said and started to string yellow crime-scene tape around the trees and old cabin.

Mickey and R.O. got back on the snowmobile and drove down to the convenience store, where they found Jack, Chris, Heather, and Roy. The windows of the store had been shattered by the sonic boom of the B-1. The owner had just driven up and had a look of astonishment on his face. The clerk handed him Mickey's card. A sheriff's SUV was just leaving with Vitorio handcuffed in the back seat.

Jack, Chris, and Roy were tying down the snowmobiles while Heather stayed in the H2 trying to get warm and flipping through one of the old diaries from the mine. R.O. ran over to Jack and gave him a big hug. Mickey and Jack reintroduced themselves and talked for a minute as Mickey and R.O. told him an abbreviated version of Marlena and the terrorists. Jack stood in utter disbelief and then returned the Ruger Redhawk to Mickey and thanked him. Jack explained that Mavis was in the ambulance heading to Valdez hospital and had just called and said that the paramedics concluded that the bullet had glanced off Father Fefelov's rib and had done no real damage. R.O. was relieved.

"And Mrs. Novotski was just fine. A little bruised, but the down blanket had kept her warm. She's a tough Alaskan pioneer woman," Jack said. "She insisted on riding in the front seat of the rescue unit. She said she hadn't been up to the pass in about ten years and wanted to see it again."

"Three ricochets, a thick parka, and a rib. Those little .380s spin out pretty fast. He's a lucky priest," Mickey said.

"And you are, too," Jack said and touched the hole in the right sleeve of Mickey's parka.

"Well, it's time for me to stop tempting fate for awhile. Guess I need to get down to the sheriff's office and fill out some paperwork. Nice meeting you, folks. Take care." The

special agent turned and walked over to the jeep. He threw
the big duffle into the front seat, and then remembered
something and walked toward Jack and R.O.

"Dr. MacGregor," he said as he took the Weatherby
Mark V from over his shoulder. "I told the little guy that he
was of such great service to his country during a time of
emergency that his reward was this new hunting rifle. Been
fired only three times," Mickey said and handed it to Jack.
"He said he would have to ask you."

R.O. stood waiting for an answer.

"Absolutely, Agent Banister. From what you just told
me, my son earned it. Thank you," Jack said. "It's a little big
for him right now, but in time he'll grow into it."

"My thoughts exactly. See ya'," Mickey said and walked
back to the jeep. Soon he was on his way back through
Keystone Canyon, on his way to Amarillo.

"Dad," Heather said and walked up holding one of the
diaries from the cabin. "The Cross of Charlemagne and the
Czar of Alaska were never here in the first place," she said.

Everyone turned to her and stared.

"We're waiting. Where are they?" Chris finally said.

"On Kodiak Island, at Three Saints Bay, home of the first
Russian colony."

Epilogue
November 17, 1999

Two days after the big B-1 bomber knocked the Beech Bonanza out of the air, B.A. Luff stood waiting on the pier at the Port of Valdez. His Cessna Caravan was floating in the gentle swells as the MacGregor family, Roy, and Father Fefelov, his left arm in a sling, walked toward him.

"I hope you had a fun and restful stay in Valdez. I understand we're flying to Kodiak Island," B.A. said. "I put in my spare seat in the back so there should be plenty of space. And by the way, I'm sending your luggage on to Anchorage to reduce weight. It'll be waiting for us there later today."

"You are very efficient, Mr. Luff," Mavis said as she walked up.

"Yes, you are," Heather said and walked up to him. "Can I ride up front with you?"

"Sure," he said and smiled.

The rest of the clan got on board without much ado, and Chris helped Father Fefelov get in last since Father Kristov had decided to fly back to Anchorage and meet Father Dimitri.

"You O.K., Father?" Chris asked as he helped him buckle in.

"Yes, I'm doing well, Chris. Just sore around the stitches, that's all. I've got to keep this arm down for a few days. Those lovely nurses insisted I wear this sling, you know," he said and pulled his long red beard from under the seat belt.

In a few minutes, the Caravan was skimming across the waters of Valdez Bay and was quickly airborne. Once B.A. cleared the narrows, he set his course to Kodiak Island.

"Three Saints Bay in about two hours or less," he said over the intercom.

Heather talked his ear off as everyone else was still trying to catch up on sleep after being drained from the high emotions of the last week. Roy looked out the window and enjoyed seeing yet another part of his wonderful state as they reached the Gulf of Alaska. He had spent two hours on the telephone telling his dad about his adventures, followed by another hour with Jack, explaining how it was and apologizing for everything. Roy's dad understood and said that Roy had faced many dangers in the Arctic Ocean. He said that any new adventure was always welcomed in the life of an Inupiat.

It was around noon when the Cessna Caravan touched down gently in Three Saints Bay and powered over to the big dock next to Trader Jim's marina, exactly seven days after Chris, Heather, and Ryan had embarked on their ocean journey that nearly ended in disaster. Jim was standing on the end of the pier as the prop was shut down and the plane came to a rest. He tied a big rope around the leg of one of the pontoons and opened the door.

"Welcome back," he said as Chris stepped out and then helped Father Fefelov. "Father Fefelov, my old friend," Trader Jim said and helped him step over to the pier. "What brings you back to Kodiak?" he asked.

"The blessings of God, I must say," the priest replied.

In a short while, everyone had reached the pier and B.A. had secured his aircraft and followed everyone up to the main building. As they stepped inside, they could smell lunch cooking. Two of Trader Jim's cooks were busy in the kitchen and setting the massive wooden table in the dining room.

"This smells great," Roy said and headed to the table.

Soon they were all around the table eating smoked salmon, crab cakes, and something they hadn't had in Alaska before, steak.

"I haven't had a good steak in a long time," Chris said.

"Me either," Heather said and checked her comments about food before she embarrassed herself in front of B.A.

"It's probably reindeer," Roy said.

"Stop it, Roy," R.O. said. "I don't think I could eat Rudolf or Donner."

"Well, tell me about this adventure," Trader Jim said and dabbed his mouth with the linen napkin.

"We were waiting at the top of Thompson Pass, and Heather was flipping through an old diary in the back of the H2," Chris said and spooned more mashed potatoes into his plate.

"Then Heather revealed to us something of great importance," Jack continued. "While we were taking Father Fefelov out of the mine and Chris and Roy had gone back to get the H2, Heather was looking through some of the crates that were brought out of the mine into the cellar."

"I saw some pretty lace and thought I would hold it up to the light. That's when I spotted the diary. I like to keep a diary and since the man had been dead for over seventy years, I didn't think anyone would care if I looked through it. I wasn't going to keep it," Heather said.

"That's when she made the discovery," Mavis said. "It seems that Natasha Novotski's uncle had indeed kept the box with the artifacts in them, but later the priest returned and took them back, but not before he told him he was returning them to the site of one of the earliest churches in Alaska, here on Kodiak."

"Don't forget the $600,000 worth of gold coins we found, and it all goes to Mrs. Novotski to share with her nephews, or not," R.O. said. "May I remind you, I found the mine," he said with food in his mouth.

"Chew your food before you talk," Mavis said quickly and softly.

"So after lunch, we'll go to the old church, the one the kids call the bear cabin, and read the clues in the diary," Jack said.

"Maybe it's there and maybe it's not. But it will bring to a close an exciting chapter in my life that has lasted nearly five years and has taken me around the globe. It's not a total loss. Father Kristov and I have met many good friends in the Roman and Greek churches and, of course, wonderful people like the MacGregors and Roy Nageak," Father Fefelov said.

"I'm impressed," B.A. said and picked up another hot roll.

"I have two of my men outside with enough snowmobiles to carry us through the forest to the old church. The building is about 120 years old. It was first used as a church, then turned into a hunting lodge, then back into a church again, and then a youth camp before I bought it. I know right where it is. I used to sleep overnight there after long days out hunting. But you're right. It's in the middle of bear country deluxe. So I've brought along some big guns just in case," Trader Jim said.

Before long, everyone had finished eating, bundled up, and gone out to the snowmobiles. A light powder was falling from the early winter Alaska was experiencing. The snow along the coast was thin but just enough to get them along to the deeper snow in the forest about two miles away. Before long, they were all plowing along until they came to the remains of the bear carcass draped across the crushed sled.

"My, you weren't exaggerating," Mavis said as she got off the snowmobile and walked around what the wolves had left. The massive skull was still in place.

"Good shot, right, Dad?" R.O. said.

"Yes, I have to say it was a good shot," Jack replied.

After everyone had examined the remains of the bear, it was only a short ride to the blue onion-domed church. When they arrived, Jim handed out a couple of shovels to clear a path to the door, which was still partially open where the bear had run through after the kids. Once inside, he went over and tossed a few logs in the massive fireplace.

Father Fefelov was the last inside, with Mavis at his side.

"I'm doing fine, young lady," he said to Mavis and stepped inside on his own. "I was rejuvenated when I saw the blue dome to St. Mary. It looked as though it had been repainted over the years to keep its original beauty."

"Blue for Mary?" Mavis said.

"Yes, there are special colors for a few special people," Father Fefelov replied.

The dry wood lit up quickly and everyone gathered around the fireplace. Chris brought in two lanterns and turned them on. The old rustic room got even brighter, lighting up the icons, faded by time, which hung just below the second landing and over the fireplace. Mavis took out the diary and found the place she had marked with a yellow sticky note from the hospital. She began to read:

> When Father Adrian had come back to see me, I went down into the mine and retrieved his case. It was heavy, but not as heavy as some of my tools. I had never looked in the old case because I believe that such a man of faith should have his privacy preserved. If he wanted me to see what was there and it was meant for me to see it, I was certain he would show it to me. So when I gave it to him, he looked inside and nodded and thanked me for taking care of it for so long. I had been entrusted with it for five years. I knew that the priest was poor, so I went back into the mine and got some of my gold coins and gave him five of them. He thanked me and told me that my family would be blessed someday. When he was about to go, I asked him where his journey was finally leading him. He said he was going to All Saints Bay, one of the early Russian Orthodox colonies in Alaska, and that is where his treasure would find its final home. He said it would rest among the Saints where God would bless it and man couldn't find it.

The room was quiet. Father Fefelov walked around looking up at the icons of the Russian Orthodox Church.

"My friends, these are all the Saints. The apostles and blessed people of all of Christendom," he said.

"That one's got a beard like yours, Father," R.O. said and pointed to one high on the wall under the second landing.

"Yes, it does, R.O. It's St. James, brother of our Lord. I've always been told that I look like St. James," Fefelov said, and then frowned. "But it seems that St. James is out of place. I think he should be over here." Fefelov pointed to the opposite wall and another row of icons and then looked back to the faded wooden portrait of St. James in line with four other icons. "Yes, St. James is definitely out of place," he said.

"R.O., here," Chris said.

R.O. walked over to Chris. With a quick boost, R.O. was standing on his shoulders, leaning on the wall next to the icon of St. James.

"Carefully pull it from the wall, son," Father Fefelov said.

"Careful, honey," Mavis said.

Everyone gathered around them. R.O. reached out and tugged at the wooden picture. It wouldn't budge. He gave it another jerk and almost lost his balance. He pulled again and it came free. He reached down and handed the wooden painting of St. James to Jack.

"There's a hole up here, but I can't see in it," R.O. said.

Jack walked up to the second landing and leaned over the rail and pointed a flashlight toward the small hole. He hurried back down.

"Jim you get one side and I'll take the other," Jack said.

In five seconds, Chris was standing with one foot on each man's shoulder. He reached inside the hole and tugged on the wooden plank. It gave away from years of weather and moisture. Chris lobbed it across the room and reached for another plank. Pulling the planks one by one, he could now see inside a hidden compartment.

"Looks like there's an old leather case of some kind," he said.

Chris carefully pulled on the case, and it came part of the way out of the hole. Everyone gasped. He then gave it another tug, and it slowly cleared the hole. He carefully handed it down, and Mavis took it and walked over to the fireplace and laid it on the floor in front of the firelight. Chris jumped down and everyone gathered around. Mavis tried to unfasten a buckle but the leather crumbled in her hands, so she folded the top flap of the case back. It, too, broke free. Inside, she could see faded cloth that looked like velvet, but the years had taken its toll. She carefully pulled it out and felt a solid object inside.

"Father Fefelov, I have a feeling you should be the one to do this," she said and leaned back.

The injured priest knelt down and moaned when the stitches pulled on his side.

"I'm fine," he assured everyone and finally sat on the floor as Trader Jim and Jack held him under each arm.

Instinctively, everyone sat down in a circle. Father Fefelov tugged on the material and realized that it was a bag and found the opening. He carefully peeled back the old velvet until the firelight danced off the surface of a magnificent solid gold cross. A ruby was in the middle, and it was covered with diamonds and emeralds.

"The Cross of Charlemagne. To think a great king once wore this around his neck and conquered many lands in the name of Christ," he said. "I had given up hope two days ago of ever finding it. I'm too humbled to speak."

Mavis leaned over and pulled the remaining velvet bag from the old case. It was small, and she reached inside and pulled out the Czar of Alaska, a beautiful black pearl that was set in solid gold and ringed with diamonds and rubies.

"Oh my, this is so beautiful," Mavis said and held it up to the firelight.

No one spoke for nearly five minutes. Very few men, indeed, ever touch a single treasure, but to hold two in the same moment was truly a grand one for all of them.

Father Fefelov handed Jack the Cross of Charlemagne to examine, and Mavis handed him the Czar of Alaska. Then he spoke.

"I am sure the authorities will have a challenging time trying to decide ownership of these great artifacts," he said. "But I believe that the Czar of Alaska belongs to the people of Alaska. So on behalf of Catherine II and the Russian

Orthodox Church, I present the Czar of Alaska to Mr. Roy Nageak, who will accept it on behalf of the native peoples of this great land for whom it was originally meant to be given."

Father Fefelov handed the great pearl to Roy.

Roy paused for a moment and then spoke.

"Thank you, Father. I wish my father was here to do this. Since I am Inupiat and a native of this great land, I accept," Roy said.

R.O. started clapping and then everyone followed along until they were all clapping and cheering. Father Fefelov took the Cross of Charlemagne and passed it around until everyone had touched it. Then, when it had returned to him, he held it to his heart. Everyone looked at him.

"The Cross of Charlemagne has finally come home," he said and a smile spread across his face.

Disclaimer and Warning
to All Readers

Minors should never use firearms without professional training and supervision of their parents or legal guardians. Responsible use of any firearm, by any person, is of the utmost importance. Shooting sports and hunting should only be attempted after proper supervision by a professionally trained person or organization and within the statutes of the jurisdiction where you live.

Dog-sledding is a unique but dangerous sport and should only be attempted after professional training and under the supervision of parents or legal guardian.

The MacGregor family kids are involved in dangerous and life-threatening endeavors in all of their adventures. Children should be warned that this is a work of fiction and in real life only trained professionals are involved in these activities. At the age of adulthood, with professional training and safety precautions, many of these activities may be safely duplicated.

REVIEWS FOR THE MACGREGOR
FAMILY ADVENTURE SERIES
Cayman Gold: Lost Treasure of Devils Grotto
Book One

VOYA • *Journal for Librarians* • *August 2000*
"Science fact and fiction based on folklore intertwine in this fast-paced story of pirate gold and adventure. In an increasingly rare story line, the family is intact, with parents who are intelligent and involved in the lives of their children. . . . surely will appeal to older teens—mostly boys—looking for a blend of adventure and a bit of romance."
                                                        —Pam Carlson

KLIATT • *Journal for Librarians* • *May 2000*
"In this quick-moving adventure story, teenagers who are expert scuba divers bump up against modern-day pirates. . . . The author, an environmental biologist and college professor, shows his love and fierce protectiveness of natural resources and endangered species. This story is fun to read while making teens aware of environmental issues."
                                     —Sherri Forgash Ginsberg,
                         Duke School for Children, Chapel Hill, NC

Midwest Books Review • *"Children's Bookwatch"*
". . . *Cayman Gold* is a well crafted adventure with meticulous attention to accuracy in detail and highly recommended reading for teens and young adults."   —James Cox,
                                                    Editor-in-Chief

"Kids Books" • *Northwest Metro Times*
"This riveting story combines historical events, hurricanes, daring escapades and some nasty bad guys and puts them all together in a way that will keep you on the edge of your seat until the final page." —Dale Knowles

"Book Briefs" • *The Sunday Oklahoman* • *February 2000*
". . . Billed as a young adult-family novel, this adventure story offers suspense and some good lessons in conservation."
                                                        —Kay Dyer

Elephant Tears: Mask of the Elephant
Book Two

"An action-packed journey for young adults through the trials and triumphs of wildlife conservation in the African bush." —Dr. Delia and Mark Owens, Zoologists, Authors of *Cry of the Kalahari, The Eye of the Elephant,* and National Geographic film, *African Odyssey*

VOYA • Journal for Librarians • December 2000
". . . portrays the teens' relationships with each other and with their parents as wholesome but realistic . . . respectfully depicts the native Africans and their tradition without glossing over their problems . . . descriptive narration is admirable—family-friendly realistic wildlife adventure."
—Leah Sparks

KLIATT • Journal for Librarians • September 2000
". . . the author weaves an exciting adventure while stressing the importance of protecting the earth's dwindling resources and endangered animals. It is a powerful, enlightening novel that remains exciting without being didactic."
—Sherri Forgash Ginsberg

Midwest Book Review • "Children's Bookwatch"
"*Elephant Tears* is a thriller adventure novel . . . superbly researched and written, *Elephant Tears* is one of those infrequent novels for young readers that are so easy to pick up, and so hard to put down! Also highly recommended is Trout's first adventure novel, *Cayman Gold.*"
—James Cox, Editor-in-Chief

"Kids Books" • Northwest Metro Times • August 2000
"This is an action-filled thriller set in the plains of East Africa that you will want to read for the excitement factor as well as gaining a lot of insight into the problems of wildlife survival. I certainly enjoyed it, and I think you will also."
—Dale Knowles

Falcon of Abydos: Oracle of the Nile
Book Three

"Written for all ages, *Falcon of Abydos* is a thrilling adventure story in which the MacGregor family becomes entangled in an ancient Egyptian mystery stretching from the heat of the Sahara to beneath the surface of the Red Sea. . . . An engaging, action-packed, and memorable techno/thriller for young readers."

—*Midwest Book Review, "Children's Bookwatch"*

"This is the third adventure for the traveling MacGregor family. We find them in Cairo, unearthing secrets that could change the face of the Middle East forever. The series consists of . . . action-packed stories . . . [that] make important political and environmental statements as well as providing pure entertainment. This story is loaded with historical facts, laced with romance and humor; a definite purchase for your library."

—*KLIATT*

"While dad Jack is attending classes and speaking about environmental problems, wife Mavis, sons Chris, 17, and Ryan, 12, and daughter Heather, 14, set out to discover what secrets the desert holds. A desert storm and scorpion stings are just the start of their problems, as enemies—old and new—pursue them. These include a man out for revenge; Egyptian mobsters who may have ties with terrorists; and a couple of Russians, former secret police agents trying to steal high-tech weaponry. Along the way, the author lets the MacGregor children learn some Egyptian history and mythology, and the way some projects meant to be progressive (the Aswan Dam) could turn into ecological disasters. Most young readers will like to follow the MacGregors into these exotic lands."

—Kay Dyer, *Sunday Oklahoman*

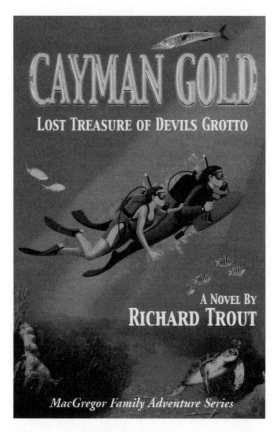

CAYMAN GOLD

LOST TREASURE OF DEVILS GROTTO

A NOVEL BY
RICHARD TROUT

MacGregor Family Adventure Series

Suddenly faced with the task of saving a lost Spanish treasure embedded in protected coral reef, the MacGregor teens rely on their courage and scuba-diving skills to explore and investigate the waters and beaches of the Cayman Islands. This first novel in the techno-thriller *MacGregor Family Adventure Series* involves sinister pirate forces, strange sea creatures, and hospitable natives, as well as issues of endangered species and environmental management. Meticulously detailed yet quick-paced, this novel is an introduction to the enterprising MacGregor clan, who have just entered what will be a full year of worldwide escapades. As with each Richard Trout book, the themes of family and wildlife conservation are apparent throughout each adventure.

In this second novel in the *MacGregor Family Adventure Series,* zoologist Dr. Jack MacGregor again strives to protect the earth's dwindling resources and endangered animals, pursuing an international cartel that is exploiting elephants in East Africa. The family's three teenagers, Chris, Heather, and Ryan, become part of the action and team up with native Africans and a seasoned American aviator to save the animals and bring the exploiters to justice. Traversing the landscape of Serengeti, Amboseli, Masai Mara, and Mount Kilimanjaro, the MacGregor teens learn about African culture and wildlife through the eyes of their new friend, native Kikuyu Samburua. This is another stimulating, action-packed journey that will appeal to all ages with its contemporary perspective of culture, environmental management, and solid family values.

FALCON OF
ABYDOS
ORACLE OF THE NILE

MacGregor Family Adventure Series

A Novel By
RICHARD TROUT

This time the globe trotting MacGregor clan lands amidst the shifting sands of the Sahara Desert to uncover a secret that could forever change the history of Egypt. Just when Egyptologists believe that the last of the great discoveries have been made, the MacGregor family's appearance at the International Environmental Conference in Cairo inspires them to pursue the truth about the Nile River. From a quaint shop in the heart of Old Cairo to Seti's exquisite temple, the mystery of the Falcon of Abydos is the third and possibly the most chilling challenge for the inimitable MacGregor family and their friends.